PRETTY JANE *and the* VIPER *of* KIDBROOKE LANE

A VICTORIAN MURDER MYSTERY SOLVED

PAUL THOMAS MURPHY

First published in the United States in 2016 by Pegasus Books LLC

First published in the UK in 2016 by Head of Zeus Ltd

This paperback edition first published in 2017 by Head of Zeus Ltd

1 3 5 7 9 8 6 4 2

A CIP catalogue record for this book is available from the British Library.

ISBN (PB): 9781784081904
ISBN (E): 9781784081881

Interior design by Maria Fernandez

Printed and bound by CPI Group (UK) Ltd, Croydon, CR0 4YY

Head of Zeus Ltd
First Floor East
5–8 Hardwick Street
London EC1R 4RG

WWW.HEADOFZEUS.COM

For Tory, of course

CONTENTS

PREFACE

J ane Maria Clouson, the subject of this book, lived her short life in the middle of the long reign of Queen Victoria, the subject of my last book. A greater separation between the obscurity of the first and the renown of the second—in their day and in ours—could hardly be imagined. Queen Victoria during her lifetime was the world's most recognized human being; since her death, no woman has been the subject of more biographies. Jane, on the other hand, lived in utter obscurity: a Deptford working-class child who spent most of the last third of her unassuming life performing the unceasing and lonely duties of a maid-of-all-work. Nothing that she did, nothing that happened to her brought her any public attention whatsoever: nothing, that is, until April 26, 1871, when she was found attacked and horribly disfigured on a quiet country lane outside of Greenwich. From the moment of that discovery to the moment of her death a week later, and for months afterward, with the investigation into her death and the trial of her alleged killer, the British public was enthralled with Jane Clouson. But after that, she was quickly forgotten.

Or, rather, she was almost forgotten.

I first heard about Jane Maria Clouson four years ago, as I was making a tour of the major archives about London—Kew, Colindale, Windsor—for some final fact-checking for my last book, *Shooting Victoria*, the story of Victoria's bedevilment by seven would-be assassins. I was at the point, in other words, where I was beginning to look past that project and to consider subjects for a new one. To celebrate *Shooting Victoria*'s near-completion, I had met with a few friends in a Greenwich brewpub, the Old Brewery—located, coincidentally, a very short walk away from the site of the home where Jane Clouson had worked until shortly before she died. Among this group was an old college friend of mine, Michael Guilfoyle, a gifted local historian who lives in Lewisham and who often conducts guided walks of nearby Brockley and Ladywell Cemeteries. (He has also, incidentally, served as a magistrate at the soon-to-be-closed Greenwich Magistrates' Court—formerly Greenwich Police Court—the site of much of the action in this book.) Hungry for possibilities, I took advantage of the moment to pick Michael's brain. "If you were to write a book about anyone buried at Brockley and Ladywell," I asked him, "who would it be?"

He answered instantly: "Jane Clouson."

I asked him to write the name down. He did, and immediately below that wrote "let me die": the words found on Jane's monument, and very likely her last words. Michael then told me what he knew of Jane, of her murder, and of her alleged killer. Jane's story was captivating on its face—a tragic domestic drama laying bare all the small-scale but explosive gender, class, and sexual strains between Jane and those who employed her, the Pook family. I told Michael I'd look into the story further, to see, as I'm afraid I put it, if the story "had legs."

It did.

In writing *Shooting Victoria*, I was guided by the principle that powerful historical insights can best be found in exploring episodes of cultural collision. In all the clashes between Queen Victoria and the seven malcontents who assailed her, that collision could hardly have been more obvious—or more dramatic. And as I dug deeper and deeper into the case of Jane Clouson, I discovered that her case offered many moments of cultural collision equally striking, and equally revealing. The crime became the subject of an exhaustive investigation by the Metropolitan Police and Scotland Yard, an investigation that exposes the strengths and weaknesses of policing at the dawn of the age of modern forensics. *Pretty Jane* is largely the story of this investigation and of the controversy that followed it.

The examination led to an arrest for murder, and not to one trial but to several: *Pretty Jane* is as much courtroom drama as it is police procedural. The year-long search for justice, both for Jane and for her alleged murderer Edmund Pook, exposes the workings of the English legal system in the years before major legal reforms swept away many, but not all, customs and procedures that dated from the Middle Ages. That world is at once familiar—and utterly alien.

In addition, *Pretty Jane* deals with cultural collision in the world outside the police station and the courtroom. The murder of Jane Clouson and the subsequent trial of Edmund Pook were among the most sensational events of the decade. Thousands flocked in pilgrimage to the site of Jane's murder; thousands gathered to revile—and later to cheer—Edmund Pook during the many journeys he made to and from the courtroom; thousands on the verge of rioting gathered in the streets of Greenwich to protest the result of his trial. *Pretty Jane*, then, is a story of a vital, Dickensian world in upheaval, divided largely along class lines, clashing over different conceptions of justice and about different conceptions of respectability: different conceptions, in particular, of the respect due to a murdered working-class girl. Thousands participated in Jane

Clouson's funeral. The town of Deptford provided the plot. And the people, with their pennies, paid for her monument. But even her burial and her monument were sources of public confrontation. And in this confrontation, as in all the others, lies true insight into the community in which Jane lived and died.

Jane was forgotten, while Queen Victoria remains unforgettable. But Jane's story, like Victoria's, reveals profoundly what it meant to live—and die—a Victorian. Jane Clouson's story deserves to be told. I only hope I have done her justice.

PRETTY JANE *and the* VIPER *of* KIDBROOKE LANE

CHAPTER ONE

LET ME DIE

H e stumbled upon her at 4:15 on Wednesday morning, April 26, 1871, half an hour before the sun rose, just as definition and color began to bleed into the amorphous black and gray. Donald Gunn, a police constable of R, or Greenwich Division of the London Metropolitan police, was at the extremity of his beat, which had taken him from Shooter's Hill southwest through the smaller town of Eltham, and then northeast to this deserted road flanked by market gardens and bisected by the little rivulet—Kid Brook—that gave this road its name—Kidbrooke Lane. Kidbrooke Lane provided a direct route between the Kent countryside and the metropolis, but few carriages or wagons traveled that way, as it was muddy, rutted— nearly impassable. The lane's adjoining footpath, however, was drier, and during the day the route was well frequented by pedestrians, particularly in the evenings: then, the area around Kidbrooke Lane became a well-known haven for lovers, the surrounding fields offering the perfect space apart for lovemaking, just minutes from the bustle of southeast London, but a world away from the relentless attentions of the city, and particularly from prying parental eyes. But the lovers had fled hours before, and PC Gunn usually trod this final part of his night beat in profound solitude; Kidbrooke Lane must have seemed to him far removed from the most populous city in the world—must have seemed in its quiet more like the place where he had grown up: distant Caithness, the northeastern tip of Scotland.

Gunn had made his first circuit of Kidbrooke Lane two and a half hours before, approaching Kidbrooke by the footpath, separated from the road by high hedges, and returning by way of the road itself. If Jane had been lying there then, he must have walked right past her. The moon had set long before this, and although Gunn carried a bull's-eye lantern with him—it was standard issue for all metropolitan police officers—he did not use it that night, instead making his way down the road guided by dim starlight and by rote memory.

Now, as he made his second circuit up the footpath to the brook, and a hundred yards down the muddy lane, he made out a sodden black-and-brown jumble of clothing that slowly resolved itself into a human body: a woman, or a girl, rising from the mud and trampled grass on her hands and knees. She faced away from him, but he could see her head bobbing up and down as she moaned softly, "piteously." He immediately concluded that she was drunk, literally dumped here in her inebriation by an ungallant lover to sleep it off alone.

Gunn walked to her, towered over her, and asked sternly what she was doing there.

"Oh, my poor head; oh, my poor head," she moaned.

He clutched her shoulder and gave her a shake. What was the matter, he asked her. How had she come by her injuries? He noticed then a smear of blood on her cheek.

The woman lifted her left hand from the ground, stretched it toward him, and in a feeble voice, asked him to take hold of it.

She slowly turned her face toward him.

Gunn recoiled as he looked at her and saw a face no longer human—a battered and bloody mass. Several gashes were cloven into her skull. Her left cheek was slashed open and smashed in. Her right eye was destroyed, and above it a chunk of the temporal bone had been bashed out, leaving a hole from which her brain clearly protruded.

He stared at her in horror for several seconds before finally reaching out his hand for hers. It was too late. The woman lost her balance and pitched face-first onto the ground.

"Let me die," she murmured, and then fell still.

Gunn, for a moment helpless, let her lie there while he surveyed the area. Four feet from the woman, behind him and toward the middle of the road, he could see a small pool of blood, cold and clotted into the mud. Around this center was grouped a mass of footprints; this was where she must have been attacked, must have fallen. From here she had crawled to the side of the road. Two feet from the woman was a pair of women's gloves, daintily placed one within the other, and two feet from them was a black bonnet, decorated with three embroidered red roses.

Gunn looked up and down the road in the wild hope that the attacker might still be near. But he and the woman were alone.

He lifted her, unconscious, from the mud and set her down gently on her back on the dry grass by the side of the road. And then he turned and ran—southeast down the lane, to the farm of the ancient manor of Well Hall: the hostler and stable boys there, he knew, would already be awake and working. But upon running into the farmyard, Gunn found better help than that: his sergeant, Frederick Haynes, happened to be there, pausing in his early-morning round of surprise inspections of his constables on their beats. Gunn hurriedly conferred with Haynes about the woman. The two men then dashed off in opposite directions: Haynes up Kidbrooke Lane

to attend to the woman and Gunn to the police station at Eltham
to assemble a stretcher party from the officers who would just then
be returning from their night beats.

Sergeant Haynes found the woman lying insensible where
Gunn had left her. In his hurry Gunn had set her down with
her skirts hiked up above her knees, and so Haynes, seeing her,
jumped to the conclusion that she must have been assaulted sexually. Sergeant Haynes looked around him and saw the marks of
a violent struggle, the trampled-down grass, and the chaotic,
indistinct footsteps. He saw the hat, picked up the gloves. The
attack, he realized, had been recent, but not all that recent: the
pool of blood in the muddy road had clotted, as had the blood on
the woman's face and matted in her hair. The blood had ceased to
flow from many of her wounds. She had obviously lain here for
several hours—four or five, at least.

He stood sentinel over the unconscious woman as the sun rose,
until Constable Gunn returned with several others. Haynes took
charge, supervising the lifting of the woman onto the stretcher,
and then ordering Gunn to remain at the scene, both in the hope
of waylaying anyone who might have witnessed the attack and
to protect the crime scene from contamination by curious pass-
ersby—if not from fellow police. The others set out, double-time,
for Eltham, Haynes taking the lead, with his ear by the woman's
head. She revived enough, he later claimed, to speak once more,
moaning, "Oh, save me!" before passing out again.

They bore her into Eltham and one of the larger houses on
the High Street, where they pounded on the door to rouse Dr.
David King. As police surgeon and medical officer of health for
the district, he would seem the best man for miles around to
treat the woman's wounds. But with a glance King realized that
her life was far beyond his—and likely anyone's—power to save.
He directed Haynes to send her on to Guy's Hospital, nine miles
to the northwest in Southwark. They could at least make her
comfortable there.

An officer quickly procured a cab. They laid the insensible woman in it, Haynes and a few others climbed in, and they set off away from the rising sun. Traveling through the dew-covered fields and the still-sleeping suburbs of Lee and New Cross, and skirting the stinking tanneries of Bermondsey, they plunged into the growing din and congestion of the metropolis, turning within sight of the Thames, and pulled up at the hospital. It was 7:15 in the morning.

They were met by the hospital's house surgeon and house physician, Michael Harris and Frederic Durham. As house doctors, Harris and Durham occupied the bottommost rung of Guy's medical ladder: both were fresh out of Guy's Hospital's medical school, and neither had encountered traumatic injuries quite like these. They had the police carry the woman into a ward. There, a nurse stripped off her clothing and passed each item to Sergeant Haynes to scrutinize. Meanwhile Harris and Durham treated the woman's wounds as best they could, using forceps to remove the several chunks and fragments of bones smashed from her skull. As they probed and cleaned her, Dr. Harris made careful notes.

She was completely unconscious and perceptibly cold from loss of blood. Most of her wounds were deep and cleanly cut, inflicted by a weapon both sharp and heavy. Most wounds were at the front of her head, but Harris observed as well several cuts on her arms and hands, particularly on the backs of her hands—clean cuts with no bruising. These wounds were obviously defensive: for some time, at least, this woman had fought her attacker face to face. The incredible number of blows to the head, however—Harris counted at least a dozen of them—indicated that after she had fallen helplessly to the ground, her attacker continued to hack at her face. Simply killing her, it seemed, was not enough: whoever smashed and slashed at her repeatedly wanted to erase her physiognomy, to obliterate her identity.

Three of the woman's head wounds were particularly grievous. On her left side, over her ear, her temporal bone was bashed inward and hung fractured within the skull. Harris easily lifted this bone to find the brain lacerated underneath. A second wound—the wound that had startled PC Gunn so greatly—was a horizontal three-inch trench of smashed bone above the woman's destroyed right eye, from which swollen brain bulged through. Another blow had sliced apart the woman's upper lip and shattered her upper jawbone: Harris and Durham removed a chunk of that. The rest of the wounds to her head might have been less severe, but were distinct, telling the story of an attacker showering her head with blows: eleven, twelve, thirteen, fourteen times.

The doctors found one further wound on the girl: a bruise on her right thigh. It was slight, but it was, like all of the other wounds, recently inflicted: within the last ten or twelve hours, at most. This was the only sign of trauma on her lower body. Despite Sergeant Haynes's suspicions at the scene, the doctors found no signs whatsoever that she had been assaulted sexually.

From the general condition of the woman's body, Harris and Durham estimated that she was between twenty-three and twenty-five years old. Her occupation was obvious: the thick calluses on her hands and knees testified to years of hard labor as a servant. And she was dying; Harris and Durham were certain that they could do nothing to prevent that. There was, however, at least the hope that the woman might regain consciousness long enough to reveal her identity and name her attacker. For that reason Dr. Harris ordered that she be placed in a ward and be watched by attendants day and night.

While the doctors cleaned and dressed her wounds, Sergeant Haynes examined her clothing. They were the walking-out clothes of a servant girl. She had worn a barège (a silky fabric made of wool) dress the color of dark chocolate, pinned to which was a common-looking brooch. Under this she wore off-white petticoats, and over, a black woolen jacket with mohair trim and with lace around the neck—pretty lace, but cheap, an imitation of fine Maltese. On the sleeves of the jacket, midway between wrist and elbow, were two jagged tears obviously inflicted by her attacker's weapon. In her small blue purse, Haynes found eleven shillings and fourpence, and two small keys to boxes or suitcases, and from her jacket pocket Haynes pulled out a handkerchief and a small silver locket, bound by a length of blue ribbon. Haynes snapped the locket open, but was disappointed to find it contained nothing—no tiny image of a loved one; no lock of hair. There was nothing there, and nothing on the woman's clothing to offer a clue to her identity.

Haynes gathered up all of the woman's possessions and returned with them to the station at Eltham. While her smaller possessions remained there, her dress, jacket, and petticoats were quickly sent on to the chief station in the subdistrict, at neighboring Lee, and there displayed to anyone who might be able to identify her by them.

It was late morning when Haynes returned to Eltham, and noon when he returned to examine Kidbrooke Lane. By that time word of the assault had spread. In Greenwich, the superintendent of R Division, James Griffin, had learned of the assault and had already come to Kidbrooke Lane to investigate the scene of the assault personally. Griffin was a twenty-five-year veteran of the Metropolitan Police who had begun his career in Greenwich Division before transferring to East London posts; he moved up relatively quickly through the ranks and had been appointed superintendent of Greenwich Division four years earlier. By all evidence he was well established, comfortable and effective in his post. But the case on which he was now embarking would challenge all of that.

Although Griffin had taken personal command of the case, he'd done very little to impose any sort of discipline upon the investigation. The scene at Kidbrooke Lane was a free-for-all. Several officers from Eltham and surrounding stations—constables, sergeants, inspectors—gravitated to the lane to make personal searches for clues and to contribute their own footprints to the muddy ground. Although the forensic value of footprint evidence was well known by 1871, and techniques existed to preserve them—most commonly plaster of paris casts—no one bothered to preserve the footprints here, all concluding that their indistinctness in the sloppy mud rendered them useless for identification.

At noon, then, when Sergeant Haynes returned, the footprint evidence had been marred. But it was not entirely obliterated. He, at least, realized that the footsteps told a story. He found a number of deep, large, and widely spaced prints leading away from the chaotic tangle of prints at the place that the woman had obviously struggled with her attacker, the strides of a man—most certainly a man—running, and Haynes thought, slipping, and dirtying himself in the mud. Haynes followed the steps north for a dozen or so yards, until they petered out on firmer ground. He walked north up the lane another three hundred yards, until he reached the point where little Kid Brook trickled across the lane. Haynes crossed the brook on a little plank, where he observed on the far bank a stone on which were three drops of blood. A yard farther away, he found another drop. The assailant, Haynes thought, had stopped on his flight northward—toward the metropolis—to wash his bloody hands, and, perhaps, his weapon and his clothing. Haynes thought this evidence important enough to remember, but not to preserve. He walked away, leaving the blood behind. No one besides him was known to have seen it.

Another of the many officers milling about the scene did find more potential evidence in the mud. PC Edwin Ovens, one of the victim's stretcher-bearers, had returned to the lane and was scrutinizing the ground fifteen yards north of where she had been found. He saw a glistening in the muck, reached down, and pulled from the ground a little metal whistle. He was not very impressed with the discovery. The whistle was cheap and very common. While audible to humans, this type of whistle was most commonly used for training dogs.* Kidbrooke Lane seemed a choice spot to train

---

* The whistle now considered a dog whistle—a whistle inaudible to humans—was invented five years after this by Francis Galton, Charles Darwin's cousin. (Galton 26; "Galton Whistle.")

dogs, and thus this whistle likely had no connection with the attack. Nevertheless, Ovens passed the whistle on to his sergeant, who, upon returning to the station house at Eltham, handed it to the officer in charge, who, equally unimpressed, slipped the whistle into a cupboard without bothering to enter it into the evidence book.

○━━━○

Another piece of potential evidence made its way to Eltham station without police help.

At eight o'clock that morning young Thomas Lazell was making his way home after spending the night in Greenwich. Lazell and his family were among the few residents of Kidbrooke Lane. They rented a cottage there and grew flowers in an adjacent market garden. Their cottage was about a third of a mile from the spot where the woman had been found. If Lazell had been at his cottage the night before, therefore, he might possibly have heard or seen something. But his family also had a home in Greenwich, and Lazell's father, prostrate with gout, had needed his son's assistance there yesterday evening—and there Thomas Lazell had slept.

Lazell this morning had just turned off the footpath that connected Blackheath with Kidbrooke and onto another footpath, one that passed through a barnfield before meeting Kidbrooke Lane itself. There, he saw a man approaching excitedly, calling out to him. Lazell knew this man by sight, at least: he was a farm laborer—a haystack-maker—out of Eltham. But Lazell did not know his name. The farm laborer reached Lazell and held out to him a ragged piece of cloth. It was, the farm laborer claimed, a bloody white handkerchief. Lazell looked at it. It wasn't white; it was blue. And it wasn't a handkerchief, but a cloth irregularly torn into something like a square—a dusting rag, Lazell thought. But Lazell agreed: the cloth was stained with what looked to him like blood.

As the assault had been discovered four hours before, Lazell had almost certainly not heard anything about it, until this farm laborer excitedly proclaimed the importance of this stained cloth. And in telling Lazell what he knew about the crime, he almost certainly stated what everyone thought at the time—that the attack had taken place during the dead of night, when Lazell was miles away in Greenwich. And therefore Lazell could have had no personal connection with the crime.

Or so he thought.

The farm laborer told Lazell that he had found the cloth off of the lane, on Kidbrooke Green, half a mile or so north from the spot where the woman had been found. He was sure this cloth was evidence crucial to the case, and he planned to deliver it in person to Eltham station that evening, right after he finished work.

Lazell, too, thought the stained cloth important evidence—important enough to tell the police about himself. Later that morning, he made his way down the lane to where a knot of officers pored over the mud. There he identified himself to a sergeant: Sergeant Willis—coincidentally, the same officer to whom PC Ovens had entrusted the dog whistle. Willis was interested in Lazell's story—interested enough to want to seek out the farm laborer immediately. But Lazell had no idea where he was to be found, and repeated the farm laborer's promise that he would bring the cloth to the station; Willis would have to be satisfied with that. And the farm laborer was as good as his word: he brought the cloth to Eltham that evening. From there it was quickly sent to the station at Lee, where Sergeant Willis saw it the next morning. Willis and the police thought the cloth far less valuable as evidence than had Lazell or the farm laborer. It appeared to them to be a dirty rag, stained with something—but not, they thought, with blood. It was found off the lane, half a mile from the place of assault, near a place where gypsies often camped. It almost certainly had no connection at all with the assault.

Nonetheless, the police kept the cloth, treating it much as they had treated the dog whistle. Someone stuffed it into a cupboard. And no one bothered to record it in the evidence book. It was, however, not forgotten.

The day after the police discovered the victim, they obtained the weapon. Thomas Brown, a gardener at Morden College, an institution adjacent to Kidbrooke, was working the grounds at two o'clock on Thursday afternoon when he spied it lying on a bed of leaves, shiny new and damp from that morning's rain. It was a plasterer's or a lathing hammer, a common enough tool, but one rendered sinister by the brutal circumstances of the attack. On one side of the cast-steel instrument was a hammerhead for driving nails; on the other, a sharp axehead for splitting laths or smashing through plaster or mortar. Its sixteen-inch handle had a hole drilled in the bottom through which a string was looped. Stamped onto the steel were the trade name "J Sorby" and a trademark immediately identifiable as the capped, grinning, hook-nosed head of Punch the puppet. Brown saw bits of rust and tiny pieces of hair on the axe blade, as well as splotches of blood on the handle, which the gardener thought had been smeared or washed.

Morden College was not a college at all, but a magnificent almshouse built in 1695, to a design attributed to Christopher Wren, by a very wealthy merchant to house his aged, distressed, and bankrupt fellows. It still served that purpose in 1871. West of Morden College lay Blackheath; east lay Kidbrooke Lane. Only a public footpath fenced off from the edge of the college grounds connected the two. Brown found the hammer five yards from that footpath. If this hammer was indeed the instrument of assault— and no one doubted that it was—then the attacker who carried it was clearly familiar with the shortcuts and byways of the area. And if the woman's attacker had thrown it here, he had held on to it for some time, running a mile and a half before jettisoning it at this point, a hundred yards before the footpath opened upon the busier precincts of Blackheath. He was obviously headed for the metropolis: for Blackheath, Greenwich, or Deptford—perhaps even across the Thames for London.

Thomas Brown carefully took up the hammer and carried it to his neighbor, Thomas Hodge, a sergeant in R Division. Hodge, however, was sleeping and so Brown entrusted the hammer to his wife, who gave it to Hodge at nine that night. Hodge then rushed it to the station at Lee, where the inspector on duty passed it quickly up the chain of command.

As of that Thursday morning, however, the chain of command had changed. Given the enormity and brutality of this crime, certain to become murder, and the public attention it attracted from the start, Commissioner of the Metropolitan Police Edmund Henderson had ordered Scotland Yard to get involved. And so Detective Superintendent Adolphus "Dolly" Williamson followed the usual protocol at the time, assigning two men—one inspector and one sergeant—to the case. Detective Inspector John Mulvany was therefore now in charge of the investigation. Mulvany, a forty-two-year-old native Londoner, the son of an Irish servant, had joined the force in 1848. He was appointed to Scotland Yard in 1864 and became an inspector in 1869. As a detective he had investigated burglaries, frauds, and mail thefts; he had helped break up a counterfeiting ring; he had chased Irish revolution-aries—Fenians—in Liverpool and Paris. But he had never been assigned to such a high-profile case as this one: Dolly Williamson was clearly offering him the opportunity to make a name for himself. Mulvany would have the full resources of R Division at his command. He and Superintendent Griffin, roughly the same age, and following similar trajectories in their Metropolitan Police careers, would quickly develop an effective working partnership with each other. Mulvany reported not to Griffin, however, but to Dolly Williamson at Scotland Yard, and through Williamson Mulvany answered to Commissioner Henderson. Assisting Mul-vany was Detective Sergeant Edward Sayer.

Mulvany had already been to Eltham that afternoon, to look over the site of the assault. He also visited Eltham police station to look over the evidence there. The woman's keys he brought back with him to Scotland Yard. He deduced that they fit boxes holding her private possessions, and he wanted to see those possessions as soon as she was identified. And he also brought with him the dog whistle, obviously finding it much more interesting as evidence than the Eltham police had. Indeed he would, the next day, show it to his supervisor, Dolly Williamson. The rest of the evidence at Eltham—hat, gloves, purse, money, locket—he left behind. The evidence at Lee, which Mulvany must also have viewed before the plasterer's hammer arrived—the dress, coat, petticoats, and the stained cloth—also remained at the station.

The hammer, on the other hand, the inspector at Lee station wrapped up in paper, carried to Scotland Yard, and personally delivered into the hands of Inspector Mulvany. Until that moment, the investigation was largely limited to facilitating the viewing of the evidence and the woman's battered and comatose body, and placarding the metropolis with descriptions of the crime and of the woman. Once Mulvany held the suspected weapon, the investigation broadened. For one thing, even though the hammer appeared not to have been used for construction, the fact that the weapon was a tool raised the possibility that the assailant was actually a plasterer who, perhaps, had come upon the woman while coming to or leaving work. As it happened, plasterers had been at work building cottages just a quarter mile from the place of assault. They would have to be questioned. Also, the hammer had quite likely been purchased someplace in or near R District. Officers quickly fanned out to inquire at every ironmonger's shop in the area. At the same time, identifying marks on the hammer allowed for a more focused search: the person or persons who supplied London with J Sorby tools could be found, through them the ironmongers they supplied—and through those ironmongers, hopefully, the names of specific purchasers. It was now possible to track down the assailant even before the victim's identity was known.

The outrage at Kidbrooke Lane quickly became national news, competing in the newspapers for public attention with the great story of early 1871—the rise, and now the fall, of the radical Commune in Paris, born in the wake of the Franco-Prussian War, and the collapse of the Second Empire (and the exile, incidentally, of ex-Emperor Napoleon III to nearby Chislehurst). In that last week of April 1871 the days of the Commune were clearly numbered, and the London newspapers flooded the public with telegraphed, and thus astoundingly current, reports of the beginnings of the Commune's death agony.

Among these pages of reports appeared first paragraphs and then columns on the Kidbrooke assault. The first reports appeared the day after PC Gunn's discovery; then and over the following days, reporters scrambled to make sense of the mystery and to identify the battered woman and her attacker or attackers.* In competing for the latest information, the newspapers couldn't help but report rumors that suggested a solution to the mystery. Rumors were particularly rife that the comatose woman fluttered into enough consciousness to attempt to identify herself or her attacker. A report in the *Daily News*, two days after she was found, held that she had said with astounding coherence to PC Gunn "take hold of my hand; Lord help me; I have been murdered; Mary Smith knows about it." Other reports had her flailing her arms in her hospital bed, as if fending off a phantom attacker, and crying out "Emily, don't beat me so cruelly," or "Oh, Emily—Oh, Ned, don't," or "Oh, Edward, don't murder me!" or simply sighing "Emily" or "Sarah." A number of newspapers claimed that when asked her identity, she weakly uttered "Mary Shru—." (Michael Harris, house surgeon at Guy's, who had placed a watch day and night on the woman, would later maintain on oath that the woman never rallied to speak while under his care.)

---

* Only the London *Times* resisted reporting the crime; its first report appeared on May 1, 1871, five days after the discovery of the victim.

Some of the earliest reports about the victim suggested her assault might somehow be connected with a nearby tragedy. The day after the victim was found, another young woman—another servant—was found dead in a little pond in Lee, less than a mile from Kidbrooke Lane. The earliest speculation held that this woman had died of poisoning, not drowning, and that she carried a number of letters from somebody named Emily—a name that the victim at Guy's was rumored to have uttered. Any fears, however, that a serial killer was on the loose in Kent and preying on working women were scotched by a speedy and effective inquest on the woman found in the pond. Her name was Ann Surridge; she had been a servant in Bromley, due south of Lee. Ann Surridge's utter despondency over a romantic relationship that had soured had so alarmed Ann's employer that she had written to the woman's parents in Peckham, demanding they fetch their daughter home. Before they could do that, however, Ann herself had set off, apparently for home, and on the way there she had thrown herself into the pond and drowned. As for the letters, they were addressed to her family, which included a sister named Emily. The coroner's jury mercifully removed the stigma of suicide by returning the verdict that Ann Surridge had killed herself while in a state of temporary insanity.

Speculations and tales about mysterious happenings on Kidbrooke Lane on the night of April 25 abounded. Most of these focused upon soldiers, a fact not surprising given the presence of nearby Woolwich Arsenal—and the low sexual reputation of the military. And so police suspicion at first centered on Woolwich: several "special officers" were sent there to investigate, and one soldier there was soon arrested in connection with the crime, and just as quickly liberated. A rifleman from Woolwich, claimed another report, had been spotted early that Wednesday morning returning from the direction of Kidbrooke. One particularly elaborate rumor, reported and repeated as fact in a number of newspapers, held that a sergeant of a Scotch regiment entered an Eltham beer shop that

Tuesday night with a young woman in a chocolate dress and a black bonnet embroidered with three roses. Waiting outside was another woman. The three soon left for Kidbrooke Lane—and there, at one in the morning, a laborer heard a woman cry out "Don't murder me, Nelly. Don't murder me, Ned." (That unnamed laborer was never heard from, or heard about, again.)

For the rest of the week, the victim's clothes were on view at Lee police station, and the woman herself on view at Guy's Hospital, for anyone who thought they might identify her as their sister, daughter, wife, or friend. Several came, but no one succeeded in recognizing her for certain. That failure surely raises a question: why hadn't a family member or acquaintance—or even an employer—come forward within hours sure that a person they knew was the one in the hospital? In reporting two possible, but far from certain, identities for the woman, the newspapers suggested one dark answer to that question. If the woman remained unidentified, that must be because she had severed all connections with polite society. She had, in other words, crossed that moral line defined so clearly and absolutely for a woman in English society in 1871: she had fallen. Recently, obviously, she had been a humble servant, respectable in her sphere, but she must have made the fatal decision to trade honest labor for the dubious pleasures of a life of vice: a life once chosen, all respectable Victorians believed, entailed a bitter and inevitable path of degradation, disease—and death.

On Thursday evening, George Evans, a butcher who lived on New Oxford Street, crossed the Thames to view the comatose woman at Guy's Hospital. Evans had read descriptions of her in the papers and thought she might be Mary Caladine, his servant. Caladine had left his home two nights before on an errand, and had never returned. Looking at the smashed, torn, and swollen face of the woman at Guy's, Evans was baffled; the injuries were simply too great to know if Evans was or was not Caladine. Later, when he saw the clothes, he thought they might belong to Caladine. But

again, he could not be certain. Admittedly, he had not known Mary
Caladine very long—two or three weeks, at most. Before that—as
demonstrated by the 1871 census, taken at the beginning of April,
just three weeks before the crime—twenty-one-year-old Mary
Caladine slept not in the attic of Evans's New Oxford Street home,
but in the adjacent slum of St. Giles, as one of the twenty-three
female inmates of the Dudley Street Working Girls' Dormitory.
That Christian charitable institution was devoted specifically to
the task of "reclamation": rescuing the poor women who had once
worked as flower sellers or watercress girls or underpaid and over-
worked seamstresses, but who had been "lured," as the founder of
the house put it, "over the line that bounds virtue from vice in an
unwary moment." The Working Girls' Dormitory offered these
women a rare second chance at respectability, and they were to find
it through a rigorous regimen of Christian rehabilitation. Inmates
were carefully guarded against dissolute behavior and expelled for
drunkenness. They engaged in prayer morning and night, went to
church on Sabbath, and underwent regular proselytizing sessions
with pious and charitable society women. In the time remaining
they trained for domestic service. Thus cleansed and reborn into
respectability, inmates were placed by the matron of the home as
servants in respectable homes. And so in early April Mary Caladine entered George Evans's service. And then, apparently, the
regular, respectable, but drudgery-filled servant's life had proved
too much for her, and she bolted: she had assuredly fallen back into
her vicious ways. And if the woman at Guy's was Mary Caladine,
then she had abruptly paid the ultimate price for her error.

George Evans was not the only one who thought the girl at
Guy's Hospital might be Mary Caladine. The matron of the Dudley
Street Home, Jeanie Kay, came to Guy's on the Friday, also having
read descriptions of the girl in the papers. She entered the ward,
looked at the horror that used to be a human face, and immediately
fainted; she could not identify anyone from that. But she, like
Evans, later thought she recognized the clothing as Mary's.

For three days the London daily newspapers surmised Mary Caladine most likely to be the victim at Guy's Hospital. And then they proffered another, with the sad story of Alice, her surname withheld—withheld, one newspaper claimed, "for the ends of justice"—but the true reason, obviously, was to shield Alice's family from the shame the news would otherwise have heaped upon them. The story of Alice—and of her older sister, Sarah—reads as a melodramatic Victorian morality tale that charts the progress of two young Victorian women as they traverse that absolute moral divide and fall from disgrace to doom. Sarah and Alice had lived with their parents in the Essex countryside, but had made the disastrous choice to move to Woolwich, near the arsenal, obviously captivated by the masculine and military excitements there. And they found in Woolwich exactly what they were looking for; newspaper accounts depict their life there as one of ceaseless temptation by several cavalier and predatory soldiers. The elder sister, Sarah, soon gained the attentions of a carpenter at the arsenal, but rejected these for the less honorable but far more exciting attractions of a soldier. As a result—an almost inevitable result, to any Briton in 1871—she "fell from the path of virtue, and was induced to leave her situation, and live at a house of ill-fame." The virtuous carpenter turned his attentions to Alice, but she, too, wanted more—or less—and rejected him for a soldier. After her sister abandoned her, Alice clung to respectability for a time, seeking shelter, much as Mary Caladine had done, in a Christian home for women, this one in Greenwich. Alice's soldier-friend fusilladed her with letters there and another soldier began to follow her about; Alice told the matron that one of these men had attempted to violate her. The matron of the home implored Alice to leave the soldiers, to wait for a "better offer," to marry a civilian. But she couldn't help it, she told the matron; she liked soldiers best. Alice did manage to find a place as a servant. But soon afterward—on the very same day that Mary Caladine disappeared from her place, as it happens—Alice was visited by a Minnie, an acquaintance of Sarah's, darkly described as "a companion of soldiers at Woolwich." That night, Alice walked away with Minnie and never returned.

The chaplain of the Alice's Greenwich home, as Mary Caladine's employer and matron had done, read the descriptions of the battered woman and went to Guy's to view her. He, like all who had so far looked at her, was baffled by the battered face, but he was half convinced by the clothing that this was the person he knew. Rumors that the victim had been calling out "Sarah," as Alice would to her sister, helped sway him. But he was not certain. The *Standard* carried the story of Alice and Sarah to the latest possible moment on Saturday, with a cliff-hanger: Alice's sister had been found. She had been sought among the "lowest dens of infamy in Woolwich," places where "sat great bloated women, with many young girls, only half-clad, over whom they seemed to exercise either a fascination or a terror." In one of these places the dark companion Minnie was found, and—after a good deal of pressing—she revealed Sarah, who had been hiding there. Sarah was asked what dress Alice had worn when she last saw her and answered "without the slightest prompting, 'a brown barège, trimmed with brown fringe'": a dead match for the victim's dress. At press time Sarah was reportedly on the next train to Guy's—en route to a dramatic denouement.

But none of the newspapers reported on the outcome of that meeting, because by the next day it became very clear that the victim at Guy's was not Alice and was not Mary Caladine. And so Alice and Sarah and Mary disappeared from the newspapers altogether. Whether the woman at Guy's had fallen or not remained an open question.

Mrs. Jane Mary Thomas was alone in the family ironmongery, Samuel Thomas's Mechanical Tool Warehouse, on Saturday evening, April 29; her husband was out on business when the officer came in. By the time the police got to this shop in Deptford, they had already scoured the shops of Lee, Blackheath, Lewisham, and Woolwich. None of them carried a J Sorby #2 plasterer's hammer. Nor was one to be had in Greenwich. The police had tracked down the London agent for J Sorby hammers and learned from him that within R District only a single ironmonger's carried them: this one in the High Street, Deptford. In fact, a Sorby #2 hammer was hanging by a string in the shop window by the door, a string looped and tied exactly like the string on the hammer found at Morden College.

Mrs. Thomas, the officer observed, was a mousy, nervous woman, seemingly unable to give a straight answer to any of his questions. Even though the assault had been all anyone had talked about in the area over the last few days, when he mentioned it to her he was surprised to find that she hadn't heard about it. And so the officer enlightened her, her uneasiness certainly growing as she understood she was somehow involved in this grisly business.

The officer asked to see the ledger. Mrs. Thomas produced it immediately—a book filled with neat entries, all of them written in her hand from receipts she and her husband had made. The two of them scanned the book, Mrs. Thomas running her finger down each page. There had been no sale of a J Sorby hammer at all from the beginning of the year until April 15—when a larger #3 hammer had been sold. Mrs. Thomas's finger slipped ahead and stopped at April 22, exactly a week before: a J Sorby #2 had been sold on that day. The ledger listed items sold and prices, and thus the officer noted the odd fact that the larger #3 hammer sold for two pennies less than the smaller #2. But the ledger did not list names: any information about the buyer would have to come from an eyewitness. Who sold it? he asked her. Either she did or her husband did, Mrs. Thomas told him. And she had absolutely no recollection of selling it herself.

At that moment they were interrupted by a woman who needed a compass saw. Mrs. Thomas went to help, leaving the officer at the counter with the book. He noted other tools sold on the twenty-second—a spoke-shave (a tool for carving wheel-spokes), a chalk-line. And then he left, planning to return in the hope of getting an account of the buyer from Mr. Thomas. But in that he was disappointed. When he poked his head into the shop a third time that evening and finally saw Samuel Thomas, he learned no more from him than from his wife.

Whether they could remember that sale or not, the Thomases were potentially important witnesses—important enough to bring Detective Inspector Mulvany to the shop the next morning to speak with the couple, accompanied by another officer—likely Sergeant Sayer. Mulvany carried with him the hammer found at Morden College. He had the new J Sorby #2 fetched from the shop window; it was a cleaner, sharper twin to the hammer Mulvany held. Mulvany promptly bought it. He then looked over the ledger and saw the entries for hammer sales on the fifteenth and the twenty-second. Mulvany was fairly certain that whoever had walked out of the Thomases's shop eight days before with the #2 J Sorby hammer had committed the assault. And if either Mr. or Mrs. Thomas had sold the hammer, then one of them had almost certainly looked into the eyes of the criminal. But the past few hours had not helped their powers of recollection: they still both claimed to have no memory of the transaction. The police, Mulvany realized, would have to find another eyewitness—if there was one—to the sale. And soon afterward, placards went up all over Deptford, and throughout the district:

Eltham Murder.

—On the evening of Saturday, the 22nd of April, a man purchased a lathing hammer at the shop of Mr. Thomas, High street, Deptford. At the time he did so two or three persons were in the shop, one of whom purchased a spoke-shave. These persons are requested to communicate at once with Superintendent Griffin, Police Station, Blackheath-road, Greenwich.

As Mulvany goaded the memories of the Thomases in Deptford that Sunday morning, something remarkable was happening in

Greenwich and at Kidbrooke Lane. The still-anonymous victim at Guy's, now just barely alive, was becoming—had indeed become—a martyr.

From the time her battered body was discovered, the sympathetic and the curious had gravitated to the crime scene. First came the locals: cottagers of Kidbrooke Lane, elderly residents of Morden College, villagers from Eltham, townspeople from Blackheath and Shooter's Hill. As the story quickly became a national one, people came from farther and farther afield. And on this Sunday, April 30—four days after the discovery—thousands came. Most made their way from London by cheap transport, on the ferry from Hungerford Pier to Greenwich, or on the train from London Bridge to Greenwich station. From there they walked, streaming south in a seemingly unending line, over Greenwich Hill and across Blackheath, by footpath around Morden College, over stiles and through fields, to Kidbrooke Lane. By Sunday, thousands of pilgrims' footprints in the slushy mud had obliterated the crime scene almost completely. Only the spots where she had lain and where she had bled were untrodden—the blood, amazingly, still visible in defiance of rainshowers of the days before. Around those spots the crowd gathered, shoving and jostling to get a look. And, having gotten it, everyone sought out a souvenir—a relic—to take with them. They stripped the landscape bare, taking twigs from the hedge, taking brambles, grass, even dabs of mud. Someone placed a rudely constructed cross at the site, but that memento too was quickly snatched away.

The press, reporting on the thousands making the journey on this day, and the even greater numbers that would come over the next few weeks, were unanimous in their disdain, even their disgust. These "pilgrims," it was obvious, were overwhelmingly working-class. And as far as the newspapers were concerned, their pilgrimage only demonstrated the debased nature of a class that would travel so far on their single day of leisure to experience the cheap thrill of standing in the shoes of a brutal assailant and gawping at a pool of blood. "There are among us," stated an affronted editorialist in the *Daily News*, "large numbers of men and women who have an unmistakable craving for this sort of ghastly stimulus," whose morbid imaginations confer a "fictitious and repulsive interest" upon the scene of the crime. The *Pall Mall Gazette* judged that "the neighborhood of Eltham at present offers a spectacle which is the reverse of hopeful for the prospects of our moral and aesthetic progress." But there was more than morbid thrill-seeking in the minds of the thousands who converged at Kidbrooke on this day, and the tens of thousands more who would come in the following weeks. There was an element of a holy day in their holiday. On this Sunday, no one knew who the woman was. But they did know something about her. They knew she was young and they thought she had been pretty. They knew that she had been decoyed to this place, knew that the hell she endured was monstrous, and knew that she had lain weltering in her own gore for hours, slipping in and out of consciousness, desiring only death. Whoever she was, what she had endured had rendered her larger than life: her overwhelming suffering alone demanded their respect. And they knew more about her than this. They knew that she was one of them, the calluses on her hands and knees the stigmata of hard manual labor. One of their own had stared down an overwhelming horror; she had suffered greatly, and soon she would die.

A writer for the *Daily News* smirked about those converging on Kidbrooke Lane, "If in other and less favoured countries Saints are canonized and relics are manufactured by authority, here in England a free people elects its own saints and manufactures its own relics." Sarcasm aside, this writer was absolutely correct. With their feet, the people had elected one of their own as their secular saint, as a martyr for their age and their condition.

Michael Harris, house surgeon at Guy's hospital, knew the moment he looked upon the woman that she would die. The only question was when, and by this Sunday morning the answer was clear she was fading quickly, and wouldn't live through the day. House surgeons served by the month at Guy's. This was the last day of April. And so Michael Harris, who had watched over her as she lay insensible, who had set watchers over her day and night, realized that morning his patient would die under his care.

Just after nine o'clock on Sunday evening, April 30, the woman—still unidentified—succumbed to her many wounds, got her wish, and died.

Michael Harris's final duty as house surgeon that month, then, was to conduct a post-mortem on her. The cause of death, of course, was obvious. Nonetheless, Dr. Harris made a discovery.

When she died, the woman was two months pregnant.

CHAPTER TWO

JANE

At the same hour, the same minute, that the victim at Guy's quietly died, William Trott sat four miles down-river in his little house in Deptford, reading *Reynolds's Weekly*, his Sunday newspaper. Trott's home was hard by the Thames and by the now-defunct Deptford Dockyard. The river was Trott's life. He was a lighterman, plying the Thames in his bargelike lighter, loading, unloading, transporting goods to and from the many merchant ships undocked and anchored in the river. His father had been a lighterman, his brother was one now, and his sons would become lightermen: throughout the nineteenth century Trott men lived off of the river. Trott *women*, on the other hand, worked on land as servants to the burghers of Greenwich, Dept-ford, and Lewisham: worked, that is, until they found husbands and raised lightermen, laborers, and servants of their own. That was the path Trott's wife, Elizabeth, had taken and the one Trott's daughters would take.

William Trott had certainly heard of the brutal assault in Kidbrooke before this evening: it had been on everyone's mind and everyone's tongue that week in Deptford and on the river. But he had not read any account of the case in the daily newspapers, and he had managed not to see any of the two thousand descriptions of the victim that the police had placarded throughout the metropolis. Now, coming to page five of *Reynolds's*, he finally read of the "Mysterious Outrage at Eltham." The article largely consisted of rumors and speculation. But in the middle was a verbatim copy of the police description of the victim. ". . . Aged about twenty-five years . . . Hair, brown; 5 feet 3 inches in height. Dressed in a chocolate ribbed barege dress, black cloth jacket trimmed with black silk braid, crochet work round the neck; black lace bonnet, with three red roses in it." As he read on, he felt the odd thrill and then horror of recognition. He *knew*. The dress, the jacket, the bonnet—braid, lace, the roses. He was reading a description of his niece, Jane. Those clothes were without question Jane's walking-out clothes. She had worn those clothes exactly a week before, when she had come to the Trotts' house for Sunday tea. And that was the last time that any of the Trotts had seen Jane alive.

"11s. 5d. in a blue leather purse, and a brass clasp and chain. . . ." Every single detail fit, except one. Jane was hardly twenty-three-years old; the police and the doctors were in error there. Jane was a girl, not a woman: sixteen years old. No, seventeen: she had passed if not celebrated her seventeenth birthday just two days before—in her coma, her uncle now knew.

Jane—Jane Maria Clouson, the daughter of his wife's sister—had been deeply attached to her cousin Trotts, and they to her. Indeed, since Jane's mother had died four years before, and since her father and sister had scattered, the Trotts had been the closest thing Jane had to a family. Jane was particularly close to her cousin Charlotte, William's daughter. And when William Trott broke the terrible news to his family that night, Charlotte must have been the most shocked of all. For Charlotte thought she knew where Jane had been last week—thought she had been miles away from Kidbrooke Lane that fatal Tuesday night.

Jane had for two years worked as a servant in Greenwich, but had abruptly left her place three weeks before. After that Jane had been miserable, but when she came to tea at the Trotts' the Sunday before, her mood had altered completely. And that evening Jane revealed to her cousin the secret of her happiness. Her lover, she told Charlotte, had proposed to her. The two were about to run away together and marry. She would therefore be out of contact for some time, but told Charlotte not to worry. Although Jane had sworn Charlotte to secrecy, Charlotte couldn't help it and told her mother. And so, as the Trotts heard the description and knew that it *had* to be Jane, any joy they had felt for her metamorphosed into black foreboding.

William and Elizabeth Trott knew that they had to go to the police in Greenwich to identify their niece, and decided to leave Charlotte behind with her six younger siblings. They sought out items with which they could positively identify Jane, and found two: a scrap of imitation Maltese lace from which Jane's jacket collar had been cut, and a recent photograph taken of her. And then, they seemed to hesitate, perhaps unsure whether or not to wait until morning to speak with the police. In the end, overcome by their need to know for certain that the victim was their niece, they set out with their two items after midnight.

They arrived at Blackheath Road Station before one o'clock and learned that Jane was dead.

If Superintendent Griffin, who lived around the corner from the station, was not awake when they arrived, the Trotts' information, combined with the lace and photograph, was important enough to rouse him, and important enough to impel him to swift action. He dispatched officers to wake the landlord and boarders at 12 Ashburnham Road in Greenwich, where, the Trotts told them, Jane had been living with a friend ever since she left her servant's place. The officers were to find out whether Jane had been living there since the previous Tuesday. She had not. But neither the landlady there, nor Jane's friend, a girl by the name of Emily Wolledge, seemed particularly concerned by her absence. For before this, when she worked, Jane had often spent her days off with her aunt and uncle Trott; everyone at Ashburnham Road simply assumed that Jane had been staying in Deptford.

Superintendent Griffin heard enough from the Trotts to ask them to identify the victim's body. But he decided to wait until morning to do that; he would meet them and their daughter Charlotte and ride with them to Guy's. Inspector Mulvany, who lived in Lambeth and near the hospital, would be there, and the two would interview the Trotts more fully. In the meantime, Griffin ordered the victim's clothes sent from the station house at Lee to Guy's, so that the Trotts could identify those as well.

And so William and Elizabeth Trott returned home, surely spent a sleepless night, and at nine in the morning of the next day—Monday, May Day—they and Charlotte arrived at Guy's with Superintendent Griffin, who asked them first to examine the clothing. There was no question that the dress and petticoats were Jane's. The scrap of imitation Maltese lace they brought matched the lace on her jacket perfectly. The three were then led into the morgue. In the morning light they gazed upon the battered and swollen face of the corpse. Again, there was no doubt: the nose, the mouth—it was Jane. To be absolutely certain, Elizabeth and Charlotte told the police of Jane's birthmark—a mole on her right breast. They looked; it was there.

There was the photograph, as well. It was a small studio portrait—a cabinet card, as it was then called.* In 1871 the cost of a

---

* A copy of a photograph of Jane Maria Clouson—almost certainly the same image that the Trotts brought to the police—exists today in the archives at the Greenwich Heritage Centre, Woolwich. Newspaper advertisements of 1870 demonstrate that at the time, cabinet cards were generally sold in bulk and at relatively low cost: for example, six for 10 shillings, or 12 shillings a dozen. [LC 11 June 1870, 4; NE 4 June 1870, 1.]

photograph had lowered to the point that a servant having her portrait taken was not unheard of. Even a high-quality set of cabinet cards would have cost only a few shillings—and Jane's portrait likely cost less than this. Even so, it would without doubt have been a luxury on a servant's wages. But it would be well within the range, perhaps, of a doting aunt and uncle. In any case, it was clearly Jane's photograph, and it matched the body before them, at least in those few places undistorted by injury. Finally, after five days, the police could assign a human face to the victim's body. From the photograph, Jane Clouson gazed calmly and steadily at them, offering up the barest hint of a Mona Lisa smile. She had dressed for her portrait in all the finery she could muster—frilly cap, lace about her neck, shiny gloves covering her roughened hands. She had obviously aimed to project a sense of independence and maturity. But the shape of her body and her face—particularly of her pudgy cheeks and thick chin—betrayed her. Aunt Trott was later to describe her—obviously approvingly—as "very stout and well-looking." And for all of Jane's poise and placidity in the photograph, there is an unmistakable sense of innocence, in the shining eyes and upon the tentative lips. Jane might pretend to be a woman in the photograph, but the pretense was obvious. The police must have realized how ridiculous they had been in thinking the victim was twenty-three or twenty-five. She was a pretty child in the photograph, and she was a pretty child when she walked to her death.

The Trotts gave Mulvany and Griffin a history to accompany that young face.

The Clousons, Jane's family, were, like the Trotts, intimately connected with the river and with the sea. Jane's father, James, had been a fisherman before taking up work closer to home, as a laborer, first on the Deptford docks, and then aboard passenger steamboats plying the Thames. James's wife, Jane Elizabeth, bore a son who died as an infant, and bore three daughters: Sarah Ann, Jane Maria, and Maria Cecilia. They grew up in Deptford near their Trott cousins. Jane was a "religious and virtuous" and "good handsome" girl, William Trott said, a diligent student both at a local day school and at Sunday school. For the three years after young Maria's birth in 1860 the Clouson family remained intact. After that it fragmented.

In 1863, tuberculosis killed Jane's thirteen-year-old sister, Sarah. In 1866, it killed her mother. And by 1868, James Clouson had abandoned his remaining daughters. He slipped across the Thames to the Isle of Dogs, moved alone into a boardinghouse, and took up employment as a night watchman at a Millwall ironworks. Jane's younger sister, Maria, not old enough to take a place as a servant, was apparently farmed out to others by her father: in the census of April 1871 she is listed as a "visitor" with a family in Croydon. Jane, on the other hand, had turned twelve in 1866; twelve was the usual age at the time for entering domestic service, and so Jane then began her working life, first for a butcher in Deptford, and soon afterward for a sea captain and his family in New Cross. There, she did well and was well liked; nevertheless, after two years, in the spring of 1869, she gave up her place—perhaps because tending to the captain's many children and grandchildren proved overwhelming for her. She quickly took up another place, at 3 London Street, in the commercial heart of Greenwich. Her employers were the Pook family—Ebenezer, Mary, their elder son, Thomas (who had married and had moved away, but often stayed at London Street); their younger son, twenty-year-old Edmund; and Mary's cousin, a woman by the name of Harriet Chaplin.

When Inspector Griffin heard of Ebenezer Pook, his world and Jane's suddenly overlapped. Griffin knew Ebenezer Pook and he knew him well. Ebenezer had been proprietor of a printer's and stationer's shop in Greenwich for the better part of a decade. Ebenezer had in that time become well known—as a successful businessman, as a Freemason in the local lodge, and as a committed member of the congregation of St. Alfege, Greenwich's central and distinctive church, which towered over the Pooks' end of London Street.

Ebenezer Pook's printer's shop occupied the ground floor of 3 London Street, and his family lived on the upper two floors. Ebenezer Pook employed, besides his sons, six men and boys in the shop. But upstairs, in the home, he had employed only a single servant: Jane Clouson. Jane, in other words, toiled at one of the most grueling, and at the same time one of the most common, of mid-Victorian occupations: she was a maid-of-all-work.

Our notions about English and even Victorian domestic service are colored indelibly by those post-Victorian domestic epics *Downton Abbey* and *Upstairs, Downstairs*, with their portrayals of large, variegated, usually busy, and generally cheerful bands of servants. In 1871, such service to the gentry was not rare. But it was not the norm; servants such as Jane Clouson were. This was the time of the rise of the middle class and its attendant cult of respectability, and no family could even begin to consider itself to be middle-class or respectable without employing at least one or two servants. And so, just like hundreds of thousands of English middle-class families, the Pooks had in their maid-of-all-work—their Jane—not simply their means of remaining respectably clean and tidy, but as the primary emblem of their social stature. Of the 1.2 million English servants recorded in the 1871 census, 780,040, or roughly two-thirds, were "general domestics," or maids-of-all-work. Most of these were girls like Jane, who began service at twelve or thirteen; most, though far from all, moved on by their twenties—to marriage, which would by custom end their careers as live-in maids-of-all-work, or to a more specialized and more remunerative level of domestic service.

For nearly all maids-of-all-work, even those lucky enough to work for generous and benevolent employers, life was solitary, poor, nasty, and brutish, if not always short. Maids-of-all-work combined the duties of cook, kitchen maid, housemaid, and even valet, footman, and boot-boy. Isabella Beeton, who with the publication of her *Book of Household Management* in 1861 had become the doyenne of Victorian domestic order, sympathized with their plight.

"The general servant, or maid-of-all work, is perhaps the only one of her class deserving of commiseration," Beeton wrote. "Her life is a solitary one, and in some places, her work is never done." Beeton was not exaggerating. Maids-of-all-work were the foot soldiers in an unceasing battle against grime in a grimy world: taking on the filth of sooty kitchens, and the dust and dirt of drawing-, dining- and bedrooms, dirtiness endlessly replenished by the belching chimneys of British industry. Their battles against dirt typically occupied a maid-of-all-work for eighty hours a week or more: fifteen to eighteen hours a day, with a few hours off on Sundays and some evenings. (The factory laborer of the time, by contrast, averaged fifty-six hours of work a week.) Her duties, as elaborated by Beeton, amounted to a daily marathon of chores: lighting fires; polishing and cleaning the stove, the grates, the windows, and, in that peculiarly Victorian ritual, the front stoop and steps; sweeping and dusting; cleaning the boots; emptying the slops and rinsing the chamber pots; making the beds, setting the table, doing much of the cooking, carrying up meals, serving the family, washing the dishes. Beeton leaves out the task of cleaning the privy or water closet, but this, too, was among the duties of a maid-of-all-work. And while the maid-of-all-work wallowed in filth to satisfy her employers' compulsion, their social imperative, to be clean, she, too, was expected to be clean and so reflect her employer's cleanliness: to be spotless whenever she appeared before master or mistress and whenever she showed herself to visitors. At the sound of her mistress's call or the doorbell, therefore, the maid-of-all-work had to stop whatever she was doing, to quickly wash hands and face, and to cover her dirty clothes with a clean apron before answering.

The maid-of-all-work lived among a family, but she was never part of it. She ate alone, after serving the family its meals; she was expected to do her work out of the family's sight. She generally interacted almost entirely with her mistress, who gave her daily orders and sometimes helped with cooking, making beds, and more delicate housework. (In Jane's case, assistance likely came from

Mary Pook, as well as Mary's cousin Harriet.) To the master and the young masters she was expected to be formal and deferential, never familiar; to remain employed she needed to understand her distinct place on the class divide that existed in every English middle-class household. In terms of knowing who gave and who obeyed orders, that divide was absolute. In terms of relative class standing, however, it was often slight. Beeton notes that the maid-of-all-work "is subject to rougher treatment than either the house- or kitchen-maid" because she has "some small tradesman's wife as her mistress, just a step above her in the social scale"—a type, Beeton asserts, that includes "some very rough specimens of the feminine gender." Whether Mary Pook was such a rough specimen remains to be seen. But it is true that the Pooks were not all that far above the Clousons on the social scale. The Pooks were relatively new to the middle class, Ebenezer having been a skilled laborer—a compositor of type for the *Times*—before moving to Greenwich to start his own business. A dozen years before, then, young Edmund and younger Jane inhabited a similar social world—and had the Pooks lived in Deptford then instead of Southwark, they might have been playmates.

No longer.

If the social distance between them was slight, then the need to observe and preserve that distance became that much greater. Keeping to one's place, to someone like Jane, meant to submitting and adopting the demeanor expected of servants, to be respectful, deferential, and self-effacing. Any hint of friendliness between Jane and Edmund was forbidden. Jane's very uniform, the universal maid's uniform in 1871—black dress, white apron, and white cap—signified her social distance from the family that employed her and demonstrated to all who saw her that she was a part of the household machinery, not a part of the family. And even when Jane had free time and could temporarily free herself from the uniform and the mask of deference, she could never free herself from the need to follow her mistress's strict moral code. Maids-of-all-work were generally prohibited from having "followers," for one thing (though many did, anyway). Any serious moral breach, inside or outside the house—the catastrophe of a pregnancy, for example— would be grounds for instant dismissal, dismissal of course without a written character reference. Indeed, any moral failing on her part could result in a month's notice or a month's pay in lieu of notice. Under these circumstances, whether a servant left a home with or without a character reference was entirely up to the mistress. Without one, a maid-of-all-work's reputation and her chance of obtaining a place with any other respectable family were destroyed. For Jane and her thousands of sisters, the perils of forgetting one's place were extreme.

And Jane Clouson had forgotten her place. Her cousin Charlotte and her aunt Elizabeth knew this.

During almost all of her time at London Street, the Trotts thought, Jane had been dutiful and hardworking, and the Pooks apparently had nothing to complain about—except perhaps about one thing, if they had known it. In the face of an almost certain prohibition against followers, Jane did have one: an otherwise eminently appropriate suitor by the name of James Harley Fletcher, whose widowed mother kept a ham and beef shop around the corner from the Pooks. James Harley Fletcher, however, had the local urge and had gone to sea. And because he was not fated to become the hero of a real-life Victorian melodrama, James Harley Fletcher had remained at sea, and had not returned in the nick of time to save Jane Clouson from her death.

With Fletcher gone, Jane's troubles began. Two or three months before this first day of May, Jane began to speak to her cousin and her aunt about Edmund Pook, not with the respectful deference of a servant, but with the courage and recklessness of a lover. She and Edmund were now keeping company, she told them, walking out whenever they could, up on Blackheath where they could find privacy. (Not surprisingly, none of the Trotts had ever actually seen the two together.) Edmund had given her gifts, she told Charlotte, and she had shown her cousin the locket she said Edmund had given her. This was apparently the locket that Sergeant Haynes had pulled from the wounded girl's jacket pocket.

Aunt Elizabeth, herself once a servant—and one who obviously held stronger ideas about a servant's place than her niece did—disapproved of Jane's behavior and tried repeatedly to dissuade Jane from seeing Edmund. It was obvious to the Trotts that Jane's new relationship did nothing to make her happy: she had been miserable for weeks. And then, on April 13, Jane abruptly left the Pooks and moved in with Emily Wolledge, a friend who had also at one time worked for the Pooks. Jane told Charlotte that she had left by choice: she had given the Pooks a month's notice in March because she had decided to find work in a Deptford factory rather than remain a servant. By hindsight, Jane's explanation didn't make sense. She had said nothing to Charlotte about leaving the Pooks before she actually left. Moreover, she certainly had said nothing about being pregnant, which she had probably realized just about the time she left the Pooks. And Jane was, if anything, even more miserable after she left.

And then her misery vanished, as the Trotts realized on the last day they saw her alive, the Sunday before when Jane had come to their house for tea. Charlotte revealed to Mulvany and Griffin the secret Jane had told her that evening, as the two walked out after tea, through Greenwich, up to Blackheath, and finally into Greenwich Park. "Charlotte," Jane had told her cousin, "you must not be surprised if I am missing for some weeks, for Edmund says I must meet him at Shooter's Hill either tomorrow night or on Tuesday night to arrange to go with him into the country. He says he will have such a deal to tell me, and we shall have to make all the arrangements. He says he is going to take me to a christening with him at St. Ives. Then we shall go somewhere else, to such a nice place, where I shall be so happy; but I am not to tell anyone where I am going or write to anyone for some time, as he does not want anyone to know where I am. You must not be surprised if you miss me for some weeks, but you shall have the first letter I shall write to anyone. Edmund says I shall not want for money, and if it's five pounds I shall have it, and I shall be so happy." Jane then told Charlotte that she was worried about her future relationship with Edmund's parents, particularly with Mary Pook. Mrs. Pook and she had not parted on good terms, Jane said, and she feared that Edmund's mother would not accept a former servant as her daughter-in-law. "I told Edmund," she said, "that after I was married to him I should never speak to his mother." But in speaking to Charlotte, she reconsidered: she knew that Edmund's brother, Thomas, had married a working girl, an apprentice in a dressmaker's shop—and Mrs. Pook had in time become a good mother to her. Perhaps she might grow to accept Jane as well.

The Trotts offered up one other scrap of information to the police—about Jane, Edmund, and about another servant who worked near the Pooks, a girl named Mary Smith. Roughly six weeks before, a childhood friend of Jane's and a neighbor of the Trotts, William Clark, had walked with Jane from the Trotts' in Deptford to the Pooks' in Greenwich. In Greenwich the two had met Mary Smith, and Edmund Pook soon joined them. Edmund, Clark could not but notice, was on very, *very* friendly terms with Mary Smith. Indeed, all three appeared to know one another—very, very well.

The insinuation behind this story was not lost upon Griffin and Mulvany, and the seed of a suspicion that Edmund Pook was a young lothario with a particular weakness for servants was duly planted in their brains. Soon, one of the two had directed their detectives to search for Mary Smith. They quickly discovered that Mary Smith had disappeared from her place of employment—had indeed been missing for at least as long as Jane had been.

Once the Trotts had given Griffin and Mulvany a full portrait of the victim as well as a prime suspect in her murder, and once they arranged that Jane's body would follow them home as soon as it had been examined by a coroner's jury, to remain in their parlor until the funeral, the Trotts returned home. Later that day, William Trott made his way to the newspapers—or, more likely, the newspapers made their way to William Trott. Trott became the first of many in this case to attempt to appeal to public sympathy and shape public opinion through the papers; he fired the first salvo in a war that would be fought as much in the court of public opinion as in a number of courts of law. His primary concern was with the reputation of his murdered niece and her family—*his* family. Since identifying Jane, William must have seen the newspapers and had learned of the many guesses and rumors about the victim's identity. He was particularly alarmed to hear about the story of Alice and Sarah, which first appeared on this day. He made the mistake of thinking that the press had conflated Jane with Alice, and were suggesting that Jane and her sisters had been prostitutes. He obviously feared the public would make the same mistake. "It is false to state," he told reporters, "that she or any of her sisters were ever prostitutes, or were ever in a house of ill fame. I wish the published statement to that effect to be contradicted, if the newspapers will be kind enough to do so, in order that the character of our family may not be damaged. She never had an elder sister a prostitute, and I am sorry that the persons who wrote in some of the papers yesterday* were misled."

To this plea Trott added two tantalizing observations. First, he claimed that he had found several letters from a young man in a box of Jane's things—letters he had handed over to the police, and the names on which he would not reveal, at the request of the police. Second, he told of Mary Smith's mysterious disappearance. With the publication of that information, rumors began to fly, helped along by the previous rumor—if it had been a rumor—that while in Guy's Hospital Jane said *"Mary Smith knows all about it."* That

---

* "Yesterday" only in terms of the time this statement was published, on May 2; the reports of Alice and Sarah actually first appeared on May 1, the same day William Trott spoke with the press.

the press reported those words before Jane's identity and connection with any Mary Smith was discovered was an astounding coincidence—even given the commonality of the girl's name. Or else Michael Harris, resident physician at Guy's, was later wrong when he swore that Jane had not spoken while at the hospital. If that is the case, then Jane Clouson had apparently attempted to point to her killer—although in a fashion both astoundingly coherent for one with her injuries and maddeningly indirect. In any case, publication of the news about Mary Smith the next day had its effect. The public, a day after the police, learned of the prime suspect—a young lothario with a particular weakness for servants, servants who subsequently disappeared.

Although the police were satisfied after the Trotts' identification that their victim was Jane Clouson, the Trotts were not Jane's next of kin: her father, James, was. And so that afternoon the police escorted James Clouson across London Bridge and into the morgue at Guy's to make his own identification of the body. While James Clouson had not seen Jane for two years, he immediately identified the body as his battered, murdered child. Whether he was devastated or rather simply baffled at the sight was left unrecorded.

Superintendent Griffin and Inspector Mulvany had in the meantime returned from the hospital in Southwark to Greenwich. Earlier this day detectives had interviewed the inhabitants of 12 Ashburnham Road, where Jane had spent her last conscious weeks. Superintendent Griffin therefore convened a meeting with Mulvany, Sergeant Sayer, and other detectives to learn of these interviews and to plot out their next steps. His choice of meeting place was surprising—and later, to some, suspicious. The police gathered at the end of London Street, at dining rooms directly across from, and directly in sight of, the Pooks' house. And while consulting, the police enjoyed at least one round of beer. Later, Griffin would tell a reporter that they chose to meet at this place purely for refreshment. But to those who saw them there, they seemed to be celebrating. The proprietor of these dining rooms, as it happens, was

William Orchard, also proprietor of the White Hart public house across the street. Orchard was Ebenezer Pook's next-door neighbor and his good friend. It was through Orchard, certainly, that the Pooks later learned of this conclave. And the Pooks couldn't help but think that the police had put them under surveillance, and that they were celebrating solving the case—before they had solved it.

Drinking their beer, Griffin and Mulvany learned that two of those at Ashburnham Road confirmed and contributed to what they had learned from the Trotts about Jane. Mrs. Matilda Wolledge, in whose room Jane had stayed, knew nothing: she was a residential nurse, and that month she attended day and night to a woman and her newborn twins; because she had been gone, Jane was able to take her space in the bed. Matilda's daughter, Emily, knew much more. She knew that Jane had been depressed, often in tears, since the day she moved in. But she knew the very moment that Jane's mood changed. On Friday, April 21, Jane received a letter in the post. Emily herself had picked it up and handed it to Jane. Emily could not, however, recognize the handwriting or recollect the postmark. Jane, Emily said, opened the letter, read it, immediately and carefully tore it to pieces and dropped the scraps to burn in the kitchen fire under the kettle. Then Jane wrote a letter of her own and went out and posted it herself. After that, she was happy—but about what, Emily did not know, for Jane was, surprisingly, reticent with her. Jane never confided to Emily the writer of the letter or the letter's contents. She never told Emily—or anyone else at Ashburnham Road, for that matter—that she was pregnant. And though Emily knew that Jane had arranged a meeting the following Tuesday evening, Jane never told her where she was going, or whom she was meeting.

Jane revealed both these things, however, to the Wolledges' landlady, Fanny Hamilton. Fanny Hamilton, too, had noted Jane's despondency, but on the Tuesday before her meeting it was long gone, replaced by a bubbling impatient excitement, a great expectation. Jane had arranged to meet someone just after seven that evening, and when she learned that Mrs. Hamilton had to run errands in Deptford just before that, Jane decided to accompany her for no other reason than to pass the time more quickly. The two had left the house at six. Jane, of course, was dressed in her walking-out clothes. They walked to Deptford High Street. There Fanny, most likely at Jane's request, stopped to ask a passing woman the time; the woman consulted a watch and told her it was twenty-three minutes before seven. Soon after that, Jane couldn't contain herself: she told Fanny Hamilton that she was going to meet Edmund Pook at his request; they would meet at the top of Crooms Hill, near Prince Arthur's House, at the edge of Greenwich Park and on the verge of Blackheath.* She and Edmund had great plans to make. Jane would no longer have to look for factory work: Edmund had promised to do for her something much better than that. And with that, three minutes after Fanny had asked the time, they parted, Jane walking toward Blackheath Road. No one in Deptford or Greenwich ever saw her alive after that.

Griffin and Mulvany must have found all of this information about Jane's final conscious days more heady than the beer that they drank. Twelve hours before, the victim's identity had been a complete mystery, but now the evidence was coming in a flood: they knew about Jane; they had a strong suspect in her murder; they had a sense of motive, of means—even of opportunity. True, they had no solid evidence—yet—establishing Pook's relationship with Jane, let alone establishing him as the one who impregnated her. And they had no evidence connecting Pook with the hammer or with Kidbrooke Lane. But they knew

---

* Prince Arthur's House was known before and after the 1860s and 1870s as the Ranger's House, because it generally served as the residence of the ranger of Greenwich Park. Between 1862 and 1873, however, Queen Victoria's third son resided here: hence Prince Arthur's House. Prince Arthur, incidentally, was not in residence at his house on May 1, the day Jane Clouson's body was identified; he was, rather, at Windsor, celebrating his coming of age—his twenty-first birthday—with his family.

enough, certainly, to interview the young man. Later, Inspector Mulvany swore that they had no intention of arresting Edmund Pook when they went to his house to speak with him. Perhaps not. But they certainly had *hopes* of arresting Edmund Pook, either by confronting him with what they knew and forcing him into an incriminating admission, or by discovering incriminating evidence in his house.

But to catch Pook, they knew they had to be careful. They would have to go in quickly, for one thing. By the next morning—perhaps even by that evening—the newspapers would report Jane Clouson's identity. Until then, the police had surprise on their side: Edmund Pook would not know how much they knew, and they could catch him off guard. They might get him to admit to a relationship with Jane, admit to being the father of the child she bore, or admit to writing the letter or to meeting Jane on the Tuesday evening. They knew, as well, that they would have to handle Edmund's father, Ebenezer, very delicately. Ebenezer would be much more valuable as their ally than as an enemy. If they could speak with him alone and convince him of his son's involvement with Jane Clouson, he might assist them in coaxing Edmund to admit to the truth. Griffin and Mulvany therefore decided that they would visit the Pooks alone, without their detectives, and would try to speak to Ebenezer before they spoke with his son. Mulvany, as detective, would do most of the talking; Griffin would do his best to maintain a familiar, sympathetic, and reassuring presence. Then, with Ebenezer's cooperation—or at least without his outright hostility—they would interview Edmund. And whether Edmund incriminated himself or not, they also planned to look at the clothes he wore the previous Tuesday night. It had been six days since the attack at Kidbrooke Lane: plenty of time for Edmund to dispose of bloody clothing. But Edmund didn't yet know he was under suspicion. And he might be careless. They had no search warrant and therefore could only examine Edmund's clothing with Ebenezer's permission, if not Edmund's.* Enlisting the cooperation of Ebenezer—if not Edmund—would therefore be essential.

•———•

At 1:50 that afternoon Superintendent Griffin and Inspector Mulvany crossed London Street and passed through the display windows and into Ebenezer Pook's shop. Griffin could at once see that Ebenezer Pook was not there, but the Pooks' assistants were at work. He asked one if he could see Mr. Pook, and in a few moments Ebenezer Pook came downstairs. Pook of course recognized Griffin but not Mulvany. Introductions were made, hands shaken, and the police asked to speak with the elder Pook privately. Vaguely surprised by the official visit, but polite, Pook asked them up to the family drawing room, where they would be alone. They followed him up. On the stairs, they could hear the chatter and laughter of the Pook family at their midday dinner. The Pook house was quite compact, they must have noticed: prominent in Greenwich by location, but not by size. The house's façade was very narrow, but the shop and the home stretched back. The Pooks resided on the floor above the shop, and slept on the floor above that. There was no garret above that and no closet off the kitchen—none of the usual places for a servant to sleep. The police later learned that sleeping space was so limited that Jane Clouson had not slept alone while working there; rather, in a true breach of decorum, she slept in the same room as a member of the family, Harriet Chaplin, Mary Pook's cousin.

When Ebenezer closed the door of the drawing room, Mulvany wasted no time in getting to the point. They were there, he said to Pook, about the dead girl, the family's former servant, Jane

---

* Search warrants had been required in England for home searches without consent since the precedent-setting decision in the case of *Entick v. Carrington,* handed down in 1765. [Law Reform Commission, 10.]

Clouson. Pook seemed genuinely shocked to hear of this; like everyone else, he knew of the assault at Eltham, but professed to have no inkling that the victim could have been Jane. He was sorry to hear it was so, he said. Mulvany then repeated to the startled and obviously incredulous man every scrap of information, every rumor—everything that they had heard in the past few hours about Edmund's relationship with Jane. People had said, Mulvany told him, that Edmund was on "terms of intimacy" with the girl. And Jane wasn't the only servant he had seduced; Edmund had also been intimate with Mary Smith. With both of them "he did as he liked." Edmund had given Jane a lover's gift, a locket found on her after the attack. Before the murder, the police had learned, Edmund had written a letter to her, and a "respectable" witness had told them that Jane was going to meet Edmund on the night of the attack. And while Mulvany heaped accusations upon Ebenezer's son, Griffin somberly—fussily, Ebenezer thought—repeated, "Ah, it is a very painful matter, but it is too true."

It was false, Ebenezer protested, ridiculous and false. His son was not as the police portrayed him. He was a good boy. And he was a homebody: suffering from epilepsy and subject to fits, he had to be. The family watched him constantly. If he was quiet in his bedroom "a minute longer than we thought he should be," someone went to see if anything was the matter. And for the past two or three weeks, he had been watched particularly carefully by his brother, Thomas. Thomas Pook was married and had his own home in Greenwich, but two or three weeks before, his wife had left him with their daughter for her parents' home in the country; during that time Thomas had stayed at London Street and had shared Edmund's bed. And during the day, according to Ebenezer, the brothers were inseparable. "I am positive it is not the case," he told them. "Edmund is a different sort of boy altogether; it is almost impossible anything of that sort could have gone on without some of us discovering it." As for Jane's abrupt departure from their home, Ebenezer had a simple explanation. Jane was a slovenly girl—very slovenly; they had warned her about it two or three times, and on the last time she herself had decided not to stay, and she left. The family, he said, had had absolutely no idea at the time that Jane was then pregnant.

Having failed utterly at enlisting Ebenezer Pook's support in establishing his son's guilt—indeed, having convinced Pook that the police bore an implacable and irrational hostility toward Edmund—Inspector Mulvany changed his tactics, and asked if he could see Edmund's room and examine his clothes. Ebenezer agreed, certain his son had nothing to hide. He led the police upstairs to a cramped bedroom at the back of the house, and he and Griffin watched Mulvany go to work. Mulvany sifted through clothes in a portmanteau, and examined some coats, trousers, and waistcoats hung on the back of a door. His inspection, Mulvany later admitted, was not as thorough as it could have been: without a search warrant he thought himself on delicate ground. He did, however, scrutinize carefully every item of clothing he saw. He found no blood on any of them.

Ebenezer led them back down to the drawing room and offered them seats while he called his son in. He returned with Edmund, who was smiling, fresh from pleasant conversation. John Mulvany—if not James Griffin—took his first look at their suspect. Edmund was a handsome young man—young, but looking more mature than his twenty years. He was slightly built and his complexion slightly dark, his hair a shock of black curls, parted down the middle. But it was his eyes that captured attention: black, steady, and piercing. He calmly looked each officer in the eye. Mulvany introduced himself and Griffin. "Good Morning, Mr. Griffin, I know you," Edmund said cheerfully, reaching over to shake the superintendent's hand.

"We have come to inform you," said Mulvany, "that the young woman who was injured, and murdered in Kidbrooke Lane, and died in the hospital, was your late servant, Jane Clouson." Both police must have watched Edmund closely, hoping for a flinch. It did not come. Edmund told them that he would answer anything they asked.

"We have heard," Mulvany told him, "that she was a sweetheart of yours, and that you have been corresponding with her."

Edmund denied it instantly. Jane had meant nothing to him, nothing. "She was a dirty girl, and left in consequence."

But, Mulvany told him, "you have corresponded with her; you have written a letter to her."

"No, I have not."

"People say you have."

"Do they? Have you the letter? If it is in my handwriting, that will prove it."

Mulvany took another tack. "You were the last person who was with her on the night she met with her injuries; she left a person to join you on the Tuesday night."

Again, Edmund denied it. He had not seen Jane Clouson since the day she had left her place at the Pooks' three weeks before. But then, he hesitated, turned to his father, whispered a few words the police could not catch, and corrected himself: "Yes, I did though, I saw her in the town, talking to a young *gent*, and I came home and mentioned it"—mentioned it to his brother, Thomas.

As for seeing the girl last week, he could account for his whereabouts every day. Monday he was with Thomas—the two were not apart for more than fifteen or twenty minutes. As usual, his family would not leave him alone because of the danger that he might have a fit. On Tuesday he left work at seven o'clock, as he usually did, and walked, alone, to Lewisham, to see a lady. "Is it necessary to mention her name?" he asked.

"Certainly not," Mulvany and Griffin replied in unison.

Griffin asked him how he walked to Lewisham. Through Greenwich Park, he told them, across by the guns.

"That would bring you by Arthur's House," Griffin pointed out, "where the girl said she would meet you."

Edmund denied arranging any meeting with her. At Lewisham, he told them, he had not actually seen the lady; rather, he had stood on a bridge next to the Plough tavern and simply watched the lady's house for a good forty minutes. He had seen nobody he knew—nobody who could prove he was there. And then he reconsidered. To his father rather than the police, he said, "By-the-bye, I saw our boy delivering a parcel." He had seen the shop's errand-boy when he was returning from Lewisham, returning not via Greenwich Park, but by taking a more direct route through the streets. He had seen the boy, but he was certain the boy had not seen him.

It seemed an unverifiable alibi, and Edmund could see that Mulvany was doubtful. "Call up my brother," he told the detective indignantly. "He will tell you where I was."

Thomas Pook was fetched from the dining room, and Edmund snapped at him, "Tom, where was I on Monday night?"

"You were about the town with me, the whole evening."

"Where was I on Tuesday night?"

"You went to Lewisham."

"What time did I return?"

"About nine o'clock, as usual."

Ebenezer then asked Thomas whether Edmund had told him he had seen Jane with somebody. Thomas instantly answered, "Yes, I remember his coming home, and saying he had seen her with a *swell*."

Mulvany sat all this time near Edmund, staring at the lower legs of his trousers. Upon the left he discerned several tiny spots. "Are those the trousers you wore on that night?" he asked Edmund.

They were. And so Mulvany asked Edmund to produce other clothes he wore that night, item by item. First, the coat. Edmund considered; he had worn an overcoat that night, he said, and then corrected himself: he had worn a blue frock coat. He went and retrieved it, and Mulvany scrutinized it: there was no blood on it that he could see. Then the hat. Edmund left the room and brought back a short-crowned, short-brimmed "wideawake" hat. On it Mulvany discerned minute spots: three of them on the band and brim. At some point while running back and forth for the police, Edmund sarcastically asked them whether they wanted to see the waistcoat and tie he had worn that night. Surprisingly, they told him that they didn't. Finally, Mulvany asked to see the shirt Pook had worn. Edmund left but returned without a shirt—it must have gone out with the wash, he said; his cousin Harriet would know for certain. He walked out and called her, and in a few moments returned and handed a shirt to Mulvany. Mulvany quickly spotted an obvious bloodstain on the right wristband—several spots in a pattern an inch long and three-quarters of an inch wide, clearly originating on the *outside* of the band, and copious enough to have soaked through two or even three folds. Mulvany handed the shirt to Griffin, who agreed it was blood. Mulvany asked Edmund how he had bloodied his shirt. Edmund looked at his hands and held up one to show a tiny scratch. That must have bled onto the cuff. But, Mulvany pointed out, the scratch is on your left hand. The bloodstain is on your right cuff.

Edmund for a moment was baffled and did not reply.

A moment later, he guessed that he must have stained the cuff while he was washing, or by crossing his hands and bleeding on his right wristband with his left hand. The police doubted that the little scratch on his wrist could have bled that much.

Mulvany looked, significantly, at Griffin. This was enough, he said, to take Edmund Pook into custody.

Griffin agreed: "Yes, there is blood on his things."

Mulvany turned to Edmund. "I shall have to take you into custody on suspicion of murdering Jane Maria Clouson."

"Very well," said Edmund. "I shall go anywhere you like with you." His calmness was uncanny, and, to the police, grounds in itself for suspicion.

They arrested him. But in doing so, the Pooks noticed, and the police later admitted, they did not give him the usual caution against self-incrimination.*

Edmund asked the police whether he could bring a book with him, something to read in his cell. The police had no objection, and so he snatched up Charles Dickens's *Pickwick Papers*. Then the police and Edmund formed a procession, Mulvany by Edmund's side, and Griffin behind, and marched downstairs, through the shop. There they paused to wrap hat and shirt into a paper parcel. (Edmund wore the coat.) The Pooks all protested the arrest. Edmund could only repeat that he knew nothing of the girl; she was nothing to him, and it was ridiculous to assert that she was. He never thought of her; he certainly never "sweet-hearted" with her. Mulvany and Griffin marched Edmund up Royal Hill to Blackheath Road Station.

At the station, Inspector Mulvany signed the sheet charging Edmund Walter Pook of London Street, Greenwich, with the willful murder of Jane Maria Clouson, at Eltham, and then they placed Edmund in a little room off of the central chamber. Five minutes later, they could hear him reading aloud his favorite passages from the *Pickwick Papers*.

Later, the metropolitan police would be attacked for their many blunders, from the beginning of their investigation of the death of Jane Clouson to the end. They would be pilloried for their ineptitude by press and public, by lawyers, magistrates, and judges, and even in Parliament. But of all the blunders committed by the police, Superintendent Griffin and Inspector Mulvany's decision to arrest Edmund Pook and charge him with murder on this first day of May was by far their greatest.

---

* Although the police caution against self-incrimination upon the arrest of a suspect was not codified as a legal requirement in England until 1912, by 1871 such a caution was customary and expected police practice, and the existence or non-existence of a police caution, as well as the wording of that caution, could affect the admissibility of a suspect's evidence at trial. [Hostettler 241; "Confessions".]

CHAPTER THREE

TITTLE-TATTLE

With every instinct, and with the benefit of forty-eight years of investigative experience between them, James Griffin and John Mulvany were convinced that the oddly calm and confident young man they had jailed was a killer. He had seduced and impregnated Jane Clouson. He had bought a plasterer's hammer at Samuel Thomas's shop. He had enticed her away from her lodgings and into the countryside with the promise of marriage. And at Kidbrooke Lane, he had smashed and battered her head beyond recognition, and had left her to die in her blood and in the mud.

But they knew as well they had next to no proof for any of this: nothing, certainly, that would ensure Edmund Pook's conviction for murder at trial. The witnesses with whom they had spoken over the past night and day had certainly told them a great deal, enough to suggest that Edmund Pook had had a powerful motive for killing the girl. Aunt Elizabeth Trott, her daughter, Charlotte, and Fanny Hamilton all claimed that the two were lovers. Charlotte further claimed that Edmund had given Jane gifts and had proposed to her; she knew that the two were to meet around the time Jane disappeared to discuss their impending elopement. Fanny Hamilton claimed that on the night of April 25, Jane had left her in Deptford to meet Edmund Pook on Crooms Hill. All of these claims, compounded with evidence that Edmund was romantically involved with another woman—possibly two other women—strongly indicated that his deeply inconvenient attachment to Jane had, most likely with her announcement that she was pregnant, reached the point of crisis. He had a strong reason to want her out of the way, and he had formulated a plan to accomplish exactly that.

But all of this evidence had been heard, not seen. And each claim had originally been made by Jane Clouson herself. Jane was now dead; she could never verify, or correct, or explain any of the statements these witnesses attributed to her. All of this evidence, in other words, was hearsay, and would quite possibly not be admitted in court if the case came to trial. What these witnesses actually had *seen* amounted to very little. William Clark had seen Edmund Pook in a friendly conversation with Jane and another servant. Emily Wolledge had seen Jane open a letter, read and then burn it, and write and send an apparent reply—to whom, Wolledge could not say. And Fanny Hamilton had seen Jane walk away from her on the evening she was attacked in the general direction of Greenwich and Kidbrooke Lane—or in the general direction of a thousand other places.

Besides this, there was Edmund's stained clothing. But that evidence, too, amounted to little at this point. It might be blood or it might not; answering that question would take expert analysis. But even if it was blood, it might well be Edmund's and not Jane's blood—from a scratch, as Edmund claimed, or from his tongue, bitten during an epileptic seizure.

Griffin and Mulvany had hoped, in surprising Edmund Pook at home that afternoon, to parlay all of the evidence they had into something much more substantial and much more likely to lead to a conviction: to an incriminating admission from Edmund, if not an outright confession. And in that, they had failed utterly. The young man from the start had declared his innocence. Worse, they had destroyed any chance of enlisting Ebenezer Pook's cooperation in obtaining an admission from Edmund. Their descending upon his home and hauling away his protesting son had only convinced him of Edmund's innocence, and of Griffin's and Mulvany's malevolence: they, and not his son, were the criminals, as far as Ebenezer Pook was concerned.

Superintendent Griffin and Detective Inspector Mulvany, in short, had rushed to judgment. They had placed themselves and all of R Division in a legally awkward position; they would have to assemble their entire case against Edmund Pook after they had arrested him. And as they assembled that case, they would at each step now be subject to the scrutiny of the press, the public, and to any lawyer Edmund Pook might engage, who, if he was worth his salt, would do his best to attack, discredit—to destroy—every aspect of their theory, and every untested witness they brought forward to support it.

And that lawyer would have an opportunity to challenge the police's case against Edmund not in one but in two courts. The first was the tiny magistrate's court within Greenwich police station. There, the next morning, magistrate Daniel Maude would commence his examination of Edmund Pook to determine whether the evidence warranted committal to Newgate for a trial at the Old Bailey. In the second court would be held the inquest upon Jane's suspicious death. Inquests took place within the jurisdiction of a death and generally in proximity to it: Southwark and not Kidbrooke in Jane's case. And so this court met in a room set aside for the purpose at Guy's Hospital. Soon after Jane died, the deputy coroner for Southwark had begun to assemble a coroner's jury; they would assemble in three days' time.* The jury's first responsibility would be to determine the cause of Jane's death. If they determined she had been murdered, and further determined that Edmund Pook was her murderer, they could commit him for trial on that charge. Edmund, therefore, could be committed for trial twice for the one crime.

But since, as it stood, the evidence the police had very likely would *not* warrant Edmund's indictment, the police needed time to find more. They could give themselves that time by obtaining remands in both courts, on the strength of promises to come up with further and stronger evidence. That would work for a while— but only for a while. Griffin and Mulvany had given the police over as hostages to the limited patience of the magistrate, and to the deputy-coroner and his jury.

For all the pressure they had brought upon themselves by arresting Edmund Pook prematurely, however, Griffin and Mulvany had helped their investigation in at least one way. They had given a name to both the victim and her likely murderer. As the news of their identities spread across town, anyone in southeast London who knew anything about Pook and Clouson was now much more likely to come forward. More than this, they now had a suspect in custody to be identified and two witnesses who might be able to identify him. They were sure that either Samuel or Jane Thomas had sold the plasterer's hammer to Jane's killer. And so James Griffin lost no time in dispatching officers to Deptford to retrieve the two, and in setting up a formal identification.

The procedure that Griffin followed had been established long before the Metropolitan Police existed and dated back to more than a century before, to the heyday of London's early detectives,

---

* The deputy coroner for the Borough of Southwark, William John Payne, would preside over this inquest because the actual coroner for the Borough of Southwark—Payne's father, also William—had by 1871 delegated every one of his responsibilities to his son, who was thus the coroner in all but name. ["Obituary: Mr. Serjeant Payne."]

the Bow Street Runners. In a room in the station Griffin placed Edmund Pook among a couple dozen men, officers in plain clothes for the most part. (If he needed more men, he had many to choose from in the angry crowd that had been growing outside the station since Edmund's arrest.) Their ages and their general appearance weren't very important. When Jane and Samuel Thomas arrived, Mulvany and Griffin both watched while one and then the other walked among the men, instructed to scrutinize every face, and then, if they could, to touch the man who had been in their shop, to make their positive identification tangible. A terrified Jane Thomas walked into the room, stared into each face, touched no one, walked out, and immediately collapsed in a faint.

Her husband bore the ordeal more resolutely, but he, too, recognized no one.

As soon as the shock of seeing the police drag his son away had passed, Ebenezer Pook sought out a lawyer. He rushed from his home on London Street to adjoining Greenwich Road and knocked on the door of Tudor House, home and office of solicitor Henry Pook. Henry Pook, in spite of his name, was not related in any way to Ebenezer Pook and his family—although, as he declared emotionally in court the next day, he would be proud to be connected to such a respectable tradesman's family. The son of an innkeeper, Henry Pook had come to practice law later in life, and had at first found little success in that profession, having suffered bankruptcy at least twice. When he had moved to Greenwich a few years before, however, his business and to some extent his reputation improved. He performed every duty a solicitor could. He handled bankruptcies—with, one assumes, a sensitivity born of experience. He argued the odd divorce case. He once pleaded for the life of a condemned man, and failed. Most of his time, however, he spent in and about Greenwich police court, defending and, more rarely, prosecuting men and women charged with a variety of petty crimes. Henry Pook was a shaggy-haired, bulky bear of a man, and he was a bear in the practice of law: ferocious, reckless, predatory. He defended by offending, lashing out at anyone—witness, opposing counsel, magistrate—whom he saw as acting against his client's interests, with a passionate bluster that made up for any ignorance of legal subtleties.

After Ebenezer Pook angrily related what the police had done that day—invading his home, bullying his son, accusing the son of a crime his father was certain he could not have committed, spiriting him off to jail—Henry Pook agreed to take on the case. He knew it was the legal opportunity of a lifetime. But more than this, Henry Pook took on this case as a sort of moral crusade. From the start, the two older Pooks united to save Edmund, forming a bond that could easily be mistaken for the familial one that their surnames suggested. For from that moment until the final verdict—and beyond—the elder Pooks appeared to the world as seemingly inseparable brothers in arms, united not only in their commitment to save Edmund Pook from the gallows but also in their opposition to the police malevolently set upon putting him there. The Pook party had come into being.

⁘

On May 2, the day after Edmund's arrest, Greenwich police court was crowded beyond capacity; hundreds had come to catch a glimpse of the handsome young monster in their midst. The crowd spilled into the corridors of the police station, out into the yard and into the street. Henry Pook blamed the police for creating this "sensational drama," which, he complained to the magistrate Daniel Maude, they could have avoided altogether by bringing Edmund Pook to Woolwich Police Court, where Maude also sat as magistrate, the day before. "The prisoner was now before him, and that was sufficient," Maude replied. Edmund Pook was far less disturbed at this menacing assembly than his solicitor; he stood in the dock, according to one reporter, with "utmost composure," and as the examination proceeded, listened calmly to each witness with genuine interest. This was, after all, his first opportunity to learn what evidence the police had gathered against him. And what he heard must surely have perplexed and then relieved him: the police had, it seemed, next to nothing.

The apparent paltriness of evidence that day was partially the fault of a timid prosecutor. In England in 1871, prosecution of criminal cases by the state was not automatic. The state could intervene in cases of special importance and appoint a prosecutor. But that took time while the commissioner of police applied to the home secretary. This was certainly an important case, and if Commissioner Edmund Henderson had not yet applied to Home Secretary Henry Bruce, he soon would. More often than not, the police themselves handled prosecutions in police court, and Superintendent Griffin, who had a great deal of courtroom experience, was certainly willing to prosecute this case. But private prosecution—prosecution by the victim or, in this case, by the victim's family—was an option as well, and it was this option that Jane Clouson's family took, engaging a local solicitor by the name of John Lenton Pulling to prosecute*—or, rather, to brief a barrister to prosecute. But since Pulling had agreed to take on the case that very morning, he had had no time to brief a barrister, and from the start he made it clear

---

* Exactly who constituted Jane Clouson's family in this case—who engaged and paid William Lenton Pulling and the barrister he later briefed—is not known for certain. Certainly, the Trotts, the family members closest to Jane by affection, if not by blood, were involved. Perhaps her father, James, was as well. Besides them, Jane had several other aunts and uncles, on both sides of the family. It is difficult to imagine, however, that the Clousons, the Hancocks (on Jane's mother's side), and the Trotts could handle this great expense on their own. In this situation, the great support shown to Jane by the working-class community of South London likely extended beyond the emotional to the financial.

to the magistrate that he was unprepared and that he planned only to present just enough evidence to justify a remand.

Most of the testimony Pulling obtained from the witnesses that day had to do with Jane's injuries, her agony, and her death. PC Gunn and Sergeant Haynes testified to finding the broken girl in Kidbrooke Lane, Thomas Brown about finding the bloody hammer; Michael Harris itemized Jane's many injuries and revealed her pregnancy. None of this connected Edmund with the murder, although Pulling did try to make that connection, asking Harris whether the spots on Edmund's clothing were blood. (Inspector Mulvany had shown him that clothing before the inquest.) But Harris could not say—not unless he examined the spots under a microscope. The magistrate quickly halted this line of questioning altogether, until an expert had had an opportunity to examine the stains.

When the several women in whom Jane had confided her relationship with Edmund came to the witness chair, John Lenton Pulling, reluctant to introduce anything that smacked of hearsay, did not know quite what to do with them. Therefore, they contributed little. Elizabeth Trott spoke of identifying Jane's body. Her daughter Charlotte did not appear at all. Fanny Hamilton spoke of Jane's leaving her on the night of the attack to go to Crooms Hill and meet Edmund. That prompted a sharp question from Henry Pook that forced Hamilton to qualify her statement: "She said she was going to Crooms Hill but I can't say whether she went there or not."

After Fanny Hamilton there appeared the first of many witnesses who came forward to the police in the wake of the discovery that the victim was Jane Clouson. Jane Prosser was a forty-eight-year-old charwoman and costermonger's wife who occasionally worked for the Pooks, assisting Jane with heavy cleaning. She had gotten to know Jane intimately, she claimed to the police. And Jane, Prosser was ready to testify, had confided in her a startling revelation she had kept from everyone else. That revelation Prosser would disclose to the coroner's jury two days later. But John Lenton Pulling was too timid to draw out that hearsay here; Prosser testified to nothing more than the fact that she and Jane were friends.

When John Mulvany took the witness chair, his evidence, which the day before had been strong enough to arrest Edmund Pook, now seemed weak. The stains on Edmund's clothing might be blood; or they might not. And even if they were, they might have come from a scratch, as Edmund Pook had claimed. Mulvany's questioning Edmund about writing a letter to Jane sounded, by Mulvany's retelling, suspiciously like entrapment, especially after Mulvany admitted to Henry Pook that he had failed to caution Edmund against self-incrimination before questioning him. And Mulvany appeared to be holding back exculpatory evidence when, after he had sworn he had told all that he knew, Henry Pook forced him to reveal the Thomases' failure to identify Edmund as the purchaser of the hammer. Mulvany did manage to contribute to the growing public revulsion against Edmund Pook simply by repeating Edmund's cold-hearted response after hearing of Jane's death: "She was a dirty girl, and left in consequence." But callous insensitivity hardly proved Edmund Pook a murderer.*

After the witnesses had testified, the magistrate could not hide his disappointment with their evidence. "There was no evidence whatever at present produced connecting the accused with the murder of the deceased," he admitted. Henry Pook waxed indignant about the police arresting Edmund without basis: If they "had power to take anyone into custody in that manner," he vociferated,

---

* Nothing stoked the public outrage against Edmund Pook and his family more than this slur on Jane Clouson's hygiene, and thus upon her character. Later that month Archibald Taylor, Jane's employer before the Pooks "decoyed" her away, dispatched an indignant letter to the newspapers in response: "I believe a cleaner, more civil, or quieter girl never could be inside a house, and my family, and all who knew her when with me, believe it was her nature to be so. I have seen her many times since she left us, and always saw her clean and respectable." [GDC May 2, 1871, 2; NC May 26, 1871, 6; WDP May 23, 1871, 3.]

"no one would be safe." The magistrate trusted the Metropolitan Police more than the solicitor did, however. He turned to Detective Inspector Mulvany and asked if the police had further evidence. They should have other and stronger evidence within a week, Mulvany assured him. Maude gave them five days, remanding Edmund without the bail that Henry Pook demanded.

And with that, Edmund Pook was removed from the courtroom, and later that day removed to one of Kent's two county jails, the one at Maidstone, thirty miles, an hour and a half by train, away. Edmund Pook would make that journey from prison to police court, where his presence was mandatory, five times. He would grow to hate it. But because of his incarceration, he would not be able to attend a single sitting of the coroner's inquest. His presence there was not required, as the inquest ostensibly focused upon the cause of Jane's death and not the question of his culpability. In actuality, Edmund's guilt or innocence became the central question of the inquest. Ebenezer Pook and Henry Pook would have to fight that battle without him.

<hr/>

The same evening that Edmund was removed to Maidstone jail, the police succeeded in tracking down the mysterious Mary Smith. Mary Smith's friendship with Jane, her alleged intimacy with Edmund Pook, her curious disappearance at the same time Jane disappeared, and even the rumors that Jane had while at Guy's Hospital uttered "Mary Smith knows all about it," had led to police to expect that Smith would prove a powerful witness for the prosecution. Their expectations were quickly dashed. They discovered Smith in Tottenham, north of London. Her sudden disappearance, they learned, had nothing to do with Jane or with Edmund; she had simply tired of her place in Greenwich and had returned home. Smith denied she had ever been intimate with Edmund Pook and she was not aware of any intimacy between Pook and Jane Clouson.

In short, she knew nothing and could testify to nothing. Mary Smith never appeared as a witness in the case.

As with Mary Smith, so with William Clark. His account of witnessing the fraternization between Edmund Pook, Jane Clouson, and Mary Smith completely lost its lurid suggestiveness with Smith's denials. William Clark, too, never testified.

But if the police lost two witnesses, they gained three.

The approaches to Guy's Hospital two days later, on May 4, might not have been as crowded with the curious and hostile as had the approaches to Greenwich Police Court. But the impromptu court-room was crowded to overflowing, the public filling whatever seats were not taken by the doctors of Guy's, whose curiosity in the case surpassed the strictly professional. The inquest began at noon, and Deputy Coroner John William Payne began it in the traditional way—with the focus squarely upon the victim. After swearing in the twenty-two members of the jury,* Payne led them out of the courtroom and down to the mortuary, where they gazed upon Jane Clouson's beaten body. Once they had seen their fill, they left Jane's body in the hands of undertaker William Billington, who set it in a small and ornately appointed elm coffin, sealed it, and conveyed it from Southwark to the Trotts' little parlor in Deptford. Jane's funeral was set for the following Monday.

As he had at police court, Henry Pook appeared in Edmund's defense. John Lenton Pulling appeared for the prosecution. But Pulling now was silent; he had briefed a barrister to undertake the

---

* Twenty-two members sounds excessive, and at the time a reporter for the *Times* deemed this jury "unusually large" [May 26, 1871, 12]. But in 1871 up to twenty-three members could sit on coroner's juries (and on grand juries). No matter how large the jury, twelve votes alone were needed to reach a decision; limiting the jury to twenty-three members would ensure that those twelve constituted the majority.

prosecution, and that barrister, William Willis, now took charge. Willis, a rising star who would become Queen's counsel, a member of Parliament, and a county judge, was altogether more capable and comfortable in a courtroom than Pulling. And he had a reputation for partisan combativeness that Henry Pook surely respected.

After PC Gunn, Sergeant Haynes, and the physician Michael Harris repeated their police court testimony, the focus of the inquest turned to the suspect. Willis, unlike Pulling, had no qualms whatsoever about introducing the hearsay evidence against him. When Elizabeth Trott took the witness box, he lost no time in leading her to declare of Jane, "I have heard her say that she was keeping company with her young master, Mr. Edmund Walter Pook." Her daughter Charlotte did testify this time, and expounded upon the elaborate promises of marriage and a trip to the countryside that Jane said Edmund had made to coax her to meet him. Fanny Hamilton repeated her conversation with Jane the evening the girl disappeared: Jane had told Hamilton that she was leaving to meet Edmund, and said, "I'm not going to work at the machine now, for he is going to do something better for me." Beyond pressing these witnesses to admit that they had never actually seen Jane together with Edmund, Henry Pook allowed all of this testimony to pass. But then Jane Prosser took the witness box and disclosed her startling revelation: Jane, she claimed, had told her three months before that she was pregnant and that Edmund was the father.* To this Henry Pook objected passionately. Deputy Coroner Payne immediately overruled him. "When he makes a preconcerted arrangement," Payne told Henry Pook, "it is evidence"—whether hearsay or not.

After Jane's confidantes spoke, a nervously grinning young man took the witness chair. This was Thomas Lazell, the market gardener who lived in a cottage on Kidbrooke Lane, and who had

---

* Prosser testified consistently that Jane had confided her pregnancy to her three months before. Her dating of Jane's revelation is, to say the least, problematic, given the physician Michael Harris's testimony that Jane Clouson was only two months pregnant at the time of her death.

on the morning after the attack stumbled upon the farm laborer with the stained cloth. At that time he thought he knew nothing about the murder. But the day before the inquest, after he had learned of Edmund Pook's arrest, Lazell had come to the police with a stunning revelation: he could place Edmund Pook near Kidbrooke Lane on the evening of the murder. At about seven o'clock, as he was making his way from Kidbrooke to Greenwich and his father's house, cutting through a barn field between the lane and Morden College, he passed them: a young couple, the man with his arm wrapped about the woman's waist. They were heading toward Kidbrooke Lane. Lazell had spent a great deal of time in Greenwich, and he had seen Edmund Pook more than once emerging from his family's printing shop: he knew Pook by name and by sight. And the man he passed in the barn field, he was positive, was Edmund Pook.

Thomas Lazell proved to be an atrocious witness. He was, for one thing, easily cowed by authority. And he was cursed by a defect of the lip that made him seem to speak with what one reporter called a "smirking sneer"; that, and a habit of chuckling while nervous, prompted William Payne to admonish him in the midst of his testimony: "Don't laugh. It's not a laughing matter."

"It's not a laugh," William Willis interposed. "It's his manner."

In spite of its presentation, however, his revelation was "the most important evidence we have had," according to the deputy coroner. Henry Pook was well aware of its danger. "You have the audacity to come here with this pretty tale," he snarled at Lazell. He attacked him for waiting so long before going to the police and for presuming to be able to identify Edmund at all: he had only seen him "twice in a twelvemonth," and had never spoken with him. For all of the solicitor's bullying, however, Thomas Lazell remained adamant: the man he had seen that night was Edmund Pook.

Two other new witnesses testified after Lazell. Elizabeth Plane, a neighbor of the Pooks and the proprietress of a confectioners' shop at the bottom of Royal Hill, had seen Edmund Pook, whom she knew well, enter her shop on an evening around the date of the murder; she was not sure about the exact day. Testifying after her was a young woman named Louisa Billington, who was also in the shop that evening. (By curious coincidence, Louisa Billington happened to be the daughter of William Billington, then undertaking the conveyance of Jane's body to Deptford.) Louisa also knew Edmund Pook, and also wasn't sure what night it was that she saw him. Edmund entered the shop panting for breath, excited. "You seem rather warm," Mrs. Plane said to him. "I have run from the Lewisham Road," he replied. He then asked for a clothes brush, which he used to brush his clothes, concentrating upon the mud on one of his trouser legs. He had little success, and told them he would wash off the rest with a sponge. Then he bought a bag of lozenges, offered them in vain to Louisa Billington, and left.

At the next sitting of the inquest at Guy's Hospital, another witness, Julius Bendixen, who entered Mrs. Plane's shop just as Edmund was leaving, would fix the time and date of this interaction to just after nine o'clock on the night of the murder. And two more witnesses—Louisa's sister, Priscilla, and the gentleman, John Barr, with whom she was walking out—would later swear that between eight-thirty and nine that evening they saw Edmund running into Greenwich from the south, down Royal Hill. The police and the prosecution obviously introduced all of this evidence to establish a plausible timeline: Edmund Pook had a good two hours to meet Jane Clouson, walk with her to Kidbrooke Lane, kill her, and rush back to Greenwich. Beyond that, however, this was evidence of dubious value, for the evidence supported Edmund's alibi—that he had been in Lewisham—as much as it supported the police's theory. A man running from Lewisham to Greenwich would also quite possibly return via Royal Hill. True, the presence of mud on Edmund's trousers might suggest that he came from perpetually muddy Kidbrooke Lane and not from Lewisham. But it would be nearly impossible to prove, a week and more after the fact, that the entire route from Lewisham to Greenwich had been bone dry.

Would-be witnesses flowed into the police station on Greenwich's Blackheath Road that first week of May in numbers that Superintendent Griffin would later declare "overwhelmed" R Division. And on May 5 Deptford ironmonger William Sparshott became one of the many, approaching the officer on duty hesitantly, not at all sure whether what he had witnessed was important or not. Sparshott was Samuel Thomas's colleague and rival, his own shop located just fifty yards up Deptford High Street from Thomas's. At around eight-thirty on the evening of Monday, April 24—the night before Jane was attacked—Sparshott was standing in his shop doorway when a young man wearing a black coat and a low-crowned hat approached from the south. He told Sparshott that he was a performer at the nearby Deptford Literary Institution, and that he needed a little axe as a prop for a performance. They went into the shop; Sparshott consulted with his wife, and she went to a drawer behind the counter, from which she pulled out a little cook's chopper. The young man looked it over and decided it would not do; it was too expensive at two shillings and sixpence, and besides it was not an axe at all. Sparshott walked with the young man to the door, suggested that he try Thomas's shop, and pointed it out. The young man set off in that direction. It was dark outside at the time, but Sparshott's gaslights were lit and were bright, and he had had an excellent look at the young man's face. He thought that he could identify the man who came into his shop, if given the chance.

But he was not given the chance. The officer on duty who listened to this tale must have been impressed by Sparshott's power of recollection, so antithetical to those of the muddleheaded Thomases. But for all its specificity, his information was worthless, the officer knew: the murder weapon, the police were sure, had not been purchased on that Monday night, but three days before. Mrs. Thomas, for all her forgetfulness, had clearly recorded Friday, April 21, as the date of its sale. More than this, another witness had come forward to corroborate that the hammer was sold on the Friday. James Conway, a young boilermaker from Deptford, claimed that he had been at Samuel Thomas's shop on the twenty-first. Both Samuel and Jane Thomas were there at the time, he had said, and Conway had then seen a young man—"something like a gentleman," not a laborer—in a bluish coat and a low-crowned hat, perusing, testing a hammer. He had not remained in the shop to see whether the man bought that hammer. But he had gotten close to the man, had brushed up against him. And he did get a glimpse of the man's face, from the side. He might be able to identify him.

James Conway corroborated the sale: he was an important witness. William Sparshott was not. James Conway had been ordered to return to the station the next day to try to identify Edmund Pook when he came up from Maidstone for the resumption of his examination. William Sparshott, on the other hand, was thanked and sent on his way.

Meanwhile, across the Thames and across the metropolis, in his home laboratory at the edge of Regent's Park, Dr. Henry Letheby scrutinized Edmund Pook's clothing. Two days before, Inspector Mulvany had personally knocked on Letheby's door bearing in a parcel Edmund's trousers, shirt, hat, and coat; yesterday Mulvany returned with his boots, the clothes brush from Mrs. Plane's that he had used to wipe his trousers, the J Sorby hammer, and two items the coroner had ordered sent from Guy's Hospital: a little packet containing a lock of Jane's hair, and, in a white jar sealed and wrapped in paper, Jane's uterus, from which the fetus had been removed.

Letheby was a natural choice to perform the analysis of the spots on Edmund's clothing. He was the chair of chemistry at London Hospital, Medical Officer of Health for the City of London, and a highly reputed expert witness, having appeared in dozens of criminal trials over the last quarter century. Letheby's forensic expertise extended to poison as well as to blood, and if there was any hint that poison was involved in this case, he would certainly have paid a great deal more attention to Jane's uterus. As it was, he simply gave it a cursory glance, noted signs of previous pregnancy and present decomposition, and set it aside. He took up Edmund's trousers and saw on them what the police had seen: a number of spots, most of them clustered on the lower front part of the left leg. He cut from the trousers seven of these and examined each one under a microscope. They appeared as a dried jelly clinging to the mesh of the fabric. If this was blood, it had, with smearing or with time, lost its corpuscular structure. He might be looking not at blood, but at rust, spores, fruit stains: any number of substances. He had a surer test for blood than this, one so innovative in 1871 that few had either the equipment or the experience to conduct it: spectroscopic analysis.

Letheby scraped a dusting of powder from one of the tiny spots onto a watch-glass, and to this added a single drop of water. The dust began to dissolve. That indicated to him that these stains, if blood, were relatively fresh; in his experience bloodstains more than two weeks old—and even less than two weeks old in the acidic atmosphere of London—would not dissolve in water. With a pipette Letheby transferred a tiny bit of this solution into a short length of glass barometer tubing. He sealed the tube at both ends and let it stand for a while so that any sediment dropped. Then he set it upon a microscope stand. The eyepiece of the microscope had been modified with a prism. Shining a bright light through the solution, Letheby adjusted a slit until he could see the rainbow-colored spectrum. Interspersed among the lines of color were a number of dark bands. These bands—absorption lines—signified, scientists had come to realize, the chemical composition of the substance through which the light passed. In this case, Letheby saw a thick band interrupting the red part of the spectrum and two more bands within the green. That suggested to him blood—blood exposed to air. But other substances could give off similar spectra. And so Letheby opened the little glass tube and added a tiny bit of ammonia to the solution. Now, the dark band in the red disappeared and the two bands in the green grew darker. Letheby then added a bit of citric acid to the solution: the dark bands in the green faded. Finally, he added a tiny crystal of protosulphate of iron to the solution and let that act upon the solution. Now, he saw a single dark band in the green. Thus ringing the changes with these chemical reagents, Letheby simulated blood in its various states: hemoglobin (*cruorin*, Letheby called it) both refreshed by and depleted of oxygen, and then, with the addition of iron, hematin. At each stage the solution changed color, from scarlet to purple to brown, each time revealing a distinct and recognizable spectrum. It was as if he had opened a safe with the correct combination: he was positive that these stains were blood.

Letheby was able to draw a further distinction by examining under the microscope the blood on Edmund's shirt and on his hat. That blood had coagulated where it had fallen, unlike the blood on Edmund's trousers. That in itself led Letheby to conclude that someone had attempted to wash or wipe away the blood on the trousers. These intact cells on the shirt and hat clearly lacked a nucleus. He realized, therefore, that this blood was from a mammal, not a fish, bird, or reptile. That he could swear to—but no more.

In both knowledge and technique, Henry Letheby was at the vanguard in forensic detection of blood in 1871. But in 1871 the separate human blood types O, A, B, and AB, as well as conclusive methods to distinguish between blood cells of different mammalian species, were still unknown; these things would not be discovered for another thirty years. As far as Henry Letheby could tell, the blood on Edmund's clothing might be Jane Clouson's blood. Then again, it might be Edmund Pook's. Or it might be the blood of a dog, or even blood splashed on Edmund's clothes from a rare cut of roast beef.

Letheby examined the other items Mulvany had brought him. He found no blood on the boots, and was not surprised: if they had been polished with blacking during the past few days, any blood on them would have been destroyed. There was no blood on the coat, either, only stains of printer's ink. Nor was there any discernible blood on the clothes brush. Letheby did, however, find blood on the hammer, both on the axe blade and on its handle. And he found more: at the hammerhead, under a layer of mud, five fragments of hair, all between a quarter and half an inch long. Letheby placed these between a thin circular glass slide and a thinner glass cover and compared them under the microscope to hairs cut from Jane Clouson's head. They were identical in color and in structure. They might not all be Jane's, but they could be. More than this, Letheby had discovered, while scrutinizing Edmund's trousers, another hair, seven and a half inches long, matted into the fabric on the inside left leg between knee and crotch. Under the microscope that hair, too, matched Jane's, both in color and in structure.

As Edmund Pook, handcuffed and under guard, made the journey from Maidstone to Greenwich Police Court on Saturday morning, May 6, he learned what it was like to be hated. At every railway station from Dartford on—Crayford, Bexley, Sidcup, Eltham, Lee, and New Cross—howling, hissing mobs assembled to taunt him. "Ah, now he is off to Calcraft," a man at Crayford station shouted at Pook, predicting his demise at the hands of Newgate's notorious executioner. In a letter he later wrote to his father that quickly found its way into the newspapers, Edmund admitted his terror at the ordeal. He was certain as well that the demonstrations were not spontaneous but concerted. "I am most certainly astonished at the people," he wrote, "as they do not know a single thing about my defense, and believe all the tissue of lies the prosecution have brought forward as gospel truth." They were being manipulated, he claimed, by the stationmasters and porters along the route, who were telegraphing the news of his journey up the line, and collecting mobs from nearby factories and neighborhoods to taunt him. Surprisingly, Edmund exempted the police, his usual enemies, from this conspiracy; indeed, he was thankful to them for protecting him. However, he wrote to his father, "I am not disposed to extend those thanks to Inspector Mulvany or to Mr. Superintendent Griffin."

After braving the howling mobs at each railway station and then plunging into the largest mob of all outside Greenwich police station, Edmund faced one more ordeal. His solicitor, Henry Pook, met him inside the police station and—ever mindful of the legal importance of a client's good appearance in the courtroom—was about to order a hairdresser to the station to give his client a shave and haircut, when the officer guarding Edmund stopped him: that could not be done without Superintendent Griffin's permission. And Superintendent Griffin was not at that moment at the station. Henry Pook instantly burst into a tirade, heaping obloquy upon Griffin and, for good measure, upon Inspector Mulvany. Word was sent to Griffin, who lived nearby, and he ordered that Edmund be locked in a cell. Henry Pook, to prevent this, lurched threateningly at the officer, and then relented.

Henry Pook's eruption later earned him his own appearance in court, charged with violent and indecent behavior.

In the courtroom, Edmund Pook learned that he had been put through all of this turmoil for nothing, for no witnesses would appear that day. The government had agreed that this case deserved a public prosecutor. And so while Pulling and Willis continued to attend the examination on behalf of Jane's family, they now ceded active prosecution to Harry Poland, acting on behalf of the Treasury. Poland was one of London's best-known prosecutors. He had an unmatched knowledge of criminal law, and his reputation for doggedness and patience in the courtroom later earned him the epithet "the sleuth-hound of the Treasury." But since he had just that morning taken on the case, he had no intention of rushing uninformed into his examination of witnesses as John Lenton Pulling had done. Instead, he asked the magistrate for an immediate remand.

At this, Henry Pook again exploded. "Ignorant constables," he fulminated, were stigmatizing Edmund Pook in jailing him for nothing—nothing besides their own suspicions and a mass of hearsay, "the tittle-tattle of one woman to another." If Poland did not have witnesses to call, Henry Pook did—witnesses, Henry Pook claimed, who would not only establish Edmund Pook's innocence, but would set the police on the track of the actual murderer.

The magistrate disregarded his outburst. Refusing to hear defense witnesses until the prosecution had made its case, Daniel Maude remanded Pook to Maidstone for another week. Henry Pook begged Maude in that case to order Superintendent Griffin to "not be running about in other directions merely to fix the guilt on this young man" and instead to investigate the claim of a witness who had come to him with knowledge about the purchaser of the murder weapon. While Henry Pook did not elaborate upon this in court, he later shared with police his knowledge of a man named Ormond Yearsley, who had come to the solicitor claiming that he had been at the ironmonger's shop on the evening of Friday, April 21, and had seen the man who bought the hammer that evening. That man was older than Edmund, between twenty-six and thirty-four; he had light hair; he was dressed as a laborer. Henry Pook had taken Yearsley to see Edmund in custody; Yearsley was positive that Pook was not the man he had seen in the shop that night. Yearsley's description of the man who purchased the hammer, Henry Pook was sure, would lead the police to Jane Clouson's actual murderer.

Harry Poland assured Henry Pook that the Treasury would pay careful attention to any information the solicitor could give them. And with that, Edmund Pook was removed from the courtroom to again endure the ordeal of transit to Maidstone.

As the courtroom emptied, Henry Pook introduced to Superintendent Griffin a man named Henry Humphreys. Humphreys had worked as a compositor for Ebenezer Pook, but had left three months before. He knew all about the locket that Sergeant Haynes had removed from the comatose girl. With some embarrassment he confessed to Griffin that it was he, and not Edmund Pook, who had bought that locket from a local Greenwich silversmith, and he who had given the locket to Jane Clouson.

Griffin could not but be surprised. Henry Humphreys was thirty years old and married; he hardly seemed the type to be proffering tokens of affection to a sixteen-year-old girl. Griffin immediately ordered Sergeant Haynes to accompany Humphreys to the silversmith's shop. There, the daughter of the proprietor immediately recognized Humphreys as the one to whom she had sold the locket.

This revelation about the little locket quickly made its way to the newspapers and amounted to a serious setback for the police theory and the prosecution's case. It hinted at another possible suspect for Jane's murder—although neither police nor prosecution nor defense seriously considered that Humphreys killed Jane Clouson. More than this, it raised serious questions about what Henry Pook had dismissed as "tittle-tattle": all that witnesses professed Jane had told them. Charlotte had sworn that Jane had told her Edmund Pook had given her that locket. Either Charlotte had misunderstood what Jane had said to her or Jane had lied to her cousin. In either case, Henry Humphreys's revelation laid bare the shortcomings of hearsay evidence. "Thus," reported one newspaper, "one link of the supposed chain of evidence against the person now in custody appears to be broken."

As Henry Pook's behavior at Blackheath Road police station demonstrated, hostility between him and the police had grown to a dangerous and debilitating intensity. To his credit, the solicitor attempted to diffuse that hostility, inviting Superintendent Griffin to come to Tudor House the next day to discuss the case. To his credit, James Griffin accepted. They met late at night, between ten and midnight—a time suggesting that their get-together was more social than professional, befitting the fact that the two men were neighbors and long-standing acquaintances, if not exactly friends. Henry Pook sat James Griffin down and offered him a glass of whiskey and water. The two conversed about the witnesses for the defense that Henry Pook had been prevented from introducing. Griffin had another whiskey and water and left Tudor House in a cab at two in the morning.

If either man parted under the impression that the two had reached a new accord, he would be fully disabused of it the next day.

On Monday, May 8, at three o'clock and under black, threatening skies, the coffin holding Jane Clouson's body was carried from the Trotts' parlor to a horse-drawn hearse. Behind that hearse at least eight mourning coaches waited to carry Jane's friends and family on the slow ride two miles south to the cemetery outside the village of Brockley. In its opulence this cortège was an unprecedented sight on run-down Old King Street, even by mid-Victorian standards, when magnificent funerals were the norm even among the working class, who, like everyone else at the time, believed that a respectable life demanded a visibly respectable final act. Even those of slight means managed to produce the pittance each week for "club" money for burial insurance—generally called "life insurance" at the time—to give them enough to support a decent ceremony. There is no record of the teenage Jane making such payments, and even if she had, any benefit she might have obtained in that way could hardly have supported the trappings now on display. That the family and friends filling up the eight mourning coaches could alone afford this expense is doubtful as well, and again suggests that Jane's community supported her memory with their pennies as well as their pity.

Thousands lined the route through Deptford, many of them practicing the workingman's ritual of Saint Monday and skipping work altogether in order to see Jane buried. Behind them, many of the shops had been shuttered against the crowds; the others, with the exception of the public houses, did little business. Policemen took up positions at intervals to control the crowds, and four mounted offers led the cortège to ensure a clear passage. As the procession made its way to the end of the High Street, the rain began to fall in torrents. But the thousands remained in place.

As they entered the cemetery, where thousands more waited chilled and dripping, the storm reached its thunderous climax. The fortunate—women and children, mostly—found shelter in the tiny and over-packed chapel, into which eight men bore Jane's coffin with difficulty. Those organizing the funeral had planned a poignant and significant ceremony at this point: eight women— eight girls—were to bear Jane's pall into and out of the chapel. Each was to wear a black hood and a black apron: each, in other words, was to present herself as a maid-of-all-work in mourning. Having peers of the deceased hold the pall was the custom for Victorian funerals. But having servants hold the pall of a fellow servant was a striking variation on that theme, one intended to pronounce forcefully that Jane Clouson's life had had meaning and value not in spite of her humble status, but because of it.* The deluge, however, put an end to this plan. The plan had been well publicized and the multitude, anticipating the show, was disappointed; many of them fled the cemetery at this point to seek shelter.

Jane had been a Baptist; a Baptist deacon performed a service "of an unusually solemn and impressive nature." Then, the eight men carried the coffin and pall down a bouquet-strewn path to a grave site—donated by the authorities of Deptford—on the non-conformist side of the cemetery. Reportedly, it was near the graves of her mother and her elder sister, Sarah, and perhaps near that of a brother who had died as an infant. After a few more words from the deacon and many more bouquets heaped upon the coffin, the

---

* Most of the national newspapers reported that this symbolic procession had taken place; the *Illustrated Police News* even illustrated it. But the reporters for the local newspapers were certain that the procession, though planned, never happened.

remnants of the crowd dispersed, many of them to local public houses, the newspapers reported. And Jane was buried.

A good two hundred of these spectators regrouped later in the evening to enact a very different ceremony, one that provided an outlet for the rage against the man they were certain had killed Jane Clouson. They converged on London Street, outside the Pooks' shop and home, and shouted obscene abuse at Edmund's family. Ebenezer Pook, genuinely afraid for his family's safety, sent off a note to Blackheath Road police station, begging for police protection. That plea, as far as he could tell, had no effect. And so he set out for the station himself, slipping past the crowd and stopping on the way at Tudor House, where he frantically told Henry Pook that he would "either go mad or do mischief to somebody." Henry Pook hurried with Ebenezer to the station and there spoke with the sergeant on duty, Sergeant Lucas, whom they found to be maddeningly unruffled by the situation: he had already sent an officer to the scene, he told the two Pooks. Henry Pook again exploded. Raising his fist menacingly, he shouted that Lucas was a rogue, a liar, and—repeating a rumor he had heard—a police snitch and spy. A single officer? Henry Pook cried: Lucas should have sent half a dozen, at least! Lucas tried to conciliate the solicitor. He had sent two more men already, he told him; now he would send another four. Henry Pook, not assuaged, followed the sergeant into the yard, continued to abuse him, and then, fists clenched, rushed upon him. Ebenezer Pook stepped between the two, pulled the solicitor away, and shoved him into a cab.

And for the second time in three days, Henry Pook was summoned to appear before a magistrate for his behavior.

○━━○

At Guy's Hospital when the inquest resumed three days later, Deputy Coroner William John Payne considered himself greatly put upon and was disposed to vent his annoyance to his jury. He had two reasons for his frustration. Harry Poland and the Treasury, for one thing, had left him in the lurch, refusing or neglecting to show up at Guy's Hospital to prosecute. "I understand," Payne complained, "that the Treasury was about to take this case up, but they appear to have left us quite alone, to do the best we can." For the last time, then, William Willis prosecuted on behalf of Jane's family.

More than this, the police had managed to render much of the evidence presented that day useless, in Payne's opinion. The police had, since the inquest jury had last sat, found three witnesses who might be able to place Edmund Pook at Kidbrooke Lane on the night of the murder. The first, William Cronk, a gas fitter from Blackheath, had been walking home on Kidbrooke Lane before nine o'clock when, peering through a gap in the hedge not more than twenty yards from where Jane's body was later found, he saw a young man and young woman, apparently in the midst of an argument. He had watched the two for some time—mostly seeing their backs. The woman, he claimed, said, "let me go, let me go" or perhaps "let us go, let us go," and then the man thrust his arm about her and propelled her, "half consentingly," south in the direction of Eltham. Then William Norton and Louisa Putman testified. Norton served as coachman to a Blackheath family, and Putman a maid-of-all-work in an Eltham public house. Though the two were barely acquainted, they were that evening walking out upon Kidbrooke's lover's lane. Between eight-thirty and nine, a few minutes after they had walked past a young couple, and about a hundred yards south of the brook, they heard a woman screaming. Minutes later, they saw through a gap in the hedge a man, out of breath and wearing a dark coat, running past them up the lane, in the direction of Morden College. Neither had a good look at the man's face, although Norton described him as clean shaven and "of about my stamp." And neither was particularly alarmed by the woman's screams, thinking they were playful cries or perhaps exclamations of sexual pleasure. "I thought it was some young man that had got down with some young woman there," William Norton stated. Louisa Putman elaborated: "You know that when you have got a young girl out with you she often screams."

The problem with all three of these witnesses, as well as with the eyewitness in the Thomases' shop, James Conway, who also testified, was that even though Edmund Pook had now been in custody ten days, not one of them had yet been given the opportunity to identify Edmund Pook as the man they had seen. Griffin and Mulvany had intended to set up an identification when Edmund had returned to Greenwich five days before, and had gone so far as to call all of these witnesses to the station that morning. But for some reason the identification did not take place. Only one witness had actually seen Edmund Pook, and that was by accident: William Norton, waiting in the station yard, happened to look through a window into the courtroom and saw a man standing in the dock. That man, those around him told him, was Edmund Pook.

Since Edmund Pook could not appear at the inquest, there was no possibility for any of these witnesses to point to him dramatically and identify him in the courtroom. The deputy coroner would have dearly appreciated that opportunity; he had gone so far as to petition the home secretary to allow Edmund Pook to be brought up from Maidstone to Southwark to attend his inquest. That petition had been denied. And so William Payne could only complain to his jury. "A great amount of difficulty might have been obviated had the witnesses been allowed to see the prisoner," he told them. "As things stood, the evidence was worthless." Later, he extracted from Inspector Mulvany the promise that he would make sure all witnesses had the opportunity to identify Edmund Pook before Payne's jury reconvened.

Before any of these witnesses testified, Henry Pook had recalled Thomas Lazell. Lazell apparently had no need to attempt to identify Pook as the man he had seen; he claimed to know Pook by sight, and the man he had seen, he was sure, was Edmund Pook. That made him a dangerous witness for the prosecution, and Henry Pook had, since the last meeting of the inquest, done a great deal of digging in order to discredit Lazell's testimony. He thus subjected Lazell to a browbeating that soon checked the man's giggling and had him trembling. Hadn't he, Pook asked him, told three law clerks who had stopped by his cottage while making the pilgrimage to the site of martyrdom at Kidbrooke Lane, that he had seen no one in the lane that night? No, Lazell replied, his mother had said that, not he. Hadn't he told some of his mates at the Barley Mow, a Greenwich public house, on the night after Edmund Pook had been arrested, that he would like to get into court and see the young man? To this, Lazell replied, in confusion, "No," then "I don't—I don't believe I did" and then "I think I did." Hadn't he also told a man by the name of Charles Eicke that he had seen no one in the lane that night? (Henry Pook had made sure that Eicke, a notoriously cantankerous resident of Morden College, attended this inquest, and the old man now glowered at Lazell from across the room.) Lazell admitted that he had said that to Eicke. But he had been lying at the time. Now, he stood by his claim: he had seen Edmund Pook in the barn field by the lane. He was sure of it.

John Mulvany and James Griffin were the last to testify that day. Both had come, as usual, to sit in the courtroom the whole day, to watch the case on behalf of the Metropolitan Police; that was a standard procedure for officers leading an investigation. But as far as Henry Pook was concerned, the two were simply witnesses for the prosecution, subjective and hostile to the defense. And so Henry Pook had, earlier that day, employed a tactic calculated to challenge any notion that they were disinterested: he had demanded that the two be ejected from the courtroom. And Deputy Coroner Payne had agreed, asking them to leave. It was a tactic that the solicitor employed repeatedly and successfully after that, in both Southwark and at Greenwich Police Court. To testify on this day, then, Mulvany and then Griffin had to be recalled to the courtroom.

Henry Pook largely let Superintendent Griffin's account of Edmund's arrest pass. But not Inspector Mulvany's. The solicitor hammered the detective with a number of questions that pointed to the officers' misconduct in arresting Edmund. They had obviously attempted to entrap Edmund Pook by pretending that they possessed a letter he had written—the letter Jane Clouson apparently had destroyed. They had shown an unfair partisanship against Edmund Pook, withholding evidence both that Samuel and Jane Thomas had failed to identify Edmund Pook, and by dropping Ormond Yearsley—the witness who was sure that the man who bought the hammer on the twenty-first of April was *not* Edmund Pook—off their list of witnesses. They had inappropriately neglected to caution Edmund Pook before interrogating him. To emphasize this last point, Henry Pook cited a remark made just two days before by no less eminent a jurist than Alexander Cockburn, the Lord Chief Justice of England. Cockburn was that week presiding over a criminal trial—*R v. Boulton and Others*—that in its sensational fascination competed with the Pook case for the attention of the newspaper-reading public. The principal defendants in that trial, Thomas Boulton and Frederick Park, were well-known transvestites who had appeared often, both in public and on the stage; they were on trial for "conspiring and inciting persons to commit an unnatural offence." When Cockburn learned that Griffin's counterpart at E Division, Superintendent James Thomson, had interrogated Boulton and Park after arresting them, he attacked Thomson's actions as illegal. "Do you interrogate prisoners then?" Cockburn chided Thomson. "Because we have not yet come to that, nor could it be authorized except by the Legislature."* Henry Pook suggested that Griffin and Mulvany were guilty of similar misconduct because they neglected to caution Edmund Pook before they questioned him. The solicitor's comparison might have had the

---

* The treatment that Boulton and Park received at the hands of the police after they were arrested was actually far more humiliating and intrusive than the papers dared report: not only were they interrogated, but a police doctor had been called in to examine both men for signs of anal penetration. Boulton and Park—and those tried with them—were acquitted.

benefit of timeliness, but it lacked entirely any legal foundation: while Thomson had interrogated Boulton and Park after they were arrested, Griffin and Mulvany had questioned Edmund Pook before arresting him. While Mulvany himself pointed this out to Henry Pook two days later, on this day Mulvany was at a loss for words. And that allowed Henry Pook to savage the police for overstepping their bounds. He hoped in the future that Mulvany and the police would remember Cockburn's words.

⚬━━⚬

In their Deptford shop the next evening, the Thomases, Samuel and Jane, once again pored over their sales ledger. Samuel had been called to Greenwich Police Court the next day, and he was, with the help of his wife, preparing to be absolutely accurate in his testimony. Once again, the two saw the entry, in Jane's handwriting as usual, which had made them central to the case: one J Sorby #2 hammer, sold on Friday, April 21.

And they read on.

It was Jane who saw it first. Below the record of the sale of a pair of scissors and of a set of table legs, there it was, again in Jane Thomas's handwriting: the record of the sale of yet another J Sorby #2 hammer—sold on Monday, April 24—sold, oddly, for two pence more than the usual price. Monday, April 24: one day before the murder.

The two realized at that moment that the police contention that Edmund must have purchased the hammer on Friday was quite possibly wrong. And over the next few days, as customers returned to speak with them, alerted by ubiquitous police handbills seeking information about the sale, they realized that the police were certainly wrong in this contention. First, a man by the name of Thomas Wittard returned to remind them that he had purchased a hammer from the shop on April 15—a larger J Sorby #3 hammer. Samuel Thomas, speaking with him, began to remember: Ormond

Yearsley, who claimed to have been in the shop on the twenty-first, had actually been there on the fifteenth, and witnessed Wittard's purchase. And then, the purchaser of the J Sorby #2 on the twenty-first returned to the shop: he was an eighteen-year-old plasterer's assistant by the name of William Elliott; he looked nothing like Edmund Pook. Elliot still had this hammer; it was not the one found at Morden College. Speaking with him also jogged Samuel Thomas's memory: Elliott had bought the hammer around nine o'clock at night, and the shop was otherwise empty. James Conway might indeed have been in their shop that day, but he was not there then.

The day after the Thomases made this crucial discovery, Samuel Thomas attended police court, ready to reveal it. But he was not called as a witness. And he failed to share it with the police. Rather, he and his wife kept the discovery to themselves while the police continued hotly to pursue their obviously false lead.

On the morning of May 13, fresh from another harrowing journey from Maidstone and smarting from the taunts of the mob and the machinations of the porters and stationmasters, Edmund Pook was marched into the yard of Greenwich police station and placed in a line with twenty or so plain-clothed officers; Detective Mulvany had kept his promise to Deputy Coroner Payne and had set up an identification. As Mulvany and Superintendent Griffin stood to the side observing, William Norton, Louisa Putman, Thomas Lazell, James Conway, and William Cronk were one by one led into the yard, instructed, if they recognized the man they had seen, to touch him. William Norton failed to recognize Pook—even though he had just days before seen him through the courtroom window. Louisa Putman failed as well. Thomas Lazell, on the other hand, walked into the yard, recognized Pook immediately, and touched him on the shoulder. That came as no surprise to anyone, since Lazell claimed that he knew Pook by sight long before he saw him in Kidbrooke Lane. His positive identification now seemed to verify that claim, at least. James Conway, too, also touched Pook as the man he had seen in Samuel Thomas's shop.

Since William Cronk had claimed to have seen the man on Kidbrooke Lane mostly from his back, the police made a special accommodation for his identification. Before he stepped into the yard, either Griffin or Mulvany had ordered the men in the line to turn to the wall. Cronk then scrutinized the twenty men's backs. Based upon that alone, he strode up to and put a hand on Edmund Pook.

Three of these witnesses testified in court that day. Norton and Putman admitted their failure to identify Pook, and Cronk told of his success. Henry Pook immediately undercut it. "Can you say any person in court was the man you picked out from several others this morning?"

"I cannot," Cronk replied—not unless everyone turned their backs to him. Amidst the startled murmurs of spectators, Henry Pook "warmly protested" against "the most extraordinary kind of identification he had ever heard of."

The key evidence introduced this day was Dr. Henry Letheby's analysis of Edmund Pook's bloody clothing. Henry Pook did his best to minimize its importance. When Inspector Mulvany again testified, this time to describe his delivering Edmund's clothing to Letheby's home, Henry Pook hounded him, accusing him of leaving Edmund's clothing fully exposed in a room of the station where officers ate their meals and through which they passed on the way to the courtroom. Mulvany swore they had been tied up in a paper parcel, and Pook countered that he had himself seen the clothing, lying open. Those clothes were hopelessly contaminated, the solicitor concluded, before Letheby had the opportunity to analyze them. He taunted Harry Poland, making play of one of Letheby's discoveries: "If that was all the learned counsel could produce he might say that the case against the prisoner was hanging by a single hair."

Despite his ridicule, Henry Pook was well aware of the threat Letheby's testimony posed. The fact of blood-spattered clothing was in itself inflammatory. But more than this, the strength and authority of the testimony of a strong expert medical witness—and Letheby was one of the best—could go far in swaying a magistrate, and later in swaying a coroner's jury. Henry Pook therefore prepared for his confrontation with Letheby carefully, combing the medical literature on the subject. After demonstrating his own knowledge of the subject by peppering the doctor with a host of questions about the chemical composition of blood, Henry Pook forced from Letheby the crucial admission that the blood on Edmund's clothing could have come from any human being, or from any number of creatures: that blood was "common to all animals, with few exceptions, that suckle their young." The solicitor then took up the *Manual of Medical Jurisprudence*, the standard text on forensic medicine at the time, written, as it happens, by a lecturer at Guy's Hospital, Alfred Swain Taylor. Henry Pook challenged Letheby with passages from that text explaining that it was easy to confuse tobacco stains, or the pulp of lemon or orange exposed to air, for blood. Letheby brushed this off. Taylor's claims were dated; now, "such a fallacy would only be occasioned by a superficial examination of the spots, without submitting them to a microscopical or spectroscopical investigation." He was positive about the stains in this case: "They were blood."

But, Pook asked Letheby, "Wouldn't you expect to see the clothes of a person who inflicted such fearful wounds as those we have heard described completely saturated with blood?"

"It so happens," Letheby replied, "that if the temple artery is cut through it does not bleed." But, he told the solicitor, since he had not examined Jane Clouson's wounds, he could not say for sure. Michael Harris could better answer these questions.

And then Henry Pook raised what had now become the central contention of Edmund's defense concerning the blood on his clothes.

Wouldn't blood from a tongue bitten during an epileptic fit, he asked the doctor, be "similar in quality to that found?"

"It would, decidedly," Letheby replied.

Now it was the prosecutor's turn to feel the danger of an expert witness's testimony, and Harry Poland did his best to nip in the bud the theory that the blood came from Edmund's tongue. He would not expect, Letheby stated in answer to Poland's question, "blood from a self-inflicted wound to appear on the *hat* of the patient."

At the resumption of the inquest at Guy's Hospital three days later, on May 16, patient, meticulous Harry Poland, sleuth-hound of the Treasury, and a man who did not like surprises, was stunned and then enraged by the third witness he questioned. His mood could not have been helped by the first two witnesses, either: William Norton and Louisa Putman were both recalled by Henry Pook to describe their absolute failure to pick out Edmund Pook at the police identification. But it was not until Samuel Thomas took the witness chair and informed the court that the murder weapon had been sold on Monday the twenty-fourth and not on Friday the twenty-first that Poland lost his usual self-control. He turned on Thomas, alternatively hounding him to reveal details about the sale and threatening him. "I want some further particulars about this hammer sold on the Monday, and I will advise you to be careful," Poland barked at the trembling man; "the police have been put upon a wrong scent by nothing having been said to them about the hammer sold on the Monday till yesterday." Samuel Thomas only made Poland angrier when it became clear that his newfound ability to provide minute details about the sale of the hammer on Friday did not carry over to the sale of the hammer on Monday; about that, Thomas remained completely in the dark. Poland persisted, asking Thomas why he would have sold the hammer on Monday for two pence more than usual. That must have been a mistake, Thomas told him. But Poland had other ideas. "Is it not a fact that you would sell it twopence cheaper to a plasterer than to any one else not in the trade—a gentleman in a black coat, and so on?" Thomas denied that he set price by means of a customer's social standing.

Thomas did give a possible explanation for not remembering the sale on Monday: more than likely, his wife, Jane, and not he had sold the hammer. Hearing that, Poland immediately pressed the deputy coroner send officers to Deptford to retrieve Jane Thomas to testify. Poland further requested that the Thomases be kept apart until Jane Thomas appeared. As far as Harry Poland was concerned, the Thomases were obviously keeping back information they both knew, knowingly obstructing the police investigation.

While the jury waited for Mrs. Thomas to be fetched, James Conway took the witness chair in order to explain what clearly had been a false identification of Edmund Pook. Conway remained adamant on one point: he *had* been in Thomas's shop that day. But as to his positive identification of Edmund Pook, Conway now backtracked. He admitted now that he had not actually seen the face of the man in the shop. He only picked out Edmund Pook because his shoulders looked like those of that man. Upon consideration, however, he now fancied that there was a difference between the shoulders of the two, as well as a difference in hair color. Henry Pook dismissed him as a false witness, pure and simple, who had lied under oath for money. He forced Conway to admit that he had contacted Edmund's brother, Thomas. But Conway denied that he had said to Thomas Pook, "If I could get a few pence to get away to the north, I would not come to the inquest." On top of this, Conway disclosed he had been paid by the police—as was commonly done at the time—to appear as a witness: three shillings and sixpence a day.

Conway, thus having tainted both the investigation and the prosecution, stepped down. He would never testify in the case again.

Jane Thomas, who had arrived at court under police escort with her two eldest sons in tow, then took the witness chair, and soon quailed under Harry Poland's wrath, as, with the deputy coroner's encouragement, he repeatedly demanded that she reveal what she knew about the sale and disdained her claims that she knew nothing. Henry Pook, genuinely outraged at Poland's rough and "un-English" interrogation, objected: "Because the learned counsel cannot get the answers he requires he begins to browbeat the witness." But William Payne had little sympathy for Mrs. Thomas, and he overruled the solicitor. The woman was obviously keeping something back, Payne explained; she was therefore a hostile witness, and Harry Poland's aggressive, even brutal questioning was appropriate. Several members of the jury immediately concurred with the deputy coroner.

Beset, it seemed, from all sides, Mrs. Thomas held fast to her claim. She remembered absolutely nothing, and said so when she was later called and recalled both at Guy's Hospital and at Greenwich Police Court. Her steadfastness won her few admirers. Her neighbors in Deptford, reading accounts of her testimony, interpreted it, as Poland, Payne, and the jury had, as obstinacy. She began to receive anonymous, threatening letters demanding she reveal the truth. Strangers and neighbors began to harass her in their shop. It became too much for her, and she eventually relinquished all work in the shop to her husband.

When a thoroughly harrowed Jane Thomas stepped down and Henry Letheby stepped up, it was Henry Pook's turn to fume. Letheby essentially repeated the testimony he had given before Daniel Maude at Greenwich Police Court, and Henry Pook challenged him as before. But this time the solicitor went further. He had studied Letheby's formidable record as an expert witness, and had discovered one case, twenty-one years before, in which Letheby's testimony apparently had had a nearly disastrous effect. "Once," Henry Pook barked at the doctor, "a woman named Merritt was sentenced to death upon your evidence, and she was afterwards pardoned upon other scientific evidence."*

But Letheby's conscience was clear. "Yes," he replied, "and if the court wish me to tell the story of that case at great length I will do so."

Pook angrily chided Letheby for his flippant answer, but the deputy coroner defended him: "the character of Dr. Letheby is too high in this country for anything that he says to be called flippant."

The courtroom burst into applause, and Henry Pook shouted his defiance: "I will not be put down by clamour."

⚬━━⚬

A fortnight in cell 33 of Maidstone Jail had taught Edmund Pook that he faced an enemy just as insidious if not quite as perfidious as Inspector Mulvany and Superintendent Griffin: sheer mind-killing boredom. The highlights of *Pickwick* had lost their luster, and, as Edmund complained in a letter to friends, the books in the jail's library were "dry." And the police, as usual, had conspired to worsen matters; they had "needlessly" confiscated his watch, rendering the empty days measureless. Escaping that was almost worth the weekly journey north to Greenwich, though the size of the angry crowds and the abuse he took only seemed to increase each time. And there was an even greater enticement to make the trip to police court on this day, Friday, May 19: Alice Durnford, his avowed sweetheart, to whom he had written the night he was arrested, was set to testify.

---

* Ann Merritt was tried for murder in 1850 for poisoning her husband, James. Henry Letheby testified that Ann's husband had indeed been poisoned. That conclusion was never in dispute. When the poison had been ingested, on the other hand, was deeply contested. The defense argued that James Merritt had accidentally ingested arsenic in the morning; the prosecution (and Letheby) contended that Ann Merritt had given him the poison later, in a bowl of gruel. Because of doubts in this respect raised after her trial, Ann Merritt gained not a pardon but a commutation to imprisonment for life.

Her testimony was a crushing disappointment to him. She spoke, for one thing, altogether dismissively about their relationship. She had kept it a complete secret from her parents and Edmund had never entered her home. They had not met for weeks besides a very brief meeting days after the attack on Jane—not since the first week of April, when "we did not part very good friends." But worse than this, Durnford's testimony convinced the Pooks, both prisoner and solicitor, that she had betrayed Edmund and was now colluding with the police. When Edmund came calling for her outside her house, she testified, he would signal his presence to her, and to her alone, by means of a little dog whistle that he carried with him. Durnford said nothing about seeing Edmund on the night Jane was attacked. But he did stand outside her house two days later. She saw him, but could not come to him. She did not hear any dog whistle that time.

When she mentioned the whistle, Inspector Mulvany stood and held out his hand to display the pewter whistle that PC Ovens had pulled from the mud of Kidbrooke Lane. Henry Pook stood amazed at this. It was the first he had heard anything about a whistle; there was absolutely nothing about a whistle in any police records; it was certainly not listed among the evidence they had found. In cross-examining Durnford, Pook elicited the fact that she had the day before, at Superintendent Griffin's bidding, gone to the Treasury to review her testimony. The solicitor suspected she had been coached to tell this story. "A very valuable witness indeed, Mr. Poland," he uttered sarcastically, earning a reprimand from Daniel Maude, and leading to an argument that ended with the magistrate angrily and repeatedly ordering the solicitor to "sit down, sir!"

Edmund Pook, on the other hand, could hardly be surprised by Alice Durnford's revelation. He *had* often called her to him in that particularly ungallant way. But the appearance of a whistle in the palm of Mulvany's hand—whether it was or was not *the* whistle— was a shock. Later, after he had returned to Maidstone, Edmund wrote an anxious letter to Thomas Pook, genuinely or perhaps disingenuously directing him to search his bureau for whistles. And Thomas Pook found—or claimed to find—two whistles there: one of bone and the other of metal, looking very much like the one that Mulvany now possessed.

The dog whistle was the first bombshell to fall that day. The second was the appearance of Thomas Sparshott. Now convinced that the murder weapon had been purchased on Monday, April 24, the police realized the importance of Sparshott's testimony of serving in his shop that night a young man looking to buy a "chopper." Earlier that morning, they set up another identification parade in the station yard. William Sparshott had easily picked Edmund Pook from a dozen other men as the one he had seen in his shop and had directed on to the Thomases'. Sparshott proved to be a confident and convincing witness, and Henry Pook, in spite of an aggressive cross-examination, could do nothing to shake his claim. The solicitor did, however, succeed in casting a bit of doubt upon Sparshott's identification. While Sparshott swore he had never seen Edmund Pook outside his shop until the moment he identified him that morning, Henry Pook pressed him.

"Now tell us: have you not seen a photograph of the prisoner?"

"No, I have not."

"Have you not seen a portrait of him?—No, I have not."

"Why, have you not seen the *Police News* for last week?—Yes."

"And has that not a portrait of him in it?—What they call one; but I should be very sorry to judge any one by that."

Sparshott was right. The portrait in question—the first one of two to appear in the *Illustrated Police News*—was a ridiculously bad likeness of Edmund Pook. (The newspaper itself, in publishing the second portrait, had apologized for the terrible likeness of the first.) No one could have recognized Edmund Pook from that likeness. Nevertheless, Henry Pook succeeded in making Sparshott's testimony seem tainted—tainted by the intrusion of the mass media into the case.

Sparshott appeared exactly when the police and prosecution needed him. For while his star was rising, Thomas Lazell's was falling. It was not Lazell's lamentable demeanor as a witness that was the problem when he appeared on this day; it was the adamancy with which he stuck to the claim that he had seen Edmund Pook on Kidbrooke Lane no later than 6:50 on the night of the attack. That simply could not have been the case, according to the testimony of other witnesses. William Cronk, William Norton, and Louisa Putman all swore they had seen a man much later: between eight-thirty and nine o'clock. And Fanny Hamilton, Jane's landlady, swore that she had left Jane at 6:40 on Deptford High Street. It would have been physically impossible for Jane to traverse the nearly three miles between Deptford and Kidbrooke in ten minutes.

⚬────⚬

At Guy's Hospital six days later, on May 25, the police had run out of bombshells and the coroner's jury was running out of patience. Only one witness of any importance appeared: Olivia Cavell, an acquaintance and a customer of the Thomases. Cavell had been in the Thomases' shop on Monday evening, April 24, and her testimony both dovetailed with William Sparshott's and provided details about that evening that the Thomases could not—or would not—provide. She had entered the Thomases' shop between eight and eight-thirty that evening to buy a pair of scissors. (Her order was duly noted on the ledger, near the record of purchase of the J Sorby hammer.) She then remained in the parlor adjoining the shop to chat with Mrs. Thomas. Mr. Thomas was not there. Cavell thus witnessed Mrs. Thomas serve a customer—a young man in a dark coat and a low, round hat. The young man and Mrs. Thomas walked to the shop window, from which Jane Thomas fetched something that Cavell could not quite see and wrapped it up in paper. Olivia Cavell did not see the man's face, and was sure that she could not recognize him again.

88

Harry Poland recalled Jane Thomas immediately after Cavell testified, clearly hoping that Cavell's memories would jog Jane Thomas's. They did not. Harry Poland tormented Mrs. Thomas with another relentless round of questioning. Henry Pook again objected to his deplorable abuse. William Payne again overruled him, and again expressed his certainty that Jane Thomas was withholding evidence. And again, the jury agreed with him, and said so.

Soon afterward, Harry Poland gave the case over to Henry Pook to call the witnesses he had claimed would entirely exonerate Edmund Pook. But Henry Pook chose to call none of them. Clearly fearing that Edmund Pook was destined to stand trial at the Old Bailey, he elected not to show his hand at either coroner's or magistrate's court, and instead surprise the prosecution there by unleashing evidence he now claimed was "very substantial and astounding."

And so William Payne summed up the prosecution's case for his jury, and did so in a way that made it very clear he wished Edmund Pook committed for trial. There was a strong *prima facie* case of suspicion against Pook, he told the jury. Edmund had a motive: Jane had—probably truthfully—claimed that he was the father of her child. And Edmund had opportunity: Jane had said he was to meet her on the night she was attacked, and both Lazell and Cronk swore they saw Edmund Pook with a girl on Kidbrooke Lane. Norton and Putman corroborated their sightings. Letheby could not connect the blood on Edmund's clothing with Jane, but his finding of hair similar to Jane's on both the murder weapon and Edmund's trousers was more compelling. Payne also made much of the evidence that Edmund Pook purchased the murder weapon, citing both Sparshott's genuinely compelling eyewitness testimony and James Conway's—and making no mention at all of the fact that Conway's testimony had been thoroughly discredited. He could not mention the sale of the hammer without again censuring the Thomases: they had refused to speak, Payne told the jury "not because they could not, but because they would not."

If the jury thought that the evidence brought forward did not warrant committing Edmund Pook for trial, Payne told them, they could of course return the open verdict of murder by a person or persons unknown. But that, Payne told the jury, "would be very unsatisfactory, for it would to a certain extent be saying that this inquiry and all these labors had gone for nothing."

One of the more doubtful jurors here spoke up. Even if they did return an open verdict, wouldn't the magistrate still have the power to send the case for trial? "If you return an open verdict," Payne told him, "it will very much weaken the case against the prisoner, for it will be said 'the Coroner's jury has returned an open verdict,' and that will be taken as in favour of the accused." If they did that, he could not say what Daniel Maude would do. But if they named Edmund Pook as the murderer, Maude would certainly agree and indict Pook. They had the power. Clearly, Payne wished them to use it.

The jury then retired, to return thirty-five minutes later. Sixteen of the twenty-two had followed Payne's lead and held that Edmund Pook had willfully murdered Jane Maria Clouson. Six had not, and held out for an open verdict. The sixteen were more than enough to establish a verdict. A requisition was quickly drawn up; William John Payne and twelve of his jurors signed it; and Edmund Pook was committed for trial.

⌖

Although the verdict at the inquest meant that Edmund's case would certainly be decided at the Old Bailey, Magistrate Daniel Maude still had his opportunity to concur with or dissent from their verdict. And so Edmund Pook still had two turbulent journeys to make between Maidstone jail and Greenwich Police Court. He made his most chaotic and dangerous journey on May 27: then, the roiling and execration-heaping crowd through which he passed on the way to court from New Cross station had actually been able to get ahold of him, and for a few moments Edmund Pook experienced the terror of a near lynching. His coming on that day had served no purpose: Harry Poland was absent, arguing another case, and so Edmund Pook was immediately remanded back to Maidstone. Three days later, on May 30, when he returned to Greenwich, the police finally, belatedly, took steps to avoid the mob: they slipped Pook off the train at a distant station, bundled him into a cab, snuck him past the crowd and behind the station, led him up a ladder, over a wall, across the roof of the police stables, down into the yard, and into the station.

Police and prosecution on this day essentially offered up what they had offered up in Southwark five days before. Cavell repeated her testimony, and no fewer than six policemen testified, most about finding the whistle in the mud. And then Harry Poland asked Maude to commit Edmund Pook for trial as Payne's jury had done.

Henry Pook, again given the opportunity to call his witnesses, again declined. But this time he launched into a full-bore attack upon the prosecution. He was amazed, he told Maude, that the twelve men of the coroner's jury had put their names to an indict-ment on evidence so slight. It was impossible for Edmund Pook to travel from Greenwich to Kidbrooke Lane and back in the time the prosecution stated. And he would not have been foolish enough to buy the murder weapon in nearby Deptford: that would have been the act of a madman. The hair in the trousers meant nothing: thou-sands of people had similar hair. Letheby, he argued, was a hack and a legal menace: he had "been plentiful in indulging theories which had broken down." To support that contention, he mentioned, not the Ann Merritt case this time, but a more recent murder at Saffron Hill, in which a man had been found guilty of murder and sentenced to death, but was reprieved when another man confessed to the murder. Harry Poland interrupted him: Henry Letheby, he claimed, had nothing to do with that trial. (He was right—and Dr. Letheby himself shot off a letter that appeared in the *Times* the next day to say so.) In sum, the solicitor scoffed, the evidence against Edmund Pook "would not be deemed sufficient to obtain judgment for a debt of 5s. in a County Court."

For form's sake alone, Daniel Maude left the courtroom, to return five minutes later with his foregone conclusion. He was not at all sure that the evidence he had heard proved Edmund Pook's guilt. But that was not the question he had to answer. Rather, he had to decide whether the evidence he heard was enough to place the question of Pook's innocence or guilt in the hands of a jury at a criminal trial. And, he was certain, there was more than enough to do that.

The clerk told Edmund Pook he was committed to stand trial at the Old Bailey. He was cautioned and allowed to speak. "I say I am not guilty," he said—clearly; firmly. Henry Pook had only one more request to make. His defense of Edmund was already prepared, he announced. He hoped that the Crown, too, would be ready to proceed at the commencement of the next Old Bailey sessions, in a week's time.

It seemed that Henry Pook would get his wish.

But then the music hall–singing, donkey-driving cabman came forward.

CHAPTER FOUR

SOCIAL CONFUSION AND MORAL CORRUPTION

W hen Edmund Pook, now twice committed for murdering Jane Clouson, passed through the forbidding
walls of Newgate prison, he must have known
there was a chance he would never see the world outside again. All
his journeys to and from the courtroom in the Old Bailey, which
adjoined Newgate, he would make by an underground passage. If
at trial he was found guilty and condemned, and if that sentence
was carried out, he would be executed upon a gallows within
the prison, since outdoor—and crowd-pleasing—public execu-
tions had been proscribed just three years before. But even with
the specter of death before him, Pook surely found Newgate an
improvement over Maidstone. Because of reforms of the previous

two decades, Newgate was no longer an emblem of hell on earth; its notorious wards—overcrowded, unsupervised, disease-ridden stews of criminality—were no more. Prisoners now were fewer, and each had an individual cell. Moreover, Edmund Pook had a friend and protector in the prison in the Reverend Frederick Lloyd-Jones, the prison ordinary, who resided in Greenwich and had before his appointment to the prison served as curate at St. Alfege, the Pooks' church.

Lloyd-Jones apparently made sure that Pook was transferred to the more comfortable quarters of the prison infirmary when, the day after he entered the prison, he suffered a most fortunate fall. He collapsed with a *grand mal* epileptic seizure,* and reportedly bit his tongue and his lips and bled over his clothes. In terms of its influence upon the public and upon prospective jurors at his trial, this seeming corroboration of Pook's claim that the blood the police found on his clothes was his own could hardly have come at a better time, and the Pooks—most likely Henry Pook—lost no time in feeding the news to the press.

The June sessions were to begin within a week,** and as far as Edmund's defense was concerned, they could not begin soon enough; any delay would give the police time to strengthen their seemingly weak case. As a solicitor, Henry Pook could not act as Edmund Pook's advocate at the Central Criminal Court; that privilege was reserved to barristers alone. And so Henry Pook engaged for Edmund a formidable—and expensive—phalanx of defenders. As supporting counsel he engaged Joseph Miller Harrington, Edward Besley, and Douglas Straight. The last two of these were mainstays at the Old Bailey, and known for their brilliance—Besley for his solidity and Straight for his polish and acuity. To lead, Henry Pook picked Queen's Counsel John Walter

---

* Today more commonly termed a tonic-clonic epileptic seizure.

** Sittings or sessions at the Old Bailey of the Central Criminal Court were in 1871 held every month of the year.

94

Huddleston. This was an inspired choice. From the start Huddleston shared Henry Pook's perspective on the case, adopting as his own the belief that Edmund Pook was not a criminal but a victim, persecuted rather than prosecuted by an overzealous police force. But while Huddleston's passion came close to equaling the solicitor's, his forensic abilities were greatly superior. Huddleston, according to the *Times*, was "admirable in the conduct of a cause, dangerous in cross-examination, and above all things skillful in presenting his points to the jury." While Henry Pook blustered and antagonized, Huddleston won over judges and juries.

And so on the seventh of June it was with Huddleston that Edmund Pook stood at the Old Bailey before Judge Colin Blackburn to set a date for trial. Two days before this the recorder for the court had summarized the evidence against Pook to the grand jury, which then met privately and heard testimony from the prosecution's witnesses. They then returned a true bill against Pook—in effect, committing him to trial for a third time. (Had the grand jury on the other hand refused to return that bill—had they, in other words, *ignored* the bill—then Edmund Pook would have been a free man.) A trial was thus inevitable, and Huddleston declared himself eager to begin at once.

Harry Poland, however, immediately requested a postponement until July and the next sessions. Not only were the police tracking down a witness who could give "very material" evidence, he claimed, but they had already found another: one who had been to Newgate and had positively identified Edmund Pook—although identified in what context, Poland did not say. Huddleston opposed Poland's motion with a passion. Not only had Poland and the police had more than enough time to investigate the case, but five weeks' delay would prove a crushing financial burden to Pook's parents. Poland scoffed at that last argument; Ebenezer Pook, after all, was a respectable tradesman and thus a man of means. Nonetheless, Blackburn agreed to consider a delay if Poland could set out reasonable grounds in formal affidavits. Huddleston asked that these be produced quickly, and Poland submitted two of them in the court-room that afternoon. The first referred vaguely to an unnamed witness for whom the police were still searching. The second, written by Superintendent Griffin, was much more specific, and concerned the newly discovered eyewitness, a man by the name of Walter Richard Perren.

By day, twenty-six-year-old Perren managed his mother's livery stables, drove a cab, and occasionally oversaw children's donkey rides on Blackheath. (The *Times* would later disparage him as a "donkey-driver.") By night, he pursued dreams of celebrity: he sang comic songs and was master of ceremonies at the Golden Lion, a little music hall in Sydenham. Walter Perren claimed to know Edmund Pook as a fellow entertainer—and, in Perren's mind, a lesser one. Perren said that for three or four years he had known Pook slightly, only by sight and by his stage name, "Walter"; he had even seen him perform in public once. On the evening of April 24, one day before Jane Clouson was murdered, Walter Perren claimed to be in Deptford killing time before catching his train to Sydenham, when he had ducked into an ironmonger's to buy two pennies' worth of nails. That shop, he claimed, was Samuel Thomas's; Jane Thomas served him. As he left, he saw "Walter" approach him, from the south, the direction of Sparshott's shop. The two passed, recognized and nodded to each other, and for the first time, they conversed. Pook spoke first, asking Perren how he was getting along.

"Middling," Perren told him.

"Are you still at Sydenham?" Pook asked, and Perren said he was.

"I should think you will live and die there." Pook then gestured toward the Thomases' shop. I am just going in here; if you wait we'll have a liquor-up."

But Perren, late for his music hall, declined, and Edmund entered the shop. Then, Perren claimed, delayed from rushing to the station by a slow-moving van, he watched the shop window, and saw Mrs. Thomas reach into it and withdraw a hammer. Then he rushed away. He did not realize for weeks, Perren told the police, that he had apparently witnessed Pook purchasing the murder weapon. He had of course seen the ubiquitous bills posted by the police, but the purchase they described had occurred on the Saturday before the attack, not the Monday. And the torrent of newspaper reports about Edmund Pook meant nothing to Perren either, since he only knew the person he had seen as "Walter." Just a day before this hearing Perren somehow realized that he might be a crucial eyewitness and went to the police. Detective Mulvany hustled him to the Old Bailey to look at witnesses appearing before the grand jury, where Perren pointed out Jane Thomas as the woman he had seen in the ironmonger's shop. He then went to the exercise yard at Newgate, where, from the crowd of prisoners somberly trudging in circles, he picked out Edmund Pook as his acquaintance "Walter."

Edmund Pook, perusing this affidavit with his solicitor, was baffled: Perren's claims, he realized immediately, were a tissue of lies. Edmund did have ambitions as a performer, though modest ones. Once or twice, and only for charity, he had sung onstage. And he and his brother, Thomas, had put on several "penny readings" at the Greenwich Lecture Hall, for the purpose of which he had adopted the name "Edmund Walters." Possibly Walter Perren had seen him there. But Edmund had had nothing to do with the sort of music-hall life that Perren suggested he had. And Perren was an utter stranger to him. He certainly didn't invite the man to "liquor-up" with him the evening before Jane had been attacked.

He had, in other words, a "perfect answer" to Perren—and Huddleston told Judge Blackburn so. As for the other affidavit, it was vague to the point of meaninglessness. The judge sympathized; he understood that Edmund Pook might be entirely innocent; he felt, and he regretted, the hardship a delay would cause Edmund Pook and his father. Nonetheless, the affidavits clearly suggested at least the possibility that a further inquiry could yield further evidence. He granted Poland's motion for a postponement and sent Edmund back to Newgate for another six weeks.

It was an inconvenience that Edmund Pook, by all accounts, bore with perfect equanimity. "He is perfectly calm," one newspaper reported, "and spends his time chiefly in reading." The true burden of the delay fell, as Huddleston had predicted, upon Ebenezer Pook. The cost to retain counsel, and to ensure the appearance of the fifty or so witnesses the Pooks had amassed, increased the already substantial costs of a trial sure to last for several days—a thousand pounds in all, by one estimate. This, despite Harry Poland's optimistic assessment of a printer's fortune, was beyond the old man's means. He would need help, and he sought it among his friends, his neighbors—his fellow burghers: those who saw themselves as constituting the respectable population of Greenwich. A fund was quickly got up—it would come to be called the Pook Defence Fund—and £250 was gathered within days. Those participating in the fund formed the nucleus of a growing body of Pook supporters, a counterbalance to the much noisier supporters of justice for Jane Clouson. Even before Edmund's trial, the two sides in Greenwich's incipient civil war were clear.

If the police of R Division, if Detective Inspector Mulvany and Superintendent Griffin worked hard on the investigation during that June and July, they had little to show for it. Before the trial commenced, the Treasury submitted to Henry Pook a list of the witnesses they had found since Edmund's indictment. It was scant. Walter Richard Perren, of course, was on it. So were William Sparshott's wife, son, and shopboy; they could—partially— corroborate Sparshott's account of Edmund's visit to his shop. Besides these, there were two young women, Mary Ann Love and Alice Langley, whose evidence was at once deeply suggestive and utterly inconclusive. They clearly numbered among Edmund Pook's female admirers, and thus countered the image of an overprotected homebody that Edmund's family promoted. And both could testify to a curious evening out they had spent with Pook and with a cousin of his on the Sunday before the attack. The four had met next to Greenwich Park, and had strolled across Blackheath, past Morden

College, through the market fields, and into Kidbrooke Lane. The police clearly considered this a dress rehearsal for Edmund's walk two days later. The two young women also claimed to have caught Edmund in a lie, one that might be construed as an impromptu and weak alibi: he told them, as they walked, that he would be unable to meet on Monday or Tuesday, as he was engaged to sing in London. (He was, of course, not engaged to sing anywhere on the night of the attack.)

Ironically, it was Edmund Pook's defense—that is, Henry Pook—who made the best use of the trial's postponement. The solicitor conducted his own investigation in support of Edmund's alibi that he was in Lewisham at the time of the murder, on a bridge in Lewisham, gazing lovingly at the home of his true love, Alice Durnford. Although Edmund himself claimed that no one had seen him while he was there, Henry Pook found three neighbors to the Durnfords willing to testify that they had. To make sure that it was indeed Edmund Pook they had seen, Henry Pook came up with an apparently unprecedented means of identification: rather than marching them to Newgate, he invited them separately to the more comfortable confines of his home, Tudor House. There he had each one scrutinize two albums holding thirty photographs—one of Edmund Pook among them. Each one picked out that one as the image of the man they were sure they had seen on the bridge on the evening of April 25, more than ten weeks before.

Henry Pook was a busy man between his client's commitment to Newgate and his trial. He not only continued to investigate Edmund's case, but also argued a number of cases for other clients in Greenwich Police Court. And on one glorious day in the middle of that June, he experienced what surely was one of the great days of his life, when he managed to engage in a spell of international diplomacy—of a sort. Pook happened to be both an elected member of the Greenwich Board of Works and solicitor to the board's contractor for Greenwich's sewer works. In both capacities, he joined a large party of workmen on June 17 for their annual outing to Sidcup, a village southeast of Eltham. The group diverted their walk a bit to take in what had recently matched Sydenham's Crystal Palace as south London's principal tourist attraction: Camden Place in Chiselhurst, then home of the recently-deposed ex-emperor of France, Napoleon III. After the disastrous collapse of the French army at Sedan eight months before, Napoleon's wife and son had fled to England and soon took up residence there. And in mid-March, after his release from Prussian captivity, Napoleon—bowed, ailing, superfluous—joined them. And on June 17, Henry Pook and 108 workmen gathered outside the gates of Camden house to cheer Napoleon with their presence. Their brass band did their best to serenade Napoleon with "God Save the Queen" and "Auld Lang Syne." They succeeded in drawing out the ex-emperor and his family to meet them. Henry Pook was instantly delegated speaker for the group, and his outspoken conservatism was equal to the occasion. He nostalgically recalled the Empire as the high-point of Anglo-French amity; he expressed the hope that the dark clouds over France might soon be dispelled—that the Empire might rise again. Napoleon was visibly moved by Pook's extempore speech, and said so; he had, he said, always been a good friend to England. The workmen burst into cheers—three for the emperor, three for the empress, three for the prince imperial. And after handshakes all around and before the party and the triumphant solicitor left the Napoleons for Sidcup, the band struck up the then-popular tune "We May Be Happy Yet."

That hope was a forlorn one. Napoleon III of course never returned to France or to imperial glory; his chronic illness killed him in his Chislehurst exile a year and a half later.

"The interest felt in this case," the *Times* reported of Edmund Pook on June 12, "has increased rather than abated since the postponement of the trial of the accused until the next session of the Central Criminal Court." Certainly, the constant flow of visitors to Kidbrooke Lane attested to the enduring hold the crime had upon the popular imagination. The pilgrimage there reached its peak on Whit-Monday, May 29, when fully twenty thousand satisfied their curiosity, paid their respects, and tore up the landscape, transforming that generally quiet bit of London countryside into the metropolis's third-largest tourist attraction: only the Crystal Palace at Sydenham and the newly opened International Exhibition at South Kensington attracted more that day.* But while popular interest in Jane Clouson and Edmund Pook might not have abated, newspaper reports on the case, which had since the beginning of May flowed in a steady stream, dried up altogether, not to begin again until the commencement of the July sessions. The public, hungry for sensation, would temporarily have to look elsewhere for their daily serving.

The 1860s and 1870s were indeed an age of sensation, an age when the hunger for the sensational and the extraordinary was seemingly omnipresent and seemingly insatiable. And the market to feed that hunger was well developed. Sensation sold—sold books and sold newspapers. The most popular novels in 1871, and for the decade before, were sensation novels: dark revelations of the extraordinary offered up by Wilkie Collins, Mary Elizabeth Braddon, Charles Reade, and a host of others, which with their tales of murder and mayhem, duplicity and mistaken identity, forgery, theft, adultery, and bigamy, all suggested the inescapable presence of social confusion and moral entropy of everyday existence. (On a less respectable literary level, but with a similar appeal, were the ephemeral but occasionally wildly popular serials for the masses,

---

* The enormity of the crowd at Kidbrooke Lane was attributable, in part, to the fact that Parliament had just passed the Bank Holidays Act, and Whit-Monday 1871 was thus the very first legal bank holiday in England, Ireland, and Wales.

the penny dreadfuls.*) The sensation novelists shunned exotic or gothic settings, preferring the quotidian, and they looked for inspiration in everyday true crime. Newspaper publishers of the day, too, recognized the seemingly insatiable public hunger for the extraordinary. From the august *Times* to less reputable weeklies such as *Lloyd's* or *Reynolds's Weekly*, blood and skullduggery sold copy, and reports of crime—in police courts, at inquests and at trials—filled the pages of every newspaper. And in the spring and summer of 1871 there was no lack of fully reported sensational stories to compete for public attention with stories about Jane Clouson and Edmund Pook, and to sustain the public hunger during the hiatus of that case.

Coming from across the channel, for one thing, were sensational revelations on an epic scale: the vicissitudes of France, which had by that June endured a terrible year—known then and remembered in France still as *"l'année terrible,"* a time of social chaos, political uncertainty, bloodshed, and desolation. Technological innovation and the extraordinary events in France combined to change British newspapers forever. For the first time, foreign correspondents began to submit their dispatches not by post but by telegraph, and more than ever before, a paper's circulation depended upon the freshness of its news and upon its correspondents' ability to scoop the competition. And for the first time, British readers could read at breakfast about the astonishing events of the day before. In installments, then, British readers were able to follow France's yearlong descent into utter chaos, a descent that commenced with the emperor Napoleon's reckless declaration of war upon Prussia, which led to invasion, the collapse of the French army, the slaughter at Sedan; to Napoleon's capture and to his eventual exile in Chislehurst. After Sedan came the Prussian march on the

---

* Indeed, a penny dreadful—one, admittedly, atrociously written penny dreadful—appeared to capitalize upon the murder of Jane Clouson. Its title: *Pretty Jane: or, the Viper of Kidbrook Lane.*

capital, and the Siege of Paris: dire starvation and bombardment, and then surrender to the newly unified German nation. And with the formation of the French Third Republic, worse was to come, as Paris formed its Commune in opposition to the Republic, leading to a second siege of Paris, this time a bloody conflict of French against the French. And finally—as Edmund Pook was indicted and at Newgate calmly awaited trial—came absolute chaos: the *"semaine sanglante,"* the blood-saturated days that followed the collapse of the Commune, when the victorious and vindictive Army of the Republic rounded up and butchered tens of thousands of Parisians, often upon the flimsiest of pretexts.* It was the worst civil blood-letting in all of Europe and during all of the nineteenth century.

While France dominated the headlines, the papers of the time were filled as well with an unceasing succession of reports that documented London's perpetual domestic chaos. Among the daily revelations of murder and attempted murder—an inordinate number of these, incidentally, involving hammers as the weapon of choice—and of assault, robbery, counterfeiting, fraud, and forgery, three cases besides Pook's stood out. Two were criminal cases that were working their way to the Old Bailey, where they would be tried simultaneously with Pook's case; the third was a civil case fought in Westminster—a case that would become a criminal one, and had already become the most sensational case of all in that age of sensation.

The defendant in the first criminal case, fifteen-year-old Agnes Norman, first entered public consciousness on April 13 when she shyly testified at an inquest in Newington Butts investigating the death of an infant, Jessie Beer. Agnes had been the sole servant to the Beer family; Jessie Beer had died when in her care. The girl calmly declared herself baffled by the infant's death: she had always treated the child kindly, she told the coroner.

---

* The Republic admitted to killing 17,000 Parisians. Doubtless many more than that died. [Christiansen 366.]

Norman was a young, quiet, polite, hardworking and low-paid South London servant: in all those respects, she was Jane Clouson's double. But as the case proceeded from inquest and into police court, the growing mass of evidence suggested that Agnes Norman was actually Jane's moral antithesis. Jane, of course, was the victim— and, according to the theory of the police, the victim of the predatory son of her employer. Clouson personified the exploitive power of her masters played out to its darkest extreme. Her experience embodied the nightmare of working-class parents who relinquished their daughters to the unpredictable and potentially dangerous power of middle-class employers. Agnes Norman, on the other hand, embodied the corresponding nightmare for middle-class parents who entrusted the lives of their children to unpredictable and potentially dangerous care of servants—generally young, and generally, in their quick comings and quick goings, little more than strangers among them. Jane Clouson found death in her service. But Agnes Norman, by all appearances, brought death to hers.

Having returned home to find one of his children dead in her bed, and another shrieking in horror, their father, John William Beer, was instantly suspicious of his newly engaged servant. He reported the death to the Lambeth police, and managed to convince them to assign one of their detectives, Sergeant Henry Mullard, to investigate Agnes Norman's past. And what Mullard quickly pieced together about the young servant beggared belief. Either Norman was the victim of the cruelest coincidence imaginable or she was a cold-blooded and relentless killer.

Mullard revealed what he had learned at the inquest. But he had no specific evidence to prove that Norman had caused the death of Jessie Jane Beer. Neither did any of the several witnesses the Beers had brought to testify to Norman's dark past: the coroner would not let any of them speak, for they had nothing relevant to say about Jessie Jane Beer. And the surgeon who had conducted the post-mortem on the infant could not conclude for certain that she had been murdered. Jessie Jane Beer's death was ruled an accident, and Agnes Norman was free. John William Beer angrily vowed to pursue the case further. He was as good as his word; Scotland Yard was soon on the case. On April 28, as Jane Clouson lay comatose at Guy's Hospital, a detective arrested Norman for Beer's murder. There followed a month of examinations at Lambeth Police Court before Magistrate Cuthbert Ellison, one sensational revelation following another. By the second examination, the Treasury, and sleuth-hound Harry Poland, took charge of the case. At every appearance Agnes Norman stood absolutely indifferent, perhaps bored, certainly a bit confused.

Agnes Norman obtained her first place in Camberwell in January 1869, as nursemaid to Elizabeth and Ralph Milner's four children: sixteen-month-old Tommy, two-and-a-half-year-old Minnie, six-year-old Arthur, and eight-year-old Ralph. Agnes was then herself a child—no more than twelve or thirteen, though her mother had claimed she was fifteen to get her the place. Mrs. Milner worked away from home while Agnes remained alone with the children. Less than a month after she had arrived, Agnes fetched a neighbor; something was wrong with the baby. The neighbor found Tommy Milner on a bed, undressed, dead—and cold. There was an inquest; the jury ruled Tommy Milner's death natural. Two weeks later, Agnes fetched the same neighbor to see young Minnie—like Tommy, dead, on the same bed, in the same position. This time there was no inquest. After that Elizabeth Milner, with either superhuman trust or pathetic naïveté, continued to leave her two surviving children in Agnes Norman's care. Ten days after Minnie's death the Milners returned home to find their son Arthur insensible, but alive. When Arthur finally awoke the next day, he revealed to his mother what he knew about his younger sister's death. Agnes, he said, had sent him away to buy a halfpenny sweet; while he was gone, Agnes crammed Minnie into an already stuffed wardrobe. Arthur returned to witness Agnes extricate the child: her eyes, he said, were fixed and she was incapable of sitting. Agnes put her to bed. After dinner, Arthur went with Agnes to look at the girl. Agnes felt her forehead. "Minnie is dead," Agnes said to Arthur. And then she laughed. Learning of this, the Milners could not but suspect Norman of horrendous abuse, if not of outright murder. But they had little proof, nothing beyond the word of a six-year-old. And so Elizabeth Milner did all she thought she could do, under the circumstances: she lectured Agnes Norman sternly, warning her never to work with children again. And then she dismissed her—without a character reference.

A year later, in April 1870, Agnes Norman obtained—without a reference—a place in nearby Brixton, as a maid and nursemaid to Mrs. Euphemia Gardner and her fifteen-month-old son, James Alexander. Almost immediately, the Gardners' considerable menagerie of pets began to die: two cats, a favorite dog, a parrot, six or eight other birds, a dozen goldfish. And then, ten days after she arrived, another child died in her care: not James Gardner, but an unlucky infant by the name of John Stuart Taylor, who had been left with the girl while his mother visited with Mrs. Gardner. Again, there was an inquest; again, the jury ruled the death natural.

Less than three weeks after that, Mrs. Gardner discovered her own son dead in his bed.

Although all life in her household but her own had been extinguished in less than a month, Euphemia Gardner harbored no suspicion whatever against Agnes Norman. Still, she was forced to let the girl go: death had rendered her place redundant. Mrs. Gardner did her best to ensure that Agnes Norman would quickly find another place by giving her a good reference, noting her "sobriety and civility." By July Agnes had found a place as a maid-of-all-work for the Brown family in Newington. Again, the pets quickly began to die: the cat, the canary, the linnet, the goldfish. One parrot miraculously survived, though with injuries about the throat. The Browns apparently had no children, but a nephew, ten-year-old Charles Parfitt, had the misfortune to visit them on school holiday that August. One morning, the boy awoke to find Agnes Norman kneeling upon him, one of her hands clamped over his mouth and the other gripping his throat. He managed to make a noise; Norman hopped off of him and offered him a sweet if he didn't cry—and if he didn't tell. He told, and his aunt and uncle believed him. Despite their suspicions about the girl, however, Agnes remained with them for several days, until her resentment at the Browns' distrust of her became intolerable and she ran away.

Eight months later, on April 4, 1871, again with no character reference, but with the recommendation of a neighbor's servant-girl, the Beers engaged Norman for three shillings a week. Just three days later baby Jessie died. And before the inquest could take place, a cat and a canary followed. They would be the last creatures to die under her care: in the Beers Agnes Norman had finally come across a family who would not let her walk away, and who put their trust in the police and not the coroner.

Logically, the evidence against Agnes Norman was compelling. Even given the high rate of childhood mortality at the time, when nearly 30 percent of all English children never lived to see their tenth birthday, the astronomical death toll in this case with only one obvious common factor—Agnes Norman's presence—was simply too great to attribute to the workings of nature. Legally, however, the evidence against Agnes Norman was problematic, much of it quite probably inadmissible in court. Most of the deaths occurred without a witness. Only six-year-old Arthur Milner had seen Agnes—apparently—committing murder, and only ten-year-old Charles Parfitt witnessed her attempting to take a life (his own). And whether the evidence of one murder might be introduced to prove a completely different murder was, at best, an open question. The coroner at the inquest upon Jessie Jane Beer was adamant: it could not. When the infant's father attempted to introduce witnesses to detail the girl's corpse-strewn history, the coroner cut him off: "Have you witnesses to say she murdered your child?" he asked. Beer did not; none of his witnesses were allowed to testify. Magistrate Ellison, on the other hand, deemed the girl's history fully admissible, against the vehement protest of her counsel. And what Ellison learned was more than enough for him to commit the girl for trial at the Old Bailey. And so, one day after Edmund Pook entered Newgate, the perpetually perplexed girl found herself further perplexed to be in that prison. A week later, when the recorder of London, Russell Gurney, presented the case to the grand jury, he made it clear that the girl's history could not be admitted to prove a single instance of murder. "According to the laws of England," he told the jury, "every charge must rest upon the specific evidence relating to it," and further noted that very little specific evidence directly connected the girl with these deaths. The grand jury, obviously more impressed than the recorder by the transcripts of the girl's examinations, ignored his argument altogether and returned five true bills against her: four for murder* and the fifth for the attempted murder of Charles Parfitt.

Agnes Norman's trial, like Edmund Pook's, was then delayed until the July sessions. And so for another month the girl waited, a cypher in Newgate. The public might have heard enough about her case to be at least deeply suspicious that the girl was a prolific killer, but *why* she killed remained an utter mystery. Whether she harbored a motiveless malignity against her employers, or whether she was lashing out against her inescapable life of drudgery, was a question the courts could not answer, and the eerily placid girl would not. She might early on have offered the very slightest clue to her motivation, however, to an anguished Elizabeth Milner. At the moment when, two of her children already dead, Milner discovered her son Arthur comatose, she had asked Agnes Norman whether she liked children.

"No, not much," the girl calmly replied.

---

* Specifically, true bills for the murder of Tommy and Minnie Milner, John Stuart Taylor, and Jessie Jane Beer. For some reason, Norman was never charged with the murder of James Alexander Gardner.

As the examinations of both Edmund Pook and Agnes Norman were nearing their close, another killing gripped public attention—this one not south of the Thames, but in the heart of the metropolis, and at the fringe of high society in a situation, according to the *Times*, "too well known to a large part of the London world, too little known to the rest." Just before midnight on May 24 PC Charles Futerall was called by a doctor to 23 Newton Road, in Bayswater, where in the dining room he found the well-dressed corpse of Frederick Graves Moon lying faceup in a sea of blood. Moon had been stabbed in the side; a seven-inch poultry-carving knife lay beside him in a fireplace grate. Futerall asked the doctor beside him who had done this. "The person was in the house," the doctor replied. In the next room Futerall found a woman on the sofa, wildly excited and sobbing, her hair and clothing disheveled, her jacket, shirt, and skirt sodden bloody. Futerall immediately told her to consider herself under arrest. The woman gave her name as Flora Davy. She was thirty-eight years old, tall, stout, and muscular. She had been alone in the dining room with Moon when he had been stabbed; she admitted to several witnesses that they had scuffled. More than once she had stated that she thought she had done it.

It was obvious from the start that Frederick Moon had died during an altercation with Flora Davy. Nonetheless, the newspapers agreed that the Bayswater affair was a mystery—a mystery that centered upon Davy's intent at the moment of the stabbing. Was the killing outright murder, or manslaughter, or neither? Had Davy acted with cold premeditation; had Frederick Moon provoked her into a hot-blooded attack? Had she, rather, acted in self-defense— or had Moon possibly died as the result of a horrible accident? By the next morning, Flora Davy had procured the services of George Lewis, solicitor to many of London's elite—including the Prince of Wales. A soft-spoken, genial man outside the courtroom, Lewis was a tenacious battler within, and a particularly powerful cross-examiner. He appeared at Marylebone Police Court in command of the case, and from the start promoted the theory about Moon's death that best served his client: that Flora Davy had no reason to stab Frederick Moon—that indeed, she had every reason *not* to stab him—and that it was more than possible that he had died by accident, by managing somehow to fall upon the knife.

A man by the name of Captain Daniel Bishop Davy appeared in court that day and, with Lewis's help, was able to post Mrs. Davy's bail. Flora Davy returned to her home in Bayswater—the home, it turned out, that Captain Davy owned. The next day, however, at the command of the indignant magistrate, John Mansfield, the police rearrested her and hauled her back to his court. Mansfield declared he had been "grossly deceived": he had learned that Captain Davy was not Mrs. Davy's husband—that indeed, Mrs. Davy was not actually Mrs. Davy. Nor was she married to Frederick Moon. Her actual name was Hannah Newington; she had married a man named William Newington a dozen years before. Soon afterward he abandoned her and absconded to Australia. He had done so because of money problems, Davy later declared; actually, he had shunned her because she had become passionately attracted to Frederick Graves Moon, a wealthy gentleman-brewer and the son of a former Lord Mayor of London. Her husband gone, Hannah Newington came to an arrangement with Moon: he would keep and protect her as his mistress; she would retain the accoutrements of high society she had enjoyed with her marriage—while forever removing herself from that society. "I forfeited husband and character," she lamented before the magistrate, "in trying to add to his happiness." For a dozen years Flora Davy had held to this agreement with Frederick Moon; but at least three years before this she had placed herself under the protection of Captain Davy, as well, and since then she had served as the mistress to two masters, each supporting her generously. Apparently, neither man quite knew the extent of the involvement of the other in Flora Davy's life.

The true fascination of the case, as it played itself out in newspaper reports of the inquest and the police examinations that May and June, lay less in Frederick Moon's death and more in his life—or, to be more specific, in the luxurious but secret life of a metropolitan gentleman of pleasure and of the woman he kept; lives spent, as the *Times* put it, in "a sort of quicksand of social confusion and moral corruption." By outward appearance a moderately wealthy lady, Flora Davy was, in a sense, a servant—but one occupying a different sphere altogether than Jane Clouson or Agnes Norman. Testimony revealed the fine trappings of her Bayswater villa: the billiard table, the fine cut-glass decanters holding finer wines and brandy; the cigars for the gentlemen callers; the carved sideboard and the overstuffed furniture. And there were the revelations of a life both privileged and degraded: the horses she kept and the afternoons at the local riding school; the several society doctors—the future royal physician William Gull among them—who treated her maladies; the journeys she made with her "Fred," when, for a time, she could pretend to be "Mrs. Moon." But also there were the aliases she adopted to keep up her various pretenses (the Countess, Miss De Morne, Madame De Morne, Mrs. Frances S. Canning). Also there was her dubious and constant companion, Mrs. Toynbee—long separated from Mr. Toynbee—who swore she served Davy as a friend and not a hireling, but who clearly profited as well from Mr. Moon's largesse, and who swore before the magistrate, hesitantly, that she knew Mrs. Davy shared her bed with two men. And also there were the rather mysterious young ladies who were in her house to divert Mrs. Davy on the night Mr. Moon was stabbed, "found there no one knows how or why," according to the *Times*. (Actually, they were the daughter and niece of a woman with whom Flora Davy had once lodged, the niece, incidentally and coincidentally, a Pook.) These young ladies, it became clear, kept up a not quite respectable flirtation with some of the gentlemen visitors to the house—those friends of Mr. Moon who were privy to his secret life.

That secret life followed a trajectory to disaster—the inevitable trajectory, to anyone steeped in Victorian morality. Flora Davy was volatile and imperious, according to her servants; a dipsomaniac, according to her doctors—one of whom prescribed her champagne to improve her temperance. Captain Davy, for whatever reason, began to spend less and less time at 23 Newton Road; Frederick Moon too, according to his friends, was tiring of his demanding "Countess" and had vowed to pay her off and have done with her. Flora Davy, more and more, chafed at the insults she endured from Moon; soon before he was killed she had made the mistake of referring to herself as Moon's wife. "No, you are not," Moon snapped at her, "and what is more, you never will be as long as I live." In reply, she had threatened to kill him one day. And then erupted the final argument. The afternoon before the stabbing Flora Davy had ignored Moon's request to dine with him, and that evening Moon came to the house in a dark mood. He and Flora ate alone while Mrs. Toynbee and the young women entertained themselves in the billiard room, and he became querulous. He baited her with a foul remark about Mrs. Davy's mysterious and absent daughter, and when she protested, he took up a decanter and threatened to wallop her if she did not hold her tongue. She leapt up and grabbed the poultry knife—in self-defense, she claimed—and they rushed together. They scuffled and he fell, the knife having entered his side to the hilt. She screamed, desperately attempted to revive the man, sent the servants and the young ladies out to fetch doctors. The police arrived and arrested her. "He was my very all," Flora Davy sobbed on June 15, at the end of her last examination, protesting her innocence. "Without him all is a blank to me." But by then a coroner's jury had already bound her over for trial, and the magistrate could only concur with them. Whether she should be tried for manslaughter or murder Mansfield left for the grand jury to decide. That evening Davy joined Edmund Pook and Agnes Norman at Newgate. The three would be tried simultaneously during the July sessions, in the three separate courtrooms of the Old Bailey.

While Pook, Norman, and Davy awaited trial, the case of the century continued its apparently endless—but also endlessly captivating—way along in two courtrooms in Westminster Hall, both of them far too small to contain the daily floods of would-be spectators. The two trials of the Tichborne Claimant, the first—this one—civil and the second criminal, would, taken together, hold the record for the longest-lasting legal case in British history until the end of the twentieth century.* Measured by its ability to generate newspaper column-inches beyond count, its ability to generate limitless discussion and debate—in drawing rooms and servants' quarters, in the clubs and the public houses—and in its ability to generate a full-fledged popular movement that endured for well over a decade, the Tichborne saga was indisputably the legal sensation of the Victorian era. And although no one realized it as the civil case of *Tichborne v. Lushington* that gripped public attention in May and June, that case was in July to intersect dramatically with the criminal case of *R v. Pook*.

The Tichborne Claimant had first come to the attention of the public five years before, at the end of 1866, when newspapers reported that that bulky, mysterious personage was nearing the end of his voyage from Australia to England, returning to make good his claim that he was Sir Roger Charles Tichborne, heir to the Tichborne baronetcy and the Tichborne estates. From the first, he and his claim were controversial. "Great numbers of persons believe that the Tichborne family have been imposed upon by some clever schemer in Australia," the *Daily News* reported in November 1866, adding that "a few days, however, will decide the matter." Actually, it would be seven years before the matter was decided in the

---

* The Tichborne case endured for 291 days (103 days for the civil trial and 291 for the criminal). The McLibel trial, which eventually ended in 1997 after 313 days, finally eclipsed in length the Tichborne case.

courtroom. For many, doubts would linger for years after that, and for some, they would never die.

The last time that the indisputable Roger Charles Tichborne had been seen alive was in April 1854, when he—then a slender and delicate man with light-brown hair—embarked in Rio de Janeiro upon the sailing ship *Bella* for Kingston, Jamaica. That ship was never seen again; everyone presumed Roger Tichborne dead. Everyone, that is, except his mother, the dowager Lady Tichborne, a temperamental—many thought unbalanced—Frenchwoman who refused to relinquish the hope that he had somehow been saved. When her husband died in 1862, she was free to indulge in her obsession, and placed advertisements in the *Times* and then in Australian newspapers, promising "A handsome REWARD" for any information about her son. This enticing appeal was bound to get a response, and it did, in a letter from a butcher from Wagga Wagga, New South Wales, who called himself Thomas Castro, and who represented himself as the dowager's son. After the butcher convinced a couple of former retainers to the Tichbornes that he was actually the baronet, and after obtaining the financial backing of a number of Sydneyites, the Tichborne Claimant set sail with his family and landed in London on Christmas Day 1866. From there, he traveled to Paris where, as he lay sick in bed in a dark room, the dowager Lady Tichborne recognized him, and acknowledged him as her son.

The rest of the Tichbornes were far less credulous than the dowager about his claim. Almost without exception, and after several of them had had uncomfortable meetings with the Claimant, they concluded that he was a vulgar imposter bent upon stealing the Tichborne title and fortune from its rightful possessor, Roger's infant nephew Henry Tichborne. The Claimant, they believed, had nothing of Roger Tichborne's manners or attainments, and he could not speak a word of French, although the true Roger Tichborne had been born and had lived his first sixteen years in Paris. They quickly instituted an investigation of the Claimant, engaging in particular the services of the well-known detective

Jonathan Whicher. Whicher turned up a great deal of evidence to suggest that the Claimant was Arthur Orton, the son of a Wapping butcher, who had sailed from England as a young man and who had eventually disappeared into Australia.

A courtroom battle for the claim was inevitable, and became pressing for the Claimant with the death of the dowager Lady Tichborne and the loss of her financial support, in 1868. While almost every member of the Tichborne family would swear that the Claimant was not Roger Tichborne, a great many outside the family—particularly among the servants to the family, among Tichborne locals, and among the soldiers with whom Roger had served—were more than willing to swear that he was. Moreover, for what it was worth—and in the long run, it proved to be worth a great deal—the Claimant found greater and greater support among the public, and particularly among the working-class public. For, curiously, they saw the Claimant as one of them—or, more specifically, as one who *chose to be* one of them, a man who turned his back on the effete and genteel life of an English aristocrat for the rough-and-tumble life of a workingman in Australia. He was an underdog, against whom the full forces of the rich and powerful were arrayed.

Tichborne v. Lushington commenced in the tiny Court of Common Pleas, in Westminster Hall, on May 10.* As the Claimant brought the action to eject the current tenant from the Tichborne family seat, he was ostensibly the plaintiff. In a larger sense, he was the defendant, defending his entire claim. The trial promised to be one of unprecedented duration, with a hundred or so witnesses prepared to testify in favor of the Claimant's claim, and more than 250 prepared to testify against it. But key to the case was a single witness: the Claimant himself. If he could convince the jury that he was Roger Tichborne, with Tichborne's experience and Tichborne's

---

* Applications to view the trial proved so persistent and powerful that the judge was able to move the trial, for a time, across the hall to the larger Court of Queen's Bench. This did little to relieve the crush and the disappointment of would-be spectators.

memories, he would likely win the great prize. If, on the other hand, the barristers representing the Tichborne family could break him down and expose his testimony as the inventions of an opportunistic imposter, they could destroy his claim once and for all. Public interest in the case intensified on May 30—the day, incidentally, that Edmund Pook was committed to Newgate—as the Claimant lugubriously made his way to the witness box. And it soared three days later, when the great legal duel of his cross-examination began.

The Tichborne's Claimant's epic antagonist—his grand inquisitor and chief tormentor—was John Duke Coleridge. When *Tichborne v. Lushington* began, Coleridge was solicitor general of England and Wales; before the case was done, he would be attorney general. Although he was acting privately and not for the government in this case, the fact that such a high government official led the case against him only contributed to the popular feeling that the mighty were leagued to bring the Claimant down. John Duke Coleridge, son of a noted judge and grand-nephew of the more-noted poet, was known as an advocate of superhuman industry who had an ambition to match. He would eventually rise to the heights of his profession; both his prodigious talents and his political connections—he was a Liberal MP and a very good friend of Prime Minister William Gladstone—would eventually gain him the Lord Chief Justiceship of England. Coleridge's oratorical ability was legendary, his speeches saturated with classical and literary allusion and heavy with sentiment: "he would pull at the organ stop labelled 'pathos,' as readily as the one labelled 'moral indignation,'" notes one chronicler of this trial. Though his parliamentary foe, Benjamin Disraeli, dismissed his speechifying as "a stream of silvery mediocrity," it would certainly serve him well in this case, in the record-setting twenty-one-day opening speech for the defense he would later give.

Coleridge's cross-examination of the Claimant established a record for length, as well. For a full twenty-two days Coleridge sought to wear down the Claimant, forcing him beyond his relentless protestations of "I don't know" and "I have forgotten" to commit himself to assertions that he could either instantly or in time prove to be patently false. Prefacing his queries with a belittling "would it surprise you to know," words that quickly became the popular catchphrase of 1871, Coleridge laid bare the "ruffian's ignorance," as he put it in his diary. Although as a boy Roger Tichborne had studied Latin and Greek at Stonyhurst, an English public school, the Claimant could not tell him whether Caesar wrote in Latin or Greek; Greek, he thought. And he made a similar mistake when shown a page of Virgil: "It appears to me to be Greek," he told Coleridge. "It is Greek to you, anyhow," Coleridge replied, to laughter. On June 5, the Claimant made the most sensational claim of all, concerning sealed instructions that Roger Tichborne had left with his steward when he had sailed from England in 1852. Those instructions, the Claimant testified, provided for the care of Roger Tichborne's cousin and then-fiancée, Katherine Doughty, if she was pregnant.

"Do you mean to swear before the Judge and jury," Coleridge asked him, "that you seduced this lady?"

"I most solemnly to my God swear I did."

Tichborne's cousin—now Lady Radcliffe—was present in the courtroom, sitting beside her husband, and Coleridge pointed her out. "This Lady?"

"Yes, that Lady."

A "sensation," as the newspapers put it, erupted in the courtroom. In an instant, the Claimant had revealed himself to be a churl if he wasn't an outright liar, and had rendered the case more than a battle for title and property, but also one for a lady's honor. Moreover, Lady Radcliffe knew this claim to be untrue, and would in time swear to that. And Coleridge had the facts to prove that Roger Tichborne was nowhere near Katherine Doughty when this seduction was alleged to have taken place. In this despicable claim-within-a-claim lay the seeds of the Claimant's destruction.

For the few lucky spectators in the courtroom, and for the hundreds of thousands who followed the case in the newspapers, it was all pure entertainment, real-life sensation beyond the prodigious talents of Wilkie Collins or Mary Elizabeth Braddon. For the Claimant and the solicitor general, however, it was exhausting and debilitating combat. The Claimant, sickly and morbidly obese[*] when his ordeal began, only deteriorated under the strain, relentlessly pleading for, and usually obtaining, recesses and early adjournments. For Coleridge the cross involved perpetual study of a mountain of evidence. One morning Coleridge informed the court that he had been working on the case until four that morning. "I pity you, Mr. Solicitor," the judge, William Bovill, told him. "The labor devolving upon you is almost beyond human endurance." "He will kill me before I do him," Coleridge wrote about the Claimant four weeks into the cross. "I am seriously wearing out and getting ill."

Sir William Bovill, Chief Justice of the Court of Common Pleas, suffered under the strain of this case as well. When he died in 1873, at the relatively young—for a judge—age of fifty-nine, public consensus held that this trial helped kill him. In spite of his elevated position on the bench, Bovill was hardly a great judge at the best of times, and the Tichborne trial brought out his worst qualities. "On the whole," the *Law Times* noted in his obituary, "the honest opinion of lawyers concerning the lamented judge must be, that he was not great, or profoundly learned." He was notorious, for one thing, for his partiality and for his habit of premature adjudication—leaping to conclusions far ahead of the evidence. That was apparent when, in the midst of the cross-examination, Bovill gave a speech at a Lord Mayor's dinner that suggested that the Claimant's claim might be a fiction. Bovill was known as well to be querulous and irritable on the bench, with a "patent want of sympathy with the Bar"; this showed itself in his habit of interrupting and even badgering counsel in mid-examination. The marathon *Tichborne v. Lushington* demanded judicial patience, and Bovill had little.

---

[*]   Over 28 stone, or nearly 400 pounds. [McWilliam 26].

Moreover, the incredible public fascination in the case placed its own pressures on the chief justice. In one sense, Bovill enjoyed the attention: he controlled the seating about him on the bench, and allotted these to the highest and mightiest of spectators—the Prince and Princess of Wales sat by him on one day, the emperor of Brazil on another—and to a flock of society ladies, with whom he was often seen to chat during examinations. The rest of the seats in the courtroom, however, he had no control over, even though he faced relentless pressure to allot them. "I have not a moment's peace of mind from morning till night, on account of the hundreds of applications sent to me by persons who wish to hear the proceedings. From the time I left this court on Friday until I came on the bench this morning I was completely inundated with applications," he complained in the courtroom. The Claimant's chief counsel actually theorized that Bovill's health suffered not so much because of judicial strain but because of "the arduous and unaccustomed duties of master of the ceremonies." The intense public scrutiny, which only grew as the trial proceeded, proved to be a greater and greater psychological burden to him as the case tarnished his reputation. "It weighs upon me," he would later say about *Tichborne v. Lushington.*

Bovill's health, then, unsound when the trial began, only deteriorated as it proceeded. He made it known that he was continuing only with the assistance of doctors, and that he desperately needed a recess, or, as he put it, "I am only enabled to attend to this case by going down to Brighton to get a little fresh air." The law favored his desire; at the time the Court of Common Pleas could not legally sit between the end of July and the first week in November. But while judge and counsel desperately looked forward to a break, the sensation-loving public absolutely did not want a several-month suspension of the great entertainment, and the Tichborne family certainly did not want any delay whatsoever in responding to the Claimant's claims: Lady Radcliffe in particular desired to defend her honor as soon as possible. The family, then, used their mighty connections to introduce bills into both Lords and Commons to abolish the mandatory recess—bills that actually passed into law.

But in the end it was Bovill and not Parliament upon whom the decision to adjourn devolved. Bovill could not continue; on July 7 he declared himself "utterly exhausted"—and was sure that the lawyers in the case were "equally if not more fatigued than myself." He did suggest a compromise—adjourning for a few weeks and reconvening in August rather than November. But the lawyers would not hear of it; a couple threatened to quit altogether if that were the case. And so Bovill adjourned the trial that day, to recommence in November. All of the remaining sensational events of the case, then—Coleridge's triumphant opening for the defense, the collapse of the Claimant's case, and the Claimant's subsequent arrest, trial, and conviction for perjury—were therefore delayed.

Before Chief Justice Bovill could escape to breathe the salubrious air of Brighton, however, he had another judicial duty to perform. He was committed to sitting during the July sessions of the Central Criminal Court. As the most prominent judge, he would naturally take on the most prominent case. Also committed to serve at the July sessions, in his official capacity as solicitor general, was John Duke Coleridge. He, too, was assigned to the most prominent case; Harry Poland, previously in charge, would still attend, but only to support Coleridge. And that is how a fatigued William Bovill and a fatigued John Duke Coleridge, having both fatigued themselves further for five days by studying the accumulated evidence in the matter of the murder of Jane Clouson, found themselves—surely now sick to death of the sight of each other—jumping together from one sensational case to another: *R v. Pook*.

CHAPTER FIVE

TALLY-HO

The usual chaos that attended the beginning of a notable murder trial prevailed outside of the Old Bailey on the morning of July 12, as hundreds clamored for the Old Court's few public seats. But the undersheriffs of London and the City police had dealt with these crowds before, and, according to one reporter, their arrangements were as "excellent as the utterly inadequate accommodation of the Court will permit." To be admitted, respectability was key: those inside the courtroom were discernibly better dressed than those outside—and, incidentally, they were disproportionately female. Among those admitted was a man whose name would have been recognized by many, even if his portly and florid face was recognized by none. While Newton Crosland made his living as a wine merchant in the City, his wife made her living and her name as a novelist of some renown Once she had published as Camilla Toulmin, but since the two had married, twenty-three years before, she published exclusively and prolifically as "Mrs. Newton Crosland." The Croslands lived across Greenwich Park from the Pooks, in Blackheath, and Newton Crosland, captivated by the murder that had occurred so close to his home, had diligently followed reports of the case from the start. Something more than this, however, had brought him to the Old Court—although exactly what, Newton Crosland was not sure.

Newton Crosland was a devoted spiritualist, an adherent to the movement that had spread to Britain from the United States some three decades before with the central precept that the dead could—and, with surprising regularity, did—communicate with the living. It was a movement that had launched thousands of séances and the careers of a multitude of mediums; and Newton Crosland had sat in on enough of the former and had dealt with enough of the latter to reach some firm conclusions about the other side. He was certain that spirits in the millions swarmed the metropolis—dead souls making the transition to a higher plane of existence, as well as angelic beings, guarding and guiding angels. Not being blessed with a medium's powers, Crosland had never actually seen any of these. But he had *heard* them; at the properly conducted séances he had attended, he counted forty-two different spirits that had rapped out elaborate communiqués, all reiterating the living truths of the Bible. "To doubt the reality of these manifestations," Crosland had written, "would be as ridiculous and foolish as to doubt the existence of the solar system." His passionate devotion to spiritualism was matched by an equally passionate disdain for the strictly material: Newtonian physics Crosland thought "old-fashioned, clumsy, mechanical, vulgar"; the theories of Charles Darwin, whose monumental *Descent of Man* had just been published in February, were "the most colossal, dazzling, infidel mass of ignorance ever launched upon the world, and palmed off upon the credulity of mankind." He was, in other words, the sort of man who would have heeded an astrologer before a scientist. And so he did take heed when an astrologer friend had written to him three weeks before to tell him of the position of the stars on the night of April 25, the night of the attack on Kidbrooke Lane. "They are certainly very curious," he wrote to Crosland, "and I still cannot help thinking portend some evil to you." Crosland thus had come to the Old Bailey on this day certain that Jane's destiny and his own were somehow linked. And in this he was absolutely correct. Jane's death and this trial were to bring him, as he later put it, "a great deal that was very unpleasant."

Perhaps surprisingly, given his beliefs, Crosland sought to find out the truth about Jane's murder not in the séance room but in the courtroom, and he put his faith, or at least his hope, in the several legal gentleman now assembling before him: Chief Justice William Bovill on the bench, flanked on this day by the Lord Mayor of London, there to lend proper gravity to the proceedings; and on the floor, the eleven lawyers: five for the defense, with John Huddleston leading and Henry Pook instructing, and six for the prosecution—four barristers, two solicitors. Among the latter group sat Harry Poland. But the sleuth-hound had already done the bulk of his work on this case and would absent himself often over the next four days in order to prosecute Flora Davy and Agnes Norman in the Old Bailey's other courtrooms. In this case, solicitor general John Duke Coleridge would lead the prosecution, and would look for his second not to Poland but to Poland's Treasury colleague, Thomas Dickson Archibald.

Coleridge knew that this would be a difficult case to win. No one had actually witnessed Edmund Pook attack Jane Clouson; no one actually saw—or remembered seeing—Pook buy the plasterer's hammer from the Thomases' shop. The police *had* managed to gather up an abundance of evidence: evidence suggesting that Edmund Pook and Jane Clouson were sexually intimate, that he was in Deptford on the night the murder weapon was purchased, that he had lured out Jane on the evening of the murder, had walked with her to Kidbrooke Lane, had bloodied his clothes and dropped a whistle there, and had slipped in the mud and dirtied his trousers while fleeing back to Greenwich. All of this evidence was circumstantial. All of it was disputable. And much of it was hearsay and therefore quite possibly inadmissible. Coleridge knew his only chance of obtaining a guilty verdict would be in presenting the evidence as a seamless whole, as totality of circumstances that, together, would lead the jury to the one inevitable conclusion that Edmund Pook was a killer. Every bit of evidence was crucial, including the hearsay testimony: the Trotts' knowledge that Jane and Edmund were lovers; Fanny Hamilton's hearing Jane say, on the night of the attack, that she was leaving to meet Edmund.* There were exceptions to the hearsay rule; with a fight, at least some of Jane's utterances to others might be allowed as evidence. Coleridge and Archibald planned to make that fight.

Coleridge's strategy dictated the defense's—and John Huddleston's—counter-strategy. Huddleston would do his best to render Coleridge's seamless whole an out-and-out mess, disrupting witnesses and sowing doubt about their testimony. He would, in other words, adopt what had been Henry Pook's strategy before the coroner and the magistrate. But Huddleston would also do what Henry Pook had carefully refrained from doing: he would finally bring forward witnesses for the defense, who could support Edmund's alibis, contradict prosecution witnesses—and speak to Edmund's good character.

Edmund Pook would not appear as a witness in his own defense; at that time, criminal defendants were legally prohibited from doing so. Nevertheless, he played his own part in convincing jury and spectators of his innocence. As Edmund was led up by underground

---

* Jane Prosser's stunning revelation of Jane's pregnancy and Edmund's paternity, on the other hand, would not be a part of the prosecution's evidence. Either because the Treasury had found cause to discount her claims, or because they had decided that no judge would admit them, they had dropped Jane Prosser from their list of witnesses.

passage and took his place in the prisoner's dock, it was immediately clear to all that his unshakeable and well-publicized calm had not deserted him. Though prison-pale and tired, he had, according to one reporter, "nothing of the hang-dog, cowering look which the mere fact of being in the dock seems to impress upon so many faces": the very last person in that courtroom that anybody would select as a brutal murderer "was the prisoner at the bar."

With Pook in place, the trial began; the jurors' names were read over* and Pook calmly but emphatically pleaded that he was not guilty. John Duke Coleridge then delivered the opening speech for the prosecution—and his silver tongue, for the most part, failed him. Because he felt compelled to refrain from even mentioning the hearsay evidence until he was certain it would be admitted, he was hamstrung from the start, and his attempts to connect Edmund Pook with Jane's murder were hesitant, awkward, and incomplete. When, for example, he told the jury of Jane's parting from Fanny Hamilton as she walked off to her death, he did not tell them that Jane told Hamilton that she was meeting Edmund Pook; he could only say that "some observations were made by Jane Clouson . . . which at the present moment I abstain from stating to you, because, though I believe they are receivable in evidence, they may be objected to." That sort of evasiveness was sure to confuse any jury.

Coleridge was more successful in at least beginning to strip away at the aura of innocence that emanated from the prisoner in the dock. By detailing Edmund Pook's several affairs, some serious and some flirtations, with a number of young women, Coleridge anticipated and countered a central contention of Edmund's defense: that he had not the character—nor, being carefully watched, the opportunity—to engage in sexual relations with his servant. Two letters Coleridge read in court demonstrated that Edmund was at

---

* To encourage a fair verdict, and because of the civil split the case had provoked south of the Thames, no one from either Kent or Surrey was allowed to sit on this jury. [T July 13, 11.]

the same time deeply involved with two young women. The first, written to Edmund from Wales by an aunt, made it clear that Edmund was actively proposing marriage to one of his cousins. The second letter—from Edmund himself, written to Alice Durnford soon after he was arrested—suggested his equal interest in her. That letter in particular told against Edmund's character with its flippancy in the face of Jane's brutal murder, and at least hinted that his unshakeable calm might instead be sheer callousness. "If I am remanded," Edmund had written to Alice, "of course I must 'grin and bear it.'" Coleridge noted Edmund's insensitivity, as well, in his response to Griffin and Mulvany when they first told him that Jane Clouson was dead: Edmund then told them that she was "dirty in her habits" and had in consequence left his father's service. Coleridge vowed to defend Jane Clouson from that particular slur: he would, he told the jury, call witnesses to testify that the girl was clean and respectable. Finally, Coleridge revealed that Edmund was a liar, having falsely told two girls, Mary Ann Love and Alice Langley, that he could not meet them on the night Jane Clouson was murdered because he was engaged to perform in London.

But here the chief justice interrupted Coleridge for the first—and far from the last—time. Perhaps, Bovill pointed out, this was not a lie; perhaps Edmund intended to go to London and changed his mind afterward.

That, Coleridge responded, was for the jury to determine.

Having thus provided these hints of Edmund's malevolence, Coleridge called three witnesses to fix the jury's attention upon Jane Clouson's horrible death. PC Donald Gunn and Sergeant Frederick Haynes described finding her, broken and degraded, wishing only to die; physician Michael Harris offered a chilling catalog of her injuries and disclosed the fact of the dead and corrupting being in her womb. John Huddleston, in cross-examination, did his best to wrest the jury's attention away from Jane, and fix it instead upon the police and their relentless bungling. In questioning Gunn, Huddleston emphasized the curious fact that he had not discovered Jane until dawn, even though—according to the theory of the police—she had been attacked a good seven or eight hours before, and even though Gunn had *twice* passed the spot by 2:15. (Lord Chief Bovill had introduced this subject by asking Gunn why his predecessor on the Kidbrooke beat—an officer named Mortimer—had not discovered Jane earlier. "I don't think he was on duty up to ten o'clock," Gunn had answered.) Gunn now admitted to Huddleston that on that night he had, for the first part of the night, walked an entirely different beat. "So that this lonely place is left without a policeman till a quarter-past two?" the chief justice interrupted. "Yes," admitted Gunn. And Gunn admitted as well to a badly missed opportunity: neither he nor anyone else in his presence had taken a single step to preserve or to measure any of the many footprints found by the girl's body.

Sergeant Haynes, as well, admitted a missed opportunity: he had failed to take into evidence the bloody stone he (and he alone) had spotted hundreds of yards from the scene of the attack. Huddleston then pressed Haynes to reveal an even more egregious omission on the part of the police: the knowledge they had of the existence of another possible suitor for Jane. The police had originally thought that the locket found upon Jane's body had been given to her by Edmund; Jane's cousin Charlotte had told them so. But Haynes admitted that in May Henry Humphreys, the middle-aged and married former assistant in the Pooks' shop, had come forward and told police he had given the locket to Jane, and that the jeweler who had sold the locket had verified that fact. Haynes also admitted that Humphreys had never appeared before the magistrate or coroner. Although this revelation of Mr. Humphreys was hardly new—it had been reported widely in the newspapers two months before, as Huddleston was well aware—the fact that Humphreys's existence had been kept out of evidence by police and prosecution until this moment surely smacked to the jury of deliberate suppression.

Michael Harris's shocking yet clinical description of Jane's wounds and her death, on the other hand, left nothing to the imagination. But Huddleston was able to use the very grievousness of Jane's wounds to deflect suspicion from Edmund. "Where there are such wounds as these, I should expect blood to spurt forth," Harris testified. And yet only a tiny amount of blood had been discovered on Edmund Pook's clothing.

After the police and the doctor, Coleridge called the three witnesses whose most powerful evidence by far consisted of Jane Clouson's words to them: Elizabeth Trott, her daughter, Charlotte, and Fanny Hamilton. With the first two, Coleridge refrained altogether from touching upon hearsay. He might have been waiting to test the admissibility of Fanny Hamilton's hearsay evidence before he tested theirs; he might have lost his nerve and concluded that their hearsay would never be admitted. In any case, with both Elizabeth and Charlotte Trott he limited his questioning to Jane's character alone, to counter Edmund's assertion that Jane was filthy to the point of impropriety. "She was not dirty, quite different to that altogether; a very clean, respectable young woman, and a hard-working industrious one, too," Elizabeth Trott testified, and her daughter agreed.

It was with Fanny Hamilton and her hearsay that John Duke Coleridge determined to make his stand. When she and Jane parted in Deptford at exactly 6:40, Hamilton testified, "she told me where she was going."

"What did she say to you?" Coleridge asked her.

Huddleston objected immediately, citing the then-standard argument against hearsay: because Jane Clouson was dead and could not be cross-examined, anything that she might have said was now inadmissible as evidence. Coleridge countered that Jane's declaration to Fanny Hamilton accompanied an act, and was indeed so much a part of that act that it ought to be admitted as evidence. Coleridge, in other words, argued for what was known then as the *res gestae* exception to the hearsay rule. *Res gestae* statements— from the Latin for "things done"—are those uttered spontaneously concerning an event by a person caught up entirely in the excitement of that event. Such statements, it was believed, were spoken without reflection and therefore without guile or equivocation. They were, in other words, likely to be truthful explanations, and not likely to be misremembered or misrepresented by anyone hearing them. Of all Jane's words spoken in the days before her death, Coleridge and the Crown had concluded that Jane's words to Fanny Hamilton were the most likely to be admitted as *res gestae* evidence. For she excitedly, spontaneously spoke those words at the very moment of her departure from Hamilton, and her words explained her reason for departing: she was going to meet Edmund; they had much to talk about; he had made great promises to her. Her words, then, both accompanied and qualified the act of her departure; they deserved consideration in court as a part of that act.

Coleridge argued the point as if his case depended upon it, citing a host of precedents for admitting this evidence. He then turned to his second, Thomas Archibald, to bolster his argument. But Archibald added little. Newton Crosland, in the gallery, was unimpressed: "the question," he noted, "was not ably argued." And on the bench Chief Justice Bovill was equally dismissive, holding, remarkably, that Jane's words—even though they connected her with Edmund Pook on the night of the murder—suggested nothing at all about the murder. "It seems to me," he ruled, "that the question asked, and the evidence which it is intended to elicit, is entirely irrelevant to the issue, and not sustainable on any of the grounds which have been urged on behalf of the Crown. I know of no precedent for its admission, and I am unwilling to create one. It is inadmissible."

It was a devastating blow for the prosecution. In that instant, any hope they had of demonstrating a motive on Edmund Pook's part for killing Jane—their sexual involvement and the fact that she likely was pregnant by him—were dashed. All that was left to suggest any sort of motivation was meager at best: nothing more than the fact that the two had lived in the same house for nearly two years. The damage done to their case by the complete exclusion

of Jane's words from trial became glaringly evident that afternoon, when, after several witnesses appeared to testify to the
finding of the hammer at Morden College, Detective Inspector
Mulvany and then Superintendent Griffin took the witness box
to give detailed accounts of their confrontation with and arrest
of Edmund Pook. Since the Trotts and Fanny Hamilton could
not provide any basis for the allegations the officers leveled
against Edmund Pook on that day, their allegations could only
appear to be absolutely baseless—mere stabs in the dark, blind
attempts to entrap the young man. In cross-examination, John
Huddleston elicited from both officers Edmund Pook's and his
father's fervent denials that the young man had had anything
to do with Jane's death, denials that now must have seemed
more convincing to the jury than Mulvany's and Griffin's seemingly invented allegations. On the very first day of Edmund's
trial, then, John Huddleston succeeded in altering the roles of
wrongdoer and victim altogether. Edmund had come into the
courtroom the alleged predator, Jane of course his victim. But
now, the police began to take on the role of predators, and the
young man in the dock the role of their victim.

Certainly, Chief Justice Bovill saw things that way. And when
John Mulvany and James Griffin testified, Bovill proved a valuable
ally to John Huddleston in effecting this shift.

All that day Newton Crosland, observing from the gallery, had
harbored suspicions against William Bovill's fitness as a judge. "He
seemed," Crosland later wrote, "out of condition, irritable, nervous,
and disposed to quarrel with anyone who gave him a chance."
Mulvany and Griffin gave him that chance. Bovill lashed out at
John Mulvany when the detective described Edmund's alibi for the
evening of the murder—walking to Lewisham, standing outside
his lady-friend's home, and returning to Greenwich via Royal Hill.
That might have been the way Edmund had come, Mulvany added,
suggesting simply that he might have come home by other streets
as well—South Street or Crooms Hill, for example.

LEFT: A sketch of Kidbrooke Lane at the time of the murder. 'It is impossible', noted the *Greenwich and Deptford Chronicle*, 'to conceive a more retired, more secluded place in which in the gloom and darkness of the night to perpetrate a black and horrible crime.'

THE MURDER AT ELT-HAM

CENTRE AND RIGHT: Imaginative depictions of the crime from the *Illustrated Police News*. (CENTRE) The attack. To the left is an image of the murder weapon, a J Sorby #2 plasterer's hammer. (RIGHT) PC Donald Gunn stumbles upon the body of Jane Clouson.

The undermentioned Houses are situate within the Boundaries of the —

No. of Schedule	ROAD, STREET, &c., and No. or NAME of HOUSE	HOUSES Inhabited / Uninhabited / Building	NAME and Surname of each Person	RELATION to Head of Family	CON-DITION	AGE of Males / Females	Rank, Profession, or OCCUPATION	WHERE BORN	Whether 1. Deaf-and-Dumb 2. Blind 3. Imbecile or Idiot 4. Lunatic
1	1 London S'	1	Richard T. Orchard	Head	Mar	50	Licensed Victualler	Kent, Somerset	
			Eliza Do	Wife	Mar	44		Suffolk, Ipswich	
			William Jn Do	Son		14	Civil Service of the —	Parish, Greenwich	
			Vincent Do	Son		10	Scholar	Do Do	
			Leticia Do	Daur		8	Do	Do Do	
			Iris Do	Daur		6	Do	Do Do	
			Edith Do	Daur		1		Do Do	
			Irene Nicol	Serv't	Unm		Barmaid	Greatly, Robert's S'	
			Eliza Williams	Serv't	Unm		Housemaid	Surrey, Richmond	
2	3 London S'	1	George W. Pook	Head	Mar		Boneworker	Kent, Lingfield	
			Mary Ann Do	Wife	Mar			Do Do	
			Elizabeth Chaplin	Serv't	Unm		Scholar (Certificated)	Do Deptford	
			Richard Chaplin	Son			Visitor	Do Do	
			Jane Louisa Chaplin	Daur				Surrey, Greenwich	
3	5 London S'	1	William G. Penfold	Head	Mar		Visitor	Kent, Deptford	
			Do	Wife	Mar			Do Do	
			Alice Ann Robinson	Sister	Unm			Do Greenwich	
			Robertson & Penfold	Son		12		Kent, Greenwich	
			Ella Francis Do	Daur		9		Do Deptford	
4	Do	1	Joseph Greenoak	Head	Unm	30	Irishman	York, Newcastle	

Total of Houses .. 4 — Total of Males and Females .. 8

* Draw the pen through such of the words as are inappropriate.

Reg— Sheet H.

The 1871 English Census—taken just three weeks before the attack on Kidbrooke Lane—showing the inhabitants at 3 London Street, residence of Ebenezer Pook and his family, listing Jane Clouson as a domestic general servant. A week after this Jane would abruptly quit the Pooks' employ.

Jane Maria Clouson. This studio photograph was almost certainly the one used to identify her body, and the clothes she is wearing—the walking-out clothes of a servant—are almost certainly the clothes she was wearing when she was attacked. *Courtesy Greenwich Heritage Centre.*

Edmund Walter Pook and his mother, Mary. Photographed at a studio at Herne Bay, Kent, Edmund Pook's place of exile in the months after his trial for murder. *Courtesy of the McLeod family.*

'Eltham Pilgrims: Whit Monday in Kidbrooke Lane.' A satirical depiction from the *Graphic* of the floods of visitors to the murder site. Commentators presented the pilgrimage as a vulgar carnival, ignoring altogether the popular sympathy and reverence shown for Jane Clouson.

ABOVE: A portrait of Edmund Pook and principal participants at his police court examination, from the May 27 1871 issue of the *Illustrated Police News*. Clockwise from upper left: Henry Letheby, expert medical witness; Harry Poland, prosecuting on behalf of the Treasury Department; Alice Durnford, Edmund Pook's acknowledged lady friend; and Henry Pook, Edmund's fiery solicitor—and no relation to him. BELOW: An earlier and far less accurate portrait of Edmund from the *Illustrated Police News*; this portrait had been spotted by a key eyewitness, William Sparshott, in a shop window, leading to charges that Sparshott's identification had been hopelessly tainted.

ABOVE AND BELOW LEFT: The principals in the trial of *R v. Pook*: John Huddleston for the defense (ABOVE LEFT), John Duke Coleridge for the prosecution (ABOVE RIGHT), and Chief Justice William Bovill on the bench (BELOW LEFT). BELOW RIGHT: Newton Crosland. Crosland's published claims that *R v. Pook* was a travesty prompted a barrage of litigation on behalf of Edmund Pook.

SIR W. BOVILL, CHIEF JUSTICE, COMMON PLEAS.

PRETTY JANE

OR, THE

VIPER OF KIDBROOK LANE

Pretty Jane: or, the Viper of Kidbrooke Lane. The penny dreadful hastily got up to capitalize upon Jane Clouson's murder. *Courtesy The British Library.*

Jane Clouson's Monument, at Brockley and Ladywell Cemeteries.

Bovill pounced upon the detective's turn of phrase—understanding his "might" as suggesting skepticism about Edmund's claim. Newton Crosland recorded the exchange:

> The Judge (angrily): "Might have been! What do you mean by might have been? Was it not, Sir, his most direct road?"
>
> Mr. Mulvany: "It was one of the roads. I am not minutely acquainted with the locality."
>
> The Judge (with solemn irritability): "You are giving your evidence very badly, Mr. Mulvany!"

"This unjust aspersion upon Mr. Mulvany soon became epidemic," Crosland wrote. "'Abusing the Police' was at once 'the mode.' The game was started from the Bench, and the 'tantivy' and 'tally-ho' soon became fast and furious."

If anything, Superintendent Griffin's testimony drew Bovill's greater wrath. In his testimony, Griffin several times made it clear that, when confronted, Edmund Pook had vehemently and constantly denied any involvement in Jane Clouson's murder. But once, apparently, he slipped. Testifying that he had told Edmund that Jane had planned to meet him on Crooms Hill the evening of the attack, Griffin noted that Edmund "had made no reply." John Huddleston, however, watching carefully for any deviation from Griffin's testimony before the magistrate and the coroner, discerned one here: before the coroner, Huddleston asserted, Griffin had stated that Edmund *had* replied, and had denied meeting Jane. Huddleston demanded that Griffin explain the discrepancy. "I do not remember his saying 'It is not true,'" said Griffin, adding, "I will not swear he did not, because his father and he, and me, and Mulvany, five or six of us, were all talking—he may have done so." Huddleston then thrust the deposition into the officer's hands. Griffin read and was baffled; he simply could not recall that Edmund had made any such denial.* But that was what was written, and that was what he had signed. Edmund must have said it, he admitted.

It was, at worst, a lapse of memory. But the chief justice, seeing Mont Blanc in that molehill, waxed apoplectic: Griffin, he was sure, was manipulating evidence—was lying—in order to ensure Edmund Pook's conviction. "How could you possibly say upon your oath," he scolded Griffin, "when you were examined in chief, that the prisoner made no reply? The answer you first gave you now admit was entirely false; and you must have been aware of the importance of the matter referred to." The matter, as far as Bovill was concerned, was one of "life or death"—Edmund Pook's life or death, of course, and not Jane Clouson's.

And James Griffin, Bovill soon suggested, was guilty of more than this: he also had suppressed important evidence. When in his cross-examination Huddleston reintroduced the subject of the locket, the chief justice commandeered the questioning to badger Griffin:

> The Chief Justice (to Witness): You are the principal officer charged with the conduct of this case?—Witness: Inspector Mulvany was sent down to take charge of the case.
>
> The Chief Justice: But you are the principal officer in the district charged with the conduct of the case?—Witness: Yes.
>
> The Chief Justice: And it would have been your duty to make inquiries into any facts that came within your knowledge?—Witness: That is so.

---

* Griffin's bafflement was very likely justified, for his testimony at the inquest may have been mistranscribed. According to the *Telegraph*'s transcripts of Griffin's testimony at Jane Clouson's inquest, Griffin did not claim that Edmund said "It is not true"; rather, he stated much the same thing he did at trial: "he made no answer." [T May 12, 1871, 3.]

> The Chief Justice: If a fact comes within your knowledge connected with the case it is a part of your duty to make enquiry.—Witness: I put most of these matters into Inspector Mulvany's hands.
>
> The Chief Justice: But it was your duty to investigate any facts?—Witness: Yes, and I did so in this case. I sent Sergeant Haynes with Mulvany to the shop about the locket.
>
> The Chief Justice: It appears to me that it is the duty of the Crown to lay before the jury every fact whether it tells for or against the prisoner. In my humble opinion, it is the imperative duty of the police and of the inspectors to lay before the judge and jury every fact that has come within their knowledge.

Bovill's humble opinion was a patent legal absurdity. He was not, after all, calling for the police and the Crown to disclose all *relevant* facts; rather, he was calling for disclosure of *every* fact. There has never existed, nor could there exist, any criminal trial in which the police laid before judge and jury every scrap of evidence, every rumor, every false lead and dead end, with which they had dealt in the course of an investigation. (Whether the evidence of the locket and Henry Humphreys was any one of these things, of course, is a different question altogether.) But as absurd as they were, Bovill's words pleased the court immensely; the gallery burst into applause, applause that Bovill dutifully suppressed. To them, Bovill's implication was clear: the investigation of Jane Clouson's murder, by both police and Treasury, was rotten to the core. When Thomas Archibald—speaking for the prosecution since the solicitor general was at that moment outside the courtroom—had the temerity to argue that the Crown had considered the evidence of the locket immaterial, Bovill reiterated his charge: "I must say that Crown prosecutions ought not to be conducted in this manner."

Newton Crosland, for one, did not join in the general approval for the chief justice's condemnation. The trial had only reached the end of the first of four days, but already Crosland had lost any hope that the truth would come to light and that Jane Clouson would find justice in this courtroom. As Edmund Pook was removed to Newgate and the jury led to their sequestration in a local hotel, Crosland walked away from the Old Court in disgust. "I hope never again," he later wrote, "to be a spectator of a trial in which the judge was so unjudicial and sensational, the witnesses were so random, the counsel so insulting, and the police so simple. A few more such exhibitions are calculated to lower the estimate of the administration of justice in this country."*

Crosland walked away and never returned to the Old Bailey. His involvement in the case, however, was far from finished.

The next morning, John Duke Coleridge, "deeply pained," in his words, demanded he be given the opportunity to defend himself against the "perfectly intolerable" imputation that the chief justice had made in his absence. The first he had heard of the locket, he claimed, had been the day before. The police, he later learned, had dropped their inquiry into the locket when they had determined it had no connection to Edmund Pook. The locket, therefore, had never been mentioned in his brief. "I protest," he concluded, "against the idea that evidence of any shape or form has been kept back in this case."

"I did not intend to imply the slightest imputation upon you, Mr. Solicitor," Bovill assuaged him. Thomas Archibald, too, he excused. The conduct of the police, on the other hand, he would

---

* Crosland did make one "striking" exception: "The Solicitor-General was equal to the occasion, and worthy of his high vocation. He was dignified, fair, and able."

not excuse. Apparently satisfied with this partial exoneration, Coleridge proceeded to call his witnesses for the day. There were fully thirty of these, all of them able to connect Edmund Pook in some way with the murder: purchasing of the hammer, walking with Jane on Kidbrooke Lane, hurriedly returning to Greenwich afterward. But only four could actually identify Edmund Pook as the person they had seen in an incriminating position. (Five more than this could identify him—but they had seen him in Greenwich, a fact that the defense did not dispute.) Two of these four crucial eyewitnesses, William Sparshott and Walter Perren, could place Edmund Pook on Deptford High Street on the evening before the murder, and two, William Cronk and Thomas Lazell, could place him at Kidbrooke Lane the next night. Sparshott, Perren, Cronk, Lazell: those were John Huddleston's prime targets, and by discrediting their testimony he would damage irreparably what was left of the prosecution's case after the rejection of hearsay and after the many intimations that police had suppressed evidence.

William Sparshott's memory for detail, and his absolute certainty that he had seen Edmund in his shop and that he had directed him to the Thomases', made him by far the prosecution's strongest eyewitness, and Coleridge called him first. Again he identified Pook with assurance: "I have no doubt whatever that he is the man." His testimony was remarkably consistent with his testimony before both magistrate and coroner. Short of a bit of quibbling about the clothes the man he saw had worn, John Huddleston in cross-examination could do little to shake his story. And so Huddleston challenged him instead upon the identification itself, compelling Sparshott to admit that he had seen a portrait of Edmund in the *Illustrated Police News* before identifying him. Huddleston then handed Sparshott a copy of that paper—the issue with the second, and much more accurate portrait of Edmund. Sparshott denied having seen that one, but the implication was as clear as it was unfair: the *Illustrated Police News* had tainted his identification. When the issue was passed up to the bench, the chief justice eyed it curiously. He asked whether it was an official police publication.

No, Huddleston told him; it was a "sort of sensational Newgate Calendar."

"It was most improper that portraits should be given when a trial of this kind was pending," he fumed: indeed, it was, he thought illegal—or at least should be. "The attention of the government ought to be called to the fact." Coleridge, far less impressed with the danger that this penny newspaper posed to the state, blandly replied that "Her Majesty's government are now engaged in very arduous duties."

The next three witnesses—Sparshott's wife, Elizabeth; his shopboy, Rowland Renneson; and his son, Alfred—partially supported Sparshott's story. They, too, had seen a man in the shop that evening. They had not seen his face, but they did remember his clothes. "He had on a lightish pair of trousers," Renneson claimed. "Light trousers; I remember that," Alfred agreed. Before them, John Huddleston had questioned Sparshott as well about the color of the man's trousers. In earlier testimony he, too, said the person he saw wore light trousers—but he was no longer sure. That all claimed that the man in the shop wore light trousers was a point Huddleston wished clearly to impress upon the jury. (Later, Olivia Cavell, the witness in the Thomases' shop, also claimed the man she had seen had worn light trousers.) That a group of people, first questioned weeks after the fact about the apparel of a stranger they had only half noticed, in unremarkable circumstances, could have such a specific memory about the color of his trousers, was certainly remarkable—even suspicious. How many of us could specify with certainty the color of the trousers of a stranger we happened to have seen in a shop two weeks before? This remarkable claim, however, earned no remark whatsoever, from the judge, or from John Duke Coleridge.

Walter Perren, taking the witness box, did offer a very different recollection of the clothing of the man with whom he had spoken:

he had worn dark trousers. Perren seemed to have an astounding memory for detail, and gave a precise if glibly delivered account of making his way to Deptford on the Monday evening, purchasing nails from Mrs. Thomas, meeting and chatting and offering to "liquor-up" with Pook, watching him enter the Thomases' shop, and watching a hammer being retrieved from the shop window. His story buttressed the account that William Sparshott had given and would dovetail with the account Oliva Cavell was about to give. Nonetheless, Coleridge could only give Perren over to Huddleston's cross-examination with a powerful sense of foreboding, the same feeling that Superintendent Griffin had had nearly three weeks before, when he discovered that the nails Perren had given him—the nails he said he had bought from Mrs. Thomas—were not nails that the Thomases carried in their shop. Griffin then, and Coleridge now, couldn't help but wonder whether Perren had been feeding them a pack of lies.

John Huddleston confirmed those fears. He demolished Walter Perren as a witness.

Huddleston demonstrated that Perren's claims about time, for one thing, did not match Sparshott's and would not match Cavell's. According to Perren's own account, he was on a train to Sydenham by eight o'clock—but Sparshott claimed he saw Pook, and Olivia Cavell would claim she saw the man she saw, well after that time. Then there was Perren's altogether dubious character. He admitted to having been before the magistrates twice: once for assaulting a man who had insulted his wife, and a second time for the mysterious reason, according to him, of "a young woman breaking her parasol over my head." He may have been before the magistrate other times as well, but to that he refused to admit: "I won't swear it, I might have been, I don't know what my friend Mr. Pook has got up against me." He admitted that he had been discharged by his employer at the Golden Lion Music Hall—for being a liar, Huddleston claimed—but that Perren denied. Perren attributed his offering to "liquor-up" with a virtual stranger to his celebrity

("there are a great many persons who know me in the concert business, and I don't know them"). Huddleston then had a man brought
into the courtroom. That man, Huddleston made clear, was prepared
to testify that Perren told him he had never seen Pook in Deptford
that night. Perren responded that he didn't remember the man and
didn't remember saying any such thing. Perren admitted that the
nails he claimed to have bought from Jane Thomas turned out to be
nails that the Thomases never sold. When pressed as to whether he
had read an account of the trial and of those nails that very morning,
Perren's memory failed him. When Huddleston persisted, Perren
sputtered, "Well, I believe that I did. I think that I did, and I am sure
that I did. Is that what you want?" He claimed to know Edmund Pook
perfectly well by sight, but when asked why he then bothered to go
through the charade of a police identification, he hedged; he had only
seen him three or four times in three or four years. "It is a farce to
ask you any more questions," exclaimed Huddleston, triumphantly
exasperated. And yet, he asked one more, about Perren's attendance
at Edmund's examination before the magistrate. "Did you say to Mr.
Field [Perren's music-hall employer] that you had been for nearly
three hours at the police court, and that you thought they had got
him to rights then?" He could not remember saying that, Perren
replied—but if he had, he had lied.

John Duke Coleridge, re-examining, attempted to prevent the
jury from concluding Perren either an idiot or a liar or both by
exhorting Perren to make some sense out of this nonsense. But
Perren could not, and Coleridge gave up, telling him, "I have given
you every opportunity of explaining yourself."

"I think he has been shown the consequences of this evidence,"
the chief justice added. "Ample opportunity has been given him
to reconsider it."

Perren then slipped away, leaving the prosecution's case
sullied by the taint of an obviously false witness. Without his
corroboration, Olivia Cavell's testimony about the man she saw
in the Thomases' shop weakened considerably; she, after all, never

saw the face to which Perren had falsely given an identity. (She had, however, remembered his clothing: a dark coat, a low, round hat—and light trousers.)

Jane Thomas, called to appear after her, was as oblivious as ever as to the identity of the person who bought the hammer from her that night. Mrs. Thomas, attacked by Harry Poland at the inquest for withholding evidence and vilified by the townspeople of Deptford for her dogged refusal to name Edmund Pook as the hammer's purchaser, now found vindication. After again declaring she could not identify Edmund Pook as the man in her shop, she burst into tears. She had received two venomous letters attacking her for her obstinacy, she told the chief justice, and now she handed these to him. "I thought," she said, "if I brought it before you it might be the means of clearing our character." The courtroom by its applause suggested that she had succeeded. Bovill was all kindness and consideration to Mrs. Thomas, and annoyed at the police for not assisting her: "All I can say is the detectives would be doing good service to society by finding out who sends these letters." He advised Mrs. Thomas in future to have her husband open her mail. She left the witness box weeping bitterly.

After calling several witnesses to establish that the hammer purchased from the Thomases' shop almost certainly was the murder weapon, Coleridge turned to the witnesses at Kidbrooke Lane: William Norton, Louisa Putman, and William Cronk. Their testimony fell flat. Neither Norton nor Putman could swear to seeing Pook or Clouson that night; as far as they were concerned, they had witnessed *nothing* that had to do with Jane's murder. The screams they had heard were "of a person in fun, and not in pain or anguish," William Norton testified. Neither had been alarmed by the running man. And when they had walked on, toward Eltham—toward the scream—they saw nothing. They *had* passed another couple during their walk, but that meant little: the couple they had passed north of the brook; the scream and the running man had come from the south.

William Cronk, in spite of his identification of Edmund Pook as the man he saw arguing with a woman on the lane, proved to be a stronger witness for the defense than for the prosecution. The identification itself was weak: "I do not speak to his face," he admitted to Coleridge; he could only identify Edmund Pook by his back. That he had, based upon that alone, picked out Pook from fifteen or twenty other men at Greenwich police station could only raise doubts about the soundness of police procedure. Far more compelling was his evidence that pointed away from Edmund Pook's guilt. "I thought she addressed the man by the Christian name of *Charley*," he told Huddleston, "and I think so now."

After Cronk, Thomas Lazell was called—but here the chief justice and counsel conferred, agreed that Lazell's testimony would be lengthy, and postponed his appearance until the next morning. Instead, Coleridge called five police officers, an assistant solicitor to the Treasury, and Edmund Pook's lady friend, Alice Durnford, to detail the progress of the dog whistle the police had found, from the mud of Kidbrooke Lane into the hands of Detective Inspector Mulvany, and to suggest that the whistle was the one that Edmund had used to summon Miss Durnford from her house. But Coleridge's attempt to demonstrate the police's careful handling of this evidence failed completely. The whistle might, as the police testified, have been found in the mud and then passed up the chain of command. Or it might not have. Among their many evasions and excuses in response to Huddleston's cross-examination, the officers made it clear that not a single one of them had bothered to note the finding or the existence of the whistle in the station's evidence book. And because they did not, there existed absolutely no official record of the whistle until fully three weeks after PC Ovens purportedly pulled it from the mud. Given the depths to which the reputation of the police had fallen during this trial, this discrepancy gave rise to a possibility that John Huddleston now harped upon forcefully: that in their blind zeal to secure Edmund Pook's conviction, they had simply

manufactured that evidence. Even the appearance of Dolly Williamson, head of the Detective Department at Scotland Yard, to
testify that *he* had seen the whistle in Mulvany's hands soon after
the attack, could do little to scrub away this suspicion.

Coleridge failed, moreover, to convince anyone the whistle that
the police produced was actually Edmund's. When Coleridge handed
Alice Durnford that whistle, she could only say it was "something
like" the one Edmund had carried. When, moments later, Huddleston handed her another whistle—the one that Thomas Pook
would claim to have found in Edmund's drawer—Alice Durnford
claimed that that one, too, was "something like." A second whistle
that Huddleston showed her, one made of bone, Durnford claimed
she recognized as well, and noted that she had never mentioned that
fact before. "At all events," the solicitor general muttered sarcastically for the benefit of the chief justice, "the prosecution could not
be accused of suppressing that piece of evidence."

That, Bovill snapped back, "was most irregular and improper."

Thomas Lazell's testimony the next morning indeed proved to be
lengthy. John Duke Coleridge would have preferred it be brief:
enough time to impress upon the jury Lazell's dead certainty that
Edmund Pook had been the man he had passed within two or three
inches of near Kidbrooke Lane—but not enough time to impress
upon them the glaring difficulty with Lazell's testimony, that is,
his equally obdurate claim that he had seen Edmund Pook with
"a pretty, good-looking young woman" at around 6:50 that evening, nearly two hours before the other Kidbrooke Lane witnesses
saw what they saw, and only ten minutes after Fanny Hamilton
claimed Jane left her in Deptford, more than three miles away.
But of course it was that inconvenient claim and Lazell's elaborate
support for it that Huddleston did his best to bring out in cross-
examination. And thus having established Lazell's certainty to an

impossibility, Huddleston set about discrediting Lazell as a witness altogether. He was of course assisted in this by Lazell's usual tongue-tied nervousness:

"How often have you seen the prisoner before?"

"Twice, to be sure of."

"The first time, how long ago?"

"Twelve months."

"The second?"

"Eighteen months."

Huddleston caught him out repeatedly with discrepancies from his earlier testimony. He noted contradictory claims about that evening that Lazell had made to others—others whom Huddleston intended to call for the defense. And it was in quizzing Lazell about one of these men, the cantankerous gentleman pensioner from Morden College, Charles Eicke, that Huddleston unexpectedly hit upon a subject that would pay massive dividends for Edmund's defense.

Huddleston asked Lazell whether he had told Eicke that he had seen a laborer passing him at four in the morning after Jane's murder. Lazell denied it. He *had* seen a laborer that morning, but at eight o'clock, not four. The farm laborer had showed him something he had picked up in Kidbrooke Lane: a blue pocket handkerchief or duster with blood upon it. He had told a police sergeant all about it.

The handkerchief—the duster—the rag: that evidence had never come up before coroner or magistrate. This was the first time that the chief justice had heard of it, and he was livid at this further instance of suppressed—and to his mind, crucial—evidence. "If the duster has been found with blood upon it, and the fact concealed from everyone, it is the most outrageous thing in the world." And he vowed to get to the bottom of the matter immediately, ordering that every one of the sergeants of R Division, then waiting outside the courtroom, be ushered in. From them Lazell immediately picked out William Willis as the sergeant with whom he had spoken. Bovill ordered Willis into the witness box, where he admitted he had seen the duster at Lee station. It was still there, slate-colored and stained, but not, he thought, stained with blood. "Did you send it to Dr. Letheby?" Huddleston snapped at him. "I had nothing to do with that," he replied.

Superintendent Griffin, recalled to the witness box, described the cloth as a "ragged dirty piece of rubbish" that the police had investigated and then rejected as being unconnected with the murder. The chief justice, as skeptical about this as he was about anything that came from the superintendent's mouth, ordered the cloth sent for immediately, along with the haystack-maker who had found it. ("I have not the least idea who the stackmaker is, or where he is to be found," Griffin told him.) Huddleston having thus—with the chief justice's energetic cooperation—suggested that the police had suppressed valuable evidence that they had actually considered and deemed worthless, he then pressed Griffin about yet another matter of seemingly suppressed evidence: the mysterious PC Thomas Mortimer, who should have preceded PC Gunn on the Kidbrooke Lane beat, who had never appeared before either coroner or magistrate, and who surely had vital information to impart. Griffin tried to explain: from six until ten o'clock on the night of the attack, *no one* covered the Kidbrooke Lane beat; PC Mortimer, who usually covered that beat, instead was on duty at the Eltham station house. Again Bovill was skeptical; obviously Mortimer was a "most essential witness," and "were I counsel for the defendant, I should certainly feel it be my duty to make strong observations on the fact that he was not called." He ordered Griffin to fetch Mortimer and any relevant records as to his whereabouts, along with the cloth and the farm laborer.

After seething about the evidence the prosecution and the police did not present, Chief Justice Bovill then derided the evidence they next *did* present: Mary Ann Love's and Alice Langley's testimony about walking with Edmund Pook and a cousin to Kidbrooke Lane two days before the attack. Any notion that their ramble might have been some sort of dress rehearsal for the murder Bovill dismissed outright. "To what does this all tend?" he scoffed in the midst of Miss Love's testimony. "Is it competent to show that a man who knows his way from St. Paul's to the Thames Embankment is guilty of a murder that is committed on the Embankment?"

Dr. Henry Letheby, the Crown's final witness, then testified, repeating his certainty that there was blood on Edmund's trousers, his shirt, and his hat—and that these bloodstains were recent. Moreover, he was sure that the hair taken from Edmund's trousers, those cut from Jane's head, and those found on the plasterer's hammer were alike both in color and in structure. But under John Huddleston's cross-examination, Letheby's uncertainties overshadowed these certainties. The blood, he admitted, could have come from any human being or any vertebrate animal. And while Letheby initially claimed that the blood could not have been on the clothes for more than two weeks before his analysis, Huddleston compelled him to revise his estimate to a month or more—an important distinction, as Huddleston planned to introduce evidence that Edmund Pook had suffered an epileptic seizure and had bled on his clothes near the beginning of April. The chief justice, in examining the holes Letheby had cut in Edmund's trousers to analyze spots of blood, was astounded: "Two of the holes are hardly perceptible unless the trousers are viewed by a glass. They are only about the size of a pin's head." To him, obviously, minuteness connoted insignificance. As for the hair, Letheby admitted that the fact they were alike hardly meant they came from the same head, and "structure" at that time meant very little more than generally similar appearance. That fact Bovill hammered home by positing to Letheby, "I suppose these points of similarity might occur in the hair of five thousand people?"

"No doubt, my lord," Letheby replied.

The solicitor general soon afterward rested for the prosecution, fully aware that the seamless case that he had hoped to present now lay in tatters.

John Huddleston rose for the defense confidently expecting that his opening speech alone would secure Edmund Pook's acquittal. He reminded the jury that it was in their power "at any time to get up and say they were satisfied that the prisoner was not guilty." And he proceeded to argue why they should do exactly that: the prosecution and their many witnesses had succeeded in proving nothing whatsoever against Edmund Pook. They had, for one thing, failed entirely at proving any sort of motive. The insinuation that he had been Jane's lover and the father of the child she carried was not supported by a tittle of evidence. Their eyewitnesses proved nothing: Cronk had only identified Pook by his back; Lazell had offered up a mass of contradictions, and his timing was impossible; Sparshott was simply wrong; and as for Walter Perren—

A jury in 1871 had every right to interrupt a trial at any time, and the jury here interrupted. The foreman stopped Huddleston, consulted with his fellows, and then announced to the chief justice that they had rejected Perren's testimony as entirely false: "I felt sure I should have the sanction of my brethren in saying that Perren and his testimony shall be, as far as we are concerned, among things forgotten."

The rest of the evidence, Huddleston argued, proved nothing. Certainly, the prosecution had hardly established its contention that the attack occurred in the evening and not late at night—and if that was true, the Crown's case "crumbled to nothing." The copious amount of blood that must have flowed from Jane Clouson when attacked would surely have saturated her attacker. If Edmund Pook had killed Jane Clouson, he should have been reeking with blood. But instead there was a tiny amount of blood on his clothes—blood for which Edmund Pook had perfectly reasonable explanations.

The police, he contended, were entirely responsible for this travesty of a case. "Like dogs after game," he declared, the police had set out with an erroneous and fixed idea, and pursued it with blind zeal, disregarding any evidence—the locket and Henry Humphreys, the bloody duster—that might have led them to the actual murderer. More than simply suppressing evidence, they had manufactured it. As proof, Huddleston cited not the whistle but the letter Griffin and Mulvany claimed Edmund had written Jane, setting up an assignation. That letter, Huddleston claimed, they invented in an effort to entrap Edmund. In short, they had employed methods "only known to the inquisitions of old." But they had failed, and Huddleston demanded the jury give the defense the victory it deserved. "It is the life of this young man," he perorated. "Victory to me, professionally, is nothing. Victory to me is rescuing you from the chance of acting contrary to the spirit of the Constitution in sacrificing the innocent. Victory to me is preventing you from imbruing your hands in the blood of a fellow creature."

The applause naturally followed, as did the chief justice's dutiful suppression of it.

This was the moment for the jury to declare themselves satisfied that Edmund Pook was innocent. But they failed to do that. And so John Huddleston proceeded to call the witnesses for the defense. There were more than two dozen of these. And since Henry Pook had wisely refrained from calling any one of them before the magistrate, every single one of them was in a sense a surprise to the prosecution. Coleridge could not catch them in discrepancies as John Huddleston had repeatedly caught the prosecution witnesses, and without investigating their claims, he could do little to rebut them.

Edmund's family members were the first to appear—father, mother, brother Thomas, and cousin Harriet. All four were emphatic that Edmund Pook would never, *could* never, carry on an improper intimacy with a servant. He was a "quiet, well-conducted man," said Ebenezer. In defending his son's character, Ebenezer managed to besmirch Jane's, restating the family's claim that she was disreputably filthy: "If I had any one call in the evening I always made it a rule to take any thing from her because she was not fit to be seen and I used to complain about her to my wife repeatedly." "I kept proper order in my house," Mary Pook proclaimed with a righteous class consciousness; "the prisoner never spoke with the girl; certainly not once a week." Besides, she added, offering up a defense and not a motive for her son,"he disliked the girl." Both parents professed to be constantly anxious about Edmund because of his epilepsy. When he went out, he was always accompanied, and in their small house—where they could always hear the slightest noise—they constantly listened for him: "even if he was in his bedroom a minute or two longer than he ought to have been," claimed Ebenezer, "inquiries were always made about him." Cousin Harriet, who shared a bedroom with Jane Clouson, was positive: "if there had been any intimacy I should certainly have discovered it at once." Even George Collins, an assistant working in the printing shop, felt confident enough about his knowledge of the Pooks' domestic comings and goings to say of Jane Clouson, "If there had been any familiarity between the prisoner and the girl, I must have seen it."

Given the hypervigilance toward Edmund that his parents professed, it is striking that neither of them offered any evidence concerning his whereabouts either on the Monday, when the hammer was purchased, or on the Tuesday, when Jane was attacked. Cousin Harriet did testify about Edmund's movements on both nights, but according to her testimony Edmund was away from home for a good hour on the Monday, and for more than two hours—from around seven o'clock until nine-thirty—on the Tuesday. The only member of the family to fully support any of Edmund's alibis was his brother, Thomas. Thomas Pook supported, it seemed, *all* of Edmund's alibis and explanations, and did so with a profusion of detail. He and Edmund, Thomas claimed, had spent most of Monday evening together, strolling about Greenwich, stopping in at the Greenwich Lecture Hall, drinking a glass of ale at the Globe Tavern. "We were not separated for five minutes," he stated. As for the Tuesday, Thomas claimed that Edmund left the house between

7:20 and 7:25, and returned at 9:05—easily enough time to go to and return from Lewisham, but barely enough time for the six-mile round-trip to Kidbrooke. As for the blood on Edmund's clothing, Thomas offered no fewer than three possible explanations. Edmund, he remembered, had suffered an epileptic fit, biting his tongue and bleeding, on the sixth of April. He had as well, on the fourteenth of that month, cut his own finger in the shop and had bled copiously; a week later an assistant in the shop had scraped the flesh off the back of his knuckles and Edmund had bound up his wounds.

More than simply supporting his brother's alibis, Thomas Pook introduced the specter of another possible lover, and possible murderer, for Jane, repeating his claim that Edmund had told him that he had seen Jane walking out with a "swell." And it was Thomas to whom Edmund had written from Maidstone jail, and who had then rummaged through Edmund's drawer to find his metal and his bone whistles.

Thomas Pook was thus his brother's best alibi witness. But he was not the only one. There were also three neighbors of Edmund's Lewisham lady friend, Alice Durnford: Joseph and Mary Anne Eagles, and their lodger, William Douglas. All three testified to seeing a man on a bridge near their house, a man whom, eleven weeks later, they identified as Edmund Pook from the photograph albums that Henry Pook showed them. Most striking about their testimony is not that two of them remembered seeing Edmund Pook in their neighborhood—after all, Edmund was a frequent visitor to the area, and Mary Anne Eagles acknowledged seeing him walking with Alice Durnford—but rather that all three were certain that they saw him on that particular evening. Joseph Eagles did offer a curious and illogical reason for connecting the sight with that date: he had obtained lotion to treat his partially blind eye earlier that day. In cross-examination the solicitor general was able to tease out some inconsistencies between their accounts. But Coleridge did little to draw the jury's attention to the implausibility of their precise recollections or cast suspicion on Henry Pook's photo identification.

Yet another witness appeared to support Edmund's alibi. Eliza Ann Merrett lived in Lewisham but had before that lived in Greenwich. She knew Edmund Pook well—indeed, she claimed, had "always" known him—and swore that Edmund had passed her that evening, about five minutes away from the bridge, walking slowly. "I thought he was waiting for somebody," she testified.

Soon after Merrett testified, Superintendent Griffin returned to court from Eltham with the mysterious cloth in his hands and with PC Mortimer in tow; the defense paused as Bovill allowed Mortimer to appear for the prosecution. Mortimer quickly dispelled any mystery about his whereabouts on the night of the attack. He acknowledged that while he regularly walked the Kidbrooke beat, that night he had not done so after six o'clock, instead serving as duty officer at the Eltham station. He was suppressing nothing because he knew nothing. That seemed to satisfy both Bovill and Huddleston; in any case, neither mentioned PC Mortimer again.

The supposedly bloody rag, however, was another matter. Superintendent Griffin again appeared in order to enter into evidence the cloth, which one reporter described as "a piece of lining full of holes, and having a number of reddish stains on it." Why, Huddleston asked him, hadn't he submitted the cloth to Dr. Letheby for analysis? Why, Bovill asked him, had he put the cloth in a cupboard in the station and said nothing about it to a Treasury solicitor? Griffin tried to explain that the cloth was insignificant: "Gypsies throw away rags, and, as it was found in a field so far away from the scene of the murder, it was thought it had nothing to do with it." Moreover, the police had not kept the cloth a secret: "the police and more than twenty people knew of it," and the newspapers had reported its finding at the time. Bovill did not accept Griffin's claim that the cloth was irrelevant. "All I can say is this," Bovill harangued him, "that you seem to have taken upon yourself a strong measure of responsibility." The chief justice was certain that the rag was a crucial link in a chain of evidence that, if pursued, might have led to the *actual* murderer. The police "ought to have investigated into the circumstance, whether it might tell for or against the prisoner, and not to have exercised their judgement as to whether it ought or ought not to be produced." Applause followed on the heels of his righteous outburst—applause that Bovill suppressed, concluding, "I cannot express my disapprobation of this conduct too strongly, and I trust that a matter of this sort will never occur again."

Mulvany testified that, far from suppressing the evidence of the cloth, the police had informed the Treasury of its existence. An assistant solicitor to the Treasury, Augustus Keppel Stephenson, appeared after him to confirm that fact. But that hardly placated the chief justice. The police, Bovill proclaimed, only *told* the assistant about the cloth; he had not *shown* it to him. Worse than this, no one had shared this evidence with Edmund's defense counsel, which therefore had no opportunity to investigate it. "That," Bovill told Mulvany, "is where the injustice lies." "It shows," Huddleston remarked, "the necessity that exists for a public prosecutor."* The stained cloth, then, worked neither to implicate nor to exculpate Edmund Pook. But the notion about it that Bovill promoted lingered: but for police incompetence, it *could have* proved valuable, likely to Edmund's benefit. And in that way, the cloth actually did work to his benefit.

⊶⊷

Edmund Pook, alternatively standing and sitting in the dock, always calm, always attentive, had surely found pleasure in repeatedly seeing his chief tormentors, James Griffin and John Mulvany,

---

* In 1871 there was in England no public prosecutor with personal power to take on fully the investigation and prosecution of important criminal cases—although the Treasury solicitor did, at least partially, take on that role. Efforts to create a public prosecutor had long been afoot and were given impetus by cases such as this one. The office of Director of Public Prosecutions was created in 1879. [Kurland and Waters 550, 570.]

censured and vilified. Now he enjoyed a pleasure of a different kind: a parade of witnesses, the burghers of Greenwich, appearing to demonstrate their unqualified support for him and to extoll the excellences of his character. Well over a dozen appeared, among them friends and fellow Freemasons of Ebenezer Pook and members of the Greenwich vestry. Mr. Price, a schoolmaster and once probably Edmund's, spoke first: he was astonished to see a young man of Edmund's character in the dock at all. Mr. William Orchard, publican and his next-door neighbor: Edmund was "an exceedingly well-conducted man at all times." Mr. Turner: "The accused had borne a character for everything that an Englishman could wish his son to bear."

Huddleston intended these witnesses to be the last ones for the defense, and with them court adjourned for the night. The next morning, however, Saturday, July 15, yet one more witness for the defense appeared in a bid to kick away the last remaining prop to the Crown's case: William Sparshott's heretofore-unchallenged eyewitness testimony that placed Edmund on Deptford High Street the night the hammer was bought. Matthew Crawford, a pastry cook, had in April and May been next-door neighbor to the Sparshotts. (He had since moved from Deptford to become a near neighbor to the Pooks in Greenwich.) He had read an account of the trial in the newspapers, was stunned by Sparshott's allegation that he had recognized Edmund Pook in his shop, and felt compelled to come forward to contradict him. Soon after Edmund Pook had been arrested, the two had had a conversation in which, Crawford claimed, Sparshott repeatedly told him that he would not be able to identify the man. Huddleston first recalled William Sparshott, who denied he had said this to Crawford and adamantly held fast to the claim that it was Edmund Pook he saw: "I could not alter my statement on any account; I consider my character is quite as much at stake as any man's in the kingdom." John Duke Coleridge, cross-examining Crawford, asked him why he had not come forward sooner, since he had read two months before that Sparshott had testified to identifying Pook. Crawford seemed stymied by the question, saying only that he didn't want to be involved. And then the chief justice intervened to nudge him toward a more reasonable answer, with a dubious parsing of Sparshott's testimony two months before. "Mr. Sparshott's evidence before the magistrate was not positive. He said he 'believed' the prisoner was the man. That is what you read, I suppose?"

"Yes, sir," Crawford replied. Why *that* should have prevented Crawford from coming forward was yet another question that Coleridge did not think to ask.

John Huddleston approached his closing argument with the spirit of a man with victory in his grasp, dismissing, point by point, the prosecution's evidence, and fervidly denouncing the police. Then he laid his own trap for his opponent. He would "wait with anxiety," he told the jury, to see whether the solicitor general, "having a father and uncle who presided with honor and dignity on the bench—would throw his aegis over the police to excuse them for cross-examining the accused before he was in custody, and suggesting facts for the purpose of entrapping him." In other words Coleridge could either abandon the police to their disgrace, leaving his case irreparably tainted, or he could sully his own reputation by defending them.

Coleridge, in his turn, lashed back at Huddleston for taking the unusual course of making his advocacy "rather a personal matter." He argued that the police had not entrapped Edmund at all. And he deplored the way the trial had descended to an out-and-out assault upon the police; "Policemen," he protested, "were not to be set up in the box like schoolboys' cockshies, for every imputation to be levied against them." But for all his celebrated oratorical ability, Coleridge's speech was, in all, subdued and defensive, words spoken in defeat. When he discussed the Lewisham alibi witnesses, for example, he simply left it up to the jury to decide whether they were credible, and weakly allowed that if they believed them, "there was an end of the case, and the prisoner ought to be acquitted." His strongest emotion and highest rhetoric he expended in a final desperate bid to return the focus of the case to the girl horribly disfigured and left to die in the mud of Kidbrooke Lane. "Outrages of this description," he concluded, "could not go unrevenged. The interests of society, and of poor girls, and the fathers and mothers of poor girls, demanded that a right and proper verdict should be returned."

His appeal fell flat. After four days of emphasis upon police persecution of Edmund Pook, Jane Clouson's agony seemed little more than a distant troubled dream. The young man in the dock was the true victim in this trial. And by now, no one doubted that the right and proper verdict would be in his favor. The jury could simply end the proceedings here and declare Edmund Pook not guilty, saving Chief Justice Bovill the trouble of summing up the case. But when Coleridge finished, they remained silent.

William Bovill likely preferred it that way, for his six-and-a-half-hour summing-up allowed him to purge the anger and frustration that had swollen within him over the past four days: anger at the prosecution and its shoddy case, even greater anger at a mistake-prone and overzealous police force, and the greatest anger of all directed at two officers in particular, John Mulvany and James Griffin, whose misrepresentations and evasions might have forced a horrible miscarriage of justice.

Chief among the offenses of the prosecution was its introduction of false witnesses to make its case. Bovill named two: James Conway and Walter Perren. The jury could not have been surprised to hear Bovill denounce Perren as "deliberately and willfully false," but his denunciation of Conway came to them as a complete surprise. For James Conway did not testify at trial; when, two months before, it became clear that Conway had mistakenly identified Edmund Pook as being in the Thomases' shop on the Saturday rather than the Monday before the attack, the police and prosecution had dropped him. But now Bovill resurrected him, paired him with Perren, and directed the jury to judge *all* of the prosecution's evidence very narrowly because of these two. He also recommended her Majesty's government prosecute both Conway and Perren for perjury.

The police, Bovill declaimed, with their fixation upon Edmund Pook's guilt and their obsession to secure a conviction, had botched the case by chasing any evidence that suggested his guilt and by disregarding any that might have proven his innocence. The cloth, the bloody stones by the brook, the locket, the footprints at the scene— all were ignored or suppressed. In an attempt to correct the errors Bovill was sure the police had made, he re-examined the evidence at length, disparaging the prosecution's case at every turn. According to Bovill, the amount of blood on Edmund's clothes was hardly enough to connect him with a vicious attack. The evidence of PC Gunn and the witnesses at Kidbrooke Lane strongly led one to believe that Jane had been killed late at night—when Edmund was proven to be home in bed—and not in the evening, as police and prosecution contended. While Bovill proclaimed that the "bloody" cloth that the police had ignored might have been crucial evidence, he dismissed the whistle and the hair found on Edmund's trousers as insignificant. And while he belittled the testimony of every eyewitness who positively connected Edmund with the murder weapon or with Kidbrooke Lane, he commended as sound the testimony of every eyewitness who supported Edmund's alibi. Fixing upon William Cronk's statement that he had seen Pook on Kidbrooke Lane at 8:45, and statements by several witnesses on Royal Hill that they had seen him before nine, Bovill suggested that Edmund Pook could not possibly have run from Kidbrooke Lane to Greenwich that evening. (Other eyewitness accounts gave him more than enough time to do this.) Finally, having successfully excluded from the trial any evidence pointing to a motive, Bovill contended that there was no evidence for a motive, and indeed, that there *was no motive* for Edmund Pook to kill Jane Clouson. And if there was no motive, he instructed the jury, "then they were left in doubt, and being in doubt, it would be their duty to acquit the prisoner of the charge."

In the midst of his summation Bovill's volatile words appeared to take on physical form when, after a short recess, the courtroom reeked with the powerful odor of gas. Bovill contributed greatly to the general consternation by nervously pointing out that a small amount of gas could "produce an explosion and blow them all up." The gas, it was discovered, had been flowing through a number of unlit jets. They were lit, windows were opened, the odor dissipated, and Bovill recommenced.

He concluded with his harshest attack of all—a lambasting of Mulvany and Griffin, who, he claimed, had tainted the case, both in their manipulation of the evidence, and in their language; they always, claimed the chief justice, gave a "tinge" to their words, in a way that was "never in favour of the accused." Mulvany, he argued, had spoken falsely in inventing a letter in order to entrap Edmund. And Griffin had suspiciously and conveniently forgotten, in recounting his questioning Edmund, that Edmund had denied meeting Jane at Crooms Hill the night she was attacked. By neglecting to mention this, Bovill contended, Griffin had suggested that Edmund tacitly admitted meeting her—creating a misimpression that might have led to disaster. "You and I," he angrily told the jury, "would have been made instruments in fixing guilt upon the prisoner by reason of a misstatement of the police—a direct, positive misstatement of the man himself."

"Sensation" enveloped the courtroom, according to one reporter. "It is cruel indeed," Bovill continued, "to those who have to administer justice, that the police should be in a condition to make such statements, to mislead judges and juries—although they did not do it intentionally—and to make them instruments perhaps in sacrificing the life of an innocent man." The applause that naturally followed, Bovill dutifully if proudly suppressed. The foreman quickly rose to acknowledge the jury's complete sympathy with his sentiments.

Bovill's passionate denunciation of James Griffin so strongly implied Edmund Pook's innocence that even if he was not quite directing the jury's verdict, they could certainly be excused for thinking that he was. When Bovill left the case in their hands, the only apparent question that remained was whether they need retire from the courtroom at all to consider that verdict. Surprisingly, they did. It was then 8:40 on that Saturday evening. Edmund Pook slipped to the back of the prisoner's dock, where for a few minutes he chatted with his guards, and was seen to smile. Then he sat in the chair provided him, rocked quietly, and waited anxiously for the entire mess to be done with.

The jury returned twenty minutes later, to finally speak the words everyone expected: not guilty. The courtroom burst into applause—applause that the chief justice was entirely unable to suppress. Bovill thanked the jury, which, before leaving, could not resist a parting shot at the police, the foreman voicing their dissatisfaction with the "loose manner" in which they had presented their case. Edmund Pook, freed from the dock, rushed to embrace his family. For him, for them all, the nightmare at the Old Bailey was over.

But in Greenwich it was just beginning.

CHAPTER SIX

ROUGH MUSIC

The cheering inside Old Court carried through corridors and windows to the crowd that had been gathering outside the Old Bailey since that morning, knowing the verdict was coming, and now several hundred strong. Although they may have passed the hours betting with one another upon Edmund Pook's guilt or innocence, they all knew what they wanted that verdict to be.

Over the next few days a flood of editorials appearing in newspapers across the nation lashed out at the "stupid" and "reprehensible" police who had suppressed and falsified evidence and had brought forward their miserable, perjuring witnesses, in a deplorable effort to convict an innocent man. In doing so, the police had surely allowed Jane Clouson's murderer to escape justice. Griffin, Mulvany, and the police of R Division had, the editorials proclaimed in choral unanimity, overstepped their proper bounds; they had become prosecutors rather than investigators. The Pook trial, then, had exposed serious flaws of English criminal justice. "It would, indeed, be hardly possible to have a more striking instance of the deficiencies of our present system," the *Times* thundered. The editorials one and all called out for the establishment in England of a public prosecutor's office to match the one that already existed in Scotland: an office with clear authority and full oversight of police investigations of serious crime. The Treasury Department—which largely held that authority—had proved itself woefully inadequate in that role during this fiasco of a trial, the newspapers agreed.

And while this crowd might not have understood, without the benefit of those coming editorials, the full extent of this broken system, they, too, had been following the progress of the case carefully from the start, and they, too, were now convinced that Edmund Pook was the victim of persecution, first by the police, and then by the Crown. They expected, they demanded, his acquittal. And when the cheers erupted from within the courtroom, they knew that acquittal had come. They burst into sustained and raucous celebration. Edmund Pook, emerging from the Old Bailey with family and solicitor after eleven weeks' imprisonment, surely paused to revel in their joy before walking away from prison and courthouse and returning home.

For two women who had also been tried that day and who were now sitting hard by the Old Bailey in their Newgate cells, the muffled sounds of celebration—celebration for *someone else*— must only have twitted them with their own misery. They, too, had been tried on this day; they had both been found guilty. They both realized that they would not walk away from prison for many years to come. If the law had failed in Edmund Pook's case, it had succeeded in theirs—at least partially.

Flora Davy could find some solace in having escaped the gallows, thanks to the grand jury. That body had in its wisdom ignored the bill for murder against her and had returned only a true bill for manslaughter. Proving manslaughter rather than murder—proving that Davy had been instrumental in killing Frederick Moon, whether or not she intended to kill him—turned out to be a relatively simple task for the Crown and its principal prosecutor, Hardinge Giffard (with Harry Poland's assistance). Giffard had a host of witnesses at his disposal—police, servants, Mrs. Davy's companion Mrs. Toynbee, her attending physicians, the two young ladies who had been visiting her—to establish beyond doubt that Davy had quarreled with Moon that evening, that she had picked up the poultry knife and rushed at him, that they had struggled before he fell dying—and that afterward, covered in Moon's blood, she had repeatedly stated, "I fear I did it."

Davy's lead counsel, John Humffreys Parry, could offer no eyewitness testimony to counter any of this. But since not one of these prosecution witnesses had actually *seen* Flora Davy stab Frederick Moon, Parry based his entire defense upon the possibility that his death came not at Flora Davy's hands but at his own: that he somehow managed to stab himself to death. Hardinge Giffard and the prosecution had anticipated this strategy and had called as expert witnesses no fewer than five physicians, all of whom had examined Moon's body, to testify that Moon had almost certainly been stabbed by another person. Parry, however, succeeded in coaxing several of these physicians to admit it at least possible that Moon died from falling upon the knife. Then Parry called as witnesses four more physicians to claim that Moon's death was likely accidental. All four of these physicians were men of stellar reputation, but not one of them had actually examined Moon. And the accident these physicians surmised did not have Frederick Moon simply and haplessly falling over and impaling himself upon the poultry knife, but rather had him struggling with Flora Davy for the knife, and equally haplessly plunging it into his own heart. That in itself, Harding Giffard argued, was enough to establish Davy's guilt: "Life in this country would not be safe if that were not manslaughter," he warned the jury.

The judge in the case, Baron William Channell, agreed, and essentially repeated the prosecutor's argument as his own sum- mation. After half an hour the jury pronounced Flora Davy guilty. Flora Davy then launched with wild-eyed distress into a semi-coherent declaration of absolute innocence of the crime and absolute devotion to Frederick Moon. What little of this outburst Baron Channell could understand, he disregarded; he sternly told Davy, as she covered her face in shame, that she was most fortunate she had been tried for manslaughter and not for murder. And then he sentenced her to eight years' penal servitude.

She collapsed and was dragged insensible to her Newgate cell.

There was no such melodramatic hysteria that day in the Old Bailey's tiny Third Court, where Agnes Norman, with her usual emotional vacancy, stood trial for murder of one child and the attempted murder of four others. Harry Poland, who had spent the last few days rushing back and forth as junior counsel in both Pook's and Davy's trials, here led the prosecution. The sleuth-hound knew from the start that his success in convicting the girl of murder depended almost entirely upon a single ruling by the judge in this case, Thomas Chambers, Common Sergeant of London. While death had attended the girl in numbers simply too great to attri- bute to coincidence, there was little to no direct proof that she had committed any one of them. If Poland were allowed to introduce that pattern of death as evidence in itself, the jury might convict. Otherwise, it likely would not. Poland, then, forced a ruling on this issue as quickly as he could, announcing during his opening that he intended to bring up the deaths of other children and of many animals in order to support the charge that Agnes Norman had murdered the infant Jessie Jane Beer.

Norman's lawyer, David Morgan Thomas, immediately barked his objection. And after Common Sergeant Chambers disputed the matter with both lawyers for some time, he declared he was simply not qualified to make the ruling on his own. He therefore suspended proceedings, left the courtroom, managed in time to steal both Chief Justice Bovill and Baron Channell away from *their* trials, and questioned them both on the issue. After this considerable recess, he returned with a decision—of sorts. Both Bovill and Channell, he announced, agreed about the evidence of the deaths of animals: that was strictly inadmissible. They were less clear about the evidence of the deaths of children. Therefore, while he would allow that evidence, if Poland pressed him to do so, he would "reserve the point." By that technical term, Chambers meant that if Poland introduced this evidence, the common sergeant would likely appeal the case to the higher court which then existed to consider such knotty legal issues: the Court for Crown Cases Reserved. Quite possibly, then, Poland could win in this court and lose on appeal: a rare outcome indeed for an Old Bailey trial in 1871.

Nonetheless, Poland pressed the point. He began to call his witnesses. Jessie Beer's father spoke of discovering his baby dead, on her back, in her bed. The child's mother spoke of Agnes Norman's oddly disconnected behavior in the wake of that discovery. The doctor that the Beers called in that night and the two doctors who conducted the infant's post-mortem all testified to the toothmarks on her lip—marks consistent with the hard and sustained pressure of deliberate suffocation, and not with accidental suffocation from a soft mattress. One of these doctors went so far as to claim that her death could not have been accidental, *if* John Beer's assertion that he found his child dead on her back was accurate. Besides this, however, the doctors refused to state with absolute certainty that the infant's death had not been an accident.

And with that—before Poland actually had a chance to bring in evidence of any other child's death—the common sergeant had had enough. Since they could not rule out an accidental cause for Jessie Jane Beer's death, Chambers told the jury, they simply did not have enough evidence to convict Agnes Norman of her murder. Thus directed, the jury quickly pronounced Agnes Norman not guilty of the infant's murder.

Seeing his most compelling case for murder fail, Harry Poland abandoned the other three murder charges and focused instead upon the one remaining charge: the attempted murder of ten-year-old Charles Parfitt. Poland's evidence in support for that charge was far more direct and compelling. There was the boy's own account of Agnes's attempt: "I was woke up in the morning by somebody strangling me—like *this*, with her hand on my throat, and her finger upon my nose—I tried to make a noise. . . ." There was also the corroborating testimony of the boy's aunts and his uncle, to whom he had revealed the attack right after it happened, and who had seen the boy's sore, swollen lips and throat. In response, Agnes Norman's counsel could only question the accuracy of a ten-year-old's recollection, and point out Agnes Norman's repeated protestations that she had done nothing, and the family's assertion that they would never have reported the case in the first place if they hadn't learned of the other, more serious charges against the girl.

The jury found Norman guilty of attempted murder. But they recommended that the common sergeant show her mercy on account of her youth. The common sergeant assured them he would consider their recommendation and deferred sentencing until the next sessions, in August, to do so.* Until then, he ordered Agnes Norman back to Newgate, where she must have wondered, as she heard the muffled sounds of celebration of someone else's freedom, how long it would be before she herself went free.

Just as the crowd outside the Old Bailey had gathered throughout the day on that Saturday, July 15, another crowd—this one more

---

* After a month's consideration, the common sergeant showed Agnes Norman very little mercy. Although he himself had caused the charges of murder against her to be thrown out, he had no doubt that she bore "moral guilt" for the deaths of four infants, and sentenced Norman to ten years' penal servitude. [TE 15 Aug. 1871, 3.]

numerous and much more ominous—had gathered in Greenwich, in the street outside the Pooks' home and shop: had gathered, then swelled, and by evening roiled with anxious anticipation. They were, according to the newspapers, a "mob of the lowest class," the "roughs of Greenwich." They, like their counterparts at the Old Bailey, had closely followed the trial; they, too, knew that a verdict was coming on this day. Unlike their Old Bailey counterparts, they anticipated that verdict with a sense of unease, and with the growing certainty that justice for Jane Clouson was about to be denied.

Within half an hour of the trial's end their fears were realized. Newsboys ran among them hawking a hastily printed special edition of the *Kentish Mercury* and announcing Edmund Pook's acquittal. A number of men and boys in the crowd had prepared for just this moment. They took up flags, all of them black, and several emblazoned with a single word: BLOOD. They formed up in a procession and, followed by a howling multitude, they paraded through the streets of Greenwich, proclaiming the deplorable verdict and attracting more to engorge the mass on London Street. Edmund Pook's return was now imminent and thousands now began to watch for him, craning their heads west in the direction of Greenwich railway station.

Edmund and his family somehow managed to evade their detection altogether and slipped into their home through a side door. Their solicitor was not as fortunate: the crowd spotted Henry Pook, mobbed him, and heaped him with execration until he managed to break free and seek sanctuary in a nearby public house, where he remained trapped for hours. Once the multitude realized that the Pooks were in their house, they unleashed their pent-up fury and frustration in a deafening and unearthly din, screaming, whistling, hooting, and shouting obscenities toward the Pooks' empty windows. They kept that up for hours, finally melting away in the early hours of the morning. The next evening, they returned—and the next. For five days they kept up their fervent and thunderous cacophony. "Greenwich is at present suffering from high fever," noted one newspaper. "Partisanship is running wild, and the usually sedate burghers are arrayed in two hostile bands, whose sympathies and antipathies are as strongly marked as were those of the Montagues and the Capulets." That description might capture the civic division that had begun with Edmund's arrest, and that had with his acquittal widened dramatically. But it did not capture the social dimension of the split: on one side, the tradesmen, the burghers, the self-consciously respectable of the town, ceding with a temporary mortification their streets to the other side—the largely working-class supporters of justice for Jane, those who had for weeks flocked to the site of her murder and had on the rainy day of her funeral lined the streets of Deptford and Lewisham. It was that side that now sought with numbers and deafening noise to impose in some way the justice that they believed had been denied the girl at the Old Bailey.

Later in the week, in a letter to the newspapers, Jane Clouson's father, James, of all people, would come closest to articulating the crowd's inchoate frustration. "I have always considered trial by jury as one of the safeguards and boasts of our English nation," Clouson wrote, "but, after this trial for the murder of my daughter, I fearlessly say—and I think it is the opinion of thousands of my fellow-countrymen—that justice has not been done. Where will they now go to look for the murderer, or what will be done? The case must not rest here; if so, murderers will carry out their designs with more impunity than ever upon our defenseless women and children, by hacking and chopping them into pieces to prevent their identification." That Clouson attributed injustice not to the police arresting the wrong man but to the court's failure to find guilty the right one was clear from his great praise for the witnesses for the prosecution "who fearlessly came forward in the cause; but who, I consider, were brow-beaten and intimidated while giving their evidence, and made appear [sic] to the world as liars and everything bad. Such disgraceful conduct to respectable witnesses has never been known in a court before." Had true justice existed in that Old Bailey courtroom, James Clouson was certain, Edmund Pook would have been convicted.

For the five days that they claimed London Street as theirs alone, however, the crowd needed no such articulation of the grievance they felt; they sought results not in reasoned reproach but in sheer, unrelenting noise. And on Monday evening, three days into their insurgence, they added street theater to that noise. At six o'clock that evening, a cart was wheeled up to the Pooks' shop windows. It bore two effigies: one of Edmund Pook raising a plasterer's hammer over his head; the other of Jane Clouson quailing under the blow. Having given the Pooks plenty of time to absorb the lessons of this tableau, the raucous multitude set off with the cart on a journey to Blackheath and back, their route lined with placards proclaiming "Pook the Butcher." As the cart was returning to London Street a group of Pook supporters, in a courageous or foolhardy sortie, rushed the cart and destroyed the effigies. (These were later resurrected and, Guy-like, employed to solicit donations: pennies for the Pook.) This challenge to their power only inflamed the crowd, now swollen to its greatest size ever. At least three thousand strong, they returned to halt all traffic and business on London Street and unleashed a "perfect Babel" against the Pooks that lasted until midnight, when, according to one report, a mock funeral for Edmund Pook was planned.

All this time, the police—led, of course, by Superintendent Griffin, who had raced back from the Old Bailey on Saturday to take charge—stood by, observed the crowd, and did nothing more. For two days the Pooks, family and solicitor, chafed helplessly at Griffin's passivity. They were certainly not surprised by it: James Griffin had become their inveterate enemy, and his passivity now struck them as yet one more manifestation of that enmity. When on Monday morning, however, the Pooks learned that the cart, the effigies, and the procession were to appear that evening, they could stand no more and took action, appealing over Griffin's head directly to Commissioner of the

Metropolitan Police Edmund Henderson. "As I have been unable to get redress from the police here," Henry Pook wrote the commissioner, "I call on you to do your duty and disperse any mob which may assemble or attempt to assemble." Henderson replied immediately through an assistant that he would give "the necessary directions to the police on the street" and sent twenty-five officers to Greenwich as a reserve force.

That reserve force remained in reserve; Griffin and the police did nothing to stop the procession. "Last night," wrote one outraged neighbor to the *Daily News* the next day, "a few policemen might be seen hovering near the spot, and from time to time vindicating the majesty of the law by calling upon a child to move on; but the mob is permitted to manifest its beery indignation unchecked, and is regarded by the paid maintainers of order with a sort of dignified imbecility."

Griffin and his officers, however, were not dignified imbeciles, and their restraint was not a product of Griffin's passive aggression toward the Pooks. The police stood in readiness to intervene when the crowd crossed the line to violence, when its verbal assault turned physical. The very few times that this happened—when, for instance, one man began to incite children to attack the Pooks' house—the police did intervene. For the most part, however, Superintendent Griffin and his police refused to treat the crowd as rioters, for the simple reason that they were *not* rioters. Underlying their chaotic outcry was self-restraint; underlying their seeming madness, method.

The crowd had no intention of inflicting physical harm upon Edmund or his home. They broke no windows, and—the tussle with Henry Pook aside—assaulted no one. Rather, they aimed to shame and stigmatize Edmund Pook—to ostracize him from their community. The court and the Crown had failed utterly to punish Edmund for his egregious violation of their social codes, and so the crowd in unconscious accord sought to do that itself, putting to use the techniques and the trappings employed for centuries by English communities driven to self-policing outrages upon its social values. The mass gathering of an aggrieved community, the flags and processions, the cart and the effigies, the mock funeral, and, above all, the raucous, ceaseless caterwaul: all were the paraphernalia of traditional *charivari*—better known, there and then, as *rough music*. Although today rough music, when it is remembered at all, tends to be associated with rural and not urban communities, the spirit of community among the working class of Greenwich and Deptford was strong, as was the urge to act when necessary in its own interests. So was the folk memory that provided them with the tools to do so. Historian E. P. Thompson notes that of in all of London in the last part of the nineteenth century, the tradition of rough music was strongest in the southeast. And on these five days in July 1871, that tradition had its most striking manifestation. One reporter, at least, predicted that the howling mob would succeed in shaming Edmund Pook away, stating of the Pooks that "none of its members can stir abroad without encountering reproach and remark," and that "the only remedy will be their removal from the neighborhood."

Ebenezer Pook, however, had no intention whatsoever of succumbing to the crowd's pressure. His son, he was certain, was not a criminal, but a victim himself of the false evidence, the false witnesses, and the malevolent and manipulative police, all of which had for months stirred up the passions of the ignorant multitude, and had made life miserable not only for Edmund but for his entire family. On the morning after the first night of rough music, Ebenezer Pook described that misery in a letter he wrote to several newspapers. "My name has been brought into most unenviable notoriety. My solicitor, my son Edmund Walter Pook, my family, my friends, and I have been hooted and yelled at in the public streets in a most frightful and disgraceful manner; and for the past 12 weeks an agony and suspense have been endured by me and my family which rarely fall to the lot of mortals." He made clear that the yowling mob had only strengthened his resolve not to fly but to fight. And on that morning, Ebenezer Pook sat down with his solicitor to plan retribution.

While Edmund Pook surely took part in this war council, he did so with far less urgency and intensity than did the two elder Pooks. Certainly, in the months to come, Edmund never demonstrated the vengeful zeal that his father did in lashing out in the press at his enemies, or that his solicitor did in the repeated courtroom tirades he directed against them. Ebenezer and Henry Pook, over the next months, would together initiate legal action and then descend upon the courtrooms of Greenwich and London with obvious vindictive relish; Edmund initiated nothing, appeared in court only when his presence was required, and, when he testified, generally did so with a stiffness that suggested he wished the entire matter over and done with. He re-entered the legal fray more the dutiful son than the ardent avenger.

The Pooks had many enemies to pursue. There was of course the mob itself. Though there was little they could do without the help of the police, they resolved to do what little they could. As it happened, the night before, one of the Pooks' neighbors, and one of their staunchest supporters, Leopold de Breanski, himself returning from the Old Bailey, had plunged into the mob on London Street, plucked out one of its better-dressed members, dragged him to the nearest constable, and demanded that the constable arrest the man for inciting the crowd to riot. The constable refused, instead advising Breanski to appear at police court and apply for a summons against the man. Remarkably, Breanski did just that, and Henry Pook, learning of the summons, agreed to prosecute. A week later, he did. The man was let go once he paid court costs. It was a paltry victory for the Pooks, and it came too late in any case to have any effect upon the howling multitude. But it did signal to all of Greenwich and Deptford that the Pooks would never dance to the crowd's discordant tune.

And then there were the witnesses that the Pooks were sure had lied at Edmund's trial. The chief justice had actually recommended the prosecution of two of them, James Conway and Walter Perren, for perjury. James Conway, who had not even testified at Edmund's trial, was so mortified by Bovill's accusation that upon hearing it he immediately wrote to the *Evening Standard* a letter protesting his innocence—a letter written in such amazingly fractured English that several newspapers republished it in full for its entertainment value alone. ("Sir I would be very much thankful if you let the publice a large know that I have been wrongfully acused of swering to the man pook has the man I see in Thomas shop. . . .") And in his letter to the press Ebenezer Pook added another name to this list of accused perjurers: "as for Perrin [sic], Conway, and Lazell, I suppose, after the remarks of the Lord Chief Justice, they will be dealt with by the Crown."

While the Pooks were willing to leave those three to the mercies of the Treasury Department, they were determined to prosecute their chief antagonists themselves. The transgressions of Superintendent Griffin and Inspector Mulvany were just too great, and too personal, to leave them to be dealt with—or possibly *not* be dealt with—by the Crown. Ebenezer and Henry resolved personally to seek summonses against the two for the willful and corrupt perjury they had committed at Edmund's trial. They would seek those summonses at London's Guildhall, in the City, as Griffin and Mulvany had testified, and allegedly committed their perjury, at the Old Bailey. If they succeeded in obtaining those summonses, the Pooks hoped to do to the officers what they had done to Edmund: have them hauled into police court, examined, committed for trial—and then, within a month, placed in the prisoners' dock of the Old Bailey to fight for *their* reputations, their careers, their freedom.

Before the Pooks could pursue this vengeful pleasure, however, Henry Pook had his own reputation to think about, having to answer to the two summonses the police had taken out against *him* for violent and indecent behavior two months before: first for his outburst when Edmund Pook was denied a haircut and a shave, and second for abusing officers while demanding police protection on the evening after Jane Clouson's funeral. On Wednesday, July 18, then, Henry Pook appeared at Greenwich Police Court not as an advocate but as a defendant. Flanking him was his barrister, Douglas Straight, who had been one of Edmund's lawyers, as well as Ebenezer Pook, his chief witness to both incidents. (Edmund Pook, who had also witnessed one of them, was on the other hand nowhere to be seen.) Eight officers of R Division testified to Henry Pook's fist-shaking and obscenity-laden conduct on both occasions. In response, Ebenezer as well as Henry (who, since he had counter-summoned two of the officers, was entitled to speak) presented a very different version of the events, with a patient and put-upon Henry Pook bullied by the police. And Douglas Straight, in cross-examining the officers, did his best to insinuate that Superintendent Griffin—who had not been present on either occasion—had concocted the entire business, trumping up the charges and coaching his officers on their testimony.

The presiding magistrate, William Partridge, remained largely unconvinced of the Pooks' perspective upon the events, and rejected outright Straight's vilification of Superintendent Griffin. He ruled to dismiss the first charge against Henry Pook—for his outburst over Edmund's missed haircut—because then, he realized, Henry Pook was acting in the interests of his client. As for his outburst on the night after Jane's funeral, however, when Edmund was not present, Partridge ruled, "with great regret," that Henry Pook was guilty of interfering with police business. He fined the solicitor two pounds and court costs.

Ebenezer Pook immediately paid the fine and hurried home to shoot off a letter to the *Standard* both castigating the police and defending his solicitor: "I feel deeply the insult to which Mr. Pook has been subjected—he having only acted as a bold and fearless advocate. . . . If I know anything of the people of Greenwich—and I believe I do—I feel sure that he will not stand less in their estimation than formerly, but, on the contrary, some marked ebullition of feeling in his favour will be evinced."

The next evening—Thursday, July 20—the Pook case became a parliamentary issue, when George Whalley, Liberal member from Peterborough, rose in the House of Commons to question Home Secretary Henry Bruce. Whalley reminded Bruce of Chief Justice Bovill's bitter attack upon police misconduct in the Pook case. What steps then, Whalley asked the home secretary, would he take to protect the public against any recurrence of that sort of misconduct?

It was a question that the home secretary could have answered in two very different ways. He could have approached it generally, as a question about government policy, an opportunity to advocate steps to reform a deficient system; in particular, it offered Bruce a chance to promote the establishment of a public prosecutor's office in England.* Or Bruce could approach it specifically and narrowly, as concerning only the objectionable conduct of James Griffin and John Mulvany: a specific question about discipline and not a general one about policy. Henry Bruce chose to approach the question that way. In doing so, he was able to dodge answering Whalley's question completely. The commissioner of the Metropolitan Police, Bruce replied to Whalley, had just informed him that summonses had been applied for against the two officers referred to. While their cases were pending, therefore, Bruce thought it best to refrain from saying anything that might prejudice them. If, of course, the summonses were not granted, Bruce told Whalley he would be happy to answer his question.

The home secretary's intelligence was accurate—almost; earlier that evening, Henry and Ebenezer Pook had marched into Guildhall police court to apply for summonses against Griffin and Mulvany. Or, at least, they had *attempted to* apply for them. They arrived

---

* A bill creating a public prosecutor had actually been introduced in Parliament during the 1871 session. But it had failed. The creation of a Director of Public Prosecutions for England and Wales would not come about for another eight years.

at Guildhall minutes after the magistrate, the highly respected Robert Carden, once Lord Mayor of London, had left for the day. Undaunted, Henry Pook expected Carden's chief clerk to take down their complaint. But he refused, instead directing the Pooks to fill out the proper forms and return to court with all witnesses; only then would their complaints be heard. The Pooks snatched up the proper forms and retired, grumbling. Four days later, they returned, this time with Edmund, and this time arriving just in time to catch Carden as he was leaving court. They convinced him to return, and they submitted and swore to the charges. Both Edmund and his father accused James Griffin of lying at his trial three times, and James Mulvany lying four times, all when testifying about their confrontation and arrest of Edmund on the first of May.

To the enraged Pooks, convinced of both officers' enmity toward them, the charges must have seemed solid. But they were not. Every one of them was less an absolute falsehood, and more a small difference in recollection between the Pooks and the police of words remembered in court two and a half months after they were spoken. The most serious claim against James Griffin, for example, was that he lied when he testified that Edmund had "made no reply" when Griffin told him Jane said she was to meet him on Crooms Hill. (Edmund and Ebenezer swore, rather, that Edmund had energetically and instantly denied meeting her there.) And the most serious charge against John Mulvany was that he denied in testimony that he had said to Edmund of Jane that "there is a letter to her in his handwriting." Both Edmund and Ebenezer swore that he used exactly those words—therefore attempting to entrap Edmund with evidence the police did not have. (Transcripts of the trial show that Mulvany did not use those words, and instead told Edmund that *people said* that he had written a letter to her.")

Two days later, Carden refused to grant the summonses. He and his chief clerk, he told the Pooks, had read the transcripts of the trial. They discovered that while Bovill had criticized the conduct of the two officers, he did not ever claim—did not even insinuate—that either one had committed perjury. And if they *had* committed perjury during the trial, Carden was sure, so "just and conscientious a judge" would certainly have called for their prosecution. Here Henry Pook interrupted to protest—Carden had surely not read Bovill's summation. (In fact, Bovill did not accuse either Griffin or Mulvany of perjury at any point during the trial.) Carden simply ignored the outraged solicitor, let his refusal of their application stand, and, while Henry Pook angrily blustered that he would take their prosecution elsewhere, turned to other business.

With that, the Pooks' dreams of placing either Griffin or Mulvany in a criminal dock died. And indeed, their dream to prosecute Mulvany died entirely. As for Griffin, they quickly adopted another strategy to make him pay for his transgressions—and make him pay literally. Since Robert Carden blocked criminal prosecution, they would simply sue him in civil court. At some time within the next few weeks, they launched that suit, seeking twenty thousand pounds' damages on two charges: that Griffin had maliciously prosecuted Edmund, and that he had made on the first of May an illegal entry into Ebenezer Pook's home.

The results of that lawsuit would not transpire for months. Meanwhile, five nights later the remote possibility that the Crown, rather than the Pooks, might prosecute either officer died as well when the Liberal member for Peterborough, Mr. Whalley, repeated his question to the home secretary. Henry Bruce gushed unqualified praise for both officers and announced that Police Commissioner Henderson had determined that neither officer had done a thing to justify dismissal from the force.

As for the supposed perjury of James Conway, Walter Perren, and Thomas Lazell, it became clear as time passed that neither police, nor Treasury Department, nor attorney general, nor home secretary had any intention whatsoever to bring any one of them to trial. The Pook Defence Committee and their secretary, Leopold de Breanski, did their best to force the matter, repeatedly writing to the home secretary to demand a meeting with him to discuss bringing Conway and Perren to justice for their lies in the witness box. (Lazell, whom Bovill never accused of perjury, had quietly slipped from the list.) Henry Bruce, however, refused to see them, and simply ignored their subsequent letters of protest.

The dying cause, then, of prosecuting the trial's supposedly false witnesses the Pooks left to the less than capable hands of their defense committee. In the meantime, a new enemy arose to torment them—torment them into mounting what would become, in the end, a frenzy of litigation.

The first letter, signed only with the letter C, appeared in the *Kentish Mercury* exactly a week after Edmund's acquittal. "As there is a general opinion abroad that there has been some miscarriage of justice in reference to this dreadful crime," it began, "I have decided to analyse some of the evidence which was produced, and the general conduct of the trial." What followed amounted to a caustic attack upon the many commentaries about the trial that had flooded the press over the previous week. While those commentaries had unanimously praised Chief Justice Bovill as a man of good sense, C castigated him as a cranky bumbler whose biases rendered him unfit to judge. While they had as one pilloried the police as inept both in detection and in testimony, C defended them. The police did not suppress evidence, he argued; rather, they set aside the locket, the "bloody" rag, the whistle, waiting until the relevance of that evidence might became clear, which is exactly what happened with the whistle. The police in their testimony were invariably clear and sensible; any confusion about their words lay entirely in the dunderheaded mind of the judge. And while the other commentaries uniformly condemned the evidence for the prosecution and commended the evidence for the defense, C did exactly the opposite. He saw nothing to exonerate Pook in the relative lack of blood on his clothing. "If the arteries were thoroughly divided" in the attack, he claimed, "they would contract, and the blood would not spurt." Minor discrepancies in the testimony of prosecution witnesses, he claimed, actually suggested their honesty, "as the testimony then appears less like a taught lesson that has been learned by rote." But testimony learned by rote was exactly what the defense witnesses seemed to speak. There was the uniform testimony of Edmund's family, for example, that because of his epilepsy he was never out of a family member's sight, a claim that was wholly belied by the proven fact that Edmund often rambled from home, alone, for hours at a time—as he did on the very night of the murder.

In short, C condemned the trial as a "burlesque of justice" in which judge and jury got it wrong. And C implicitly, but never quite explicitly, argued that Edmund Pook had murdered Jane Clouson. To the hotheaded Pooks—certainly to Ebenezer and Henry—the letter reeked of libel. And yet, with uncharacteristic reticence, the two refrained from action. They refrained, that is, until C continued his assault in the next week's issue.

After further developing his analysis in this letter, C shifted to reverie, musing about how he would go about committing the perfect murder:

> I shall prepare myself for my diabolical task, and cultivate my natural callousness and villainy by a devoted study of the popular sensation novels of the day. The girl I once loved, and who is desperately in my way, shall be my victim. I shall have studied my sensational novel to very little profit if I cannot contrive a simple plot, the simpler the better, for perpetrating my fell purpose. An evening walk down a dark unfrequented lane, and a small axe, will supply me with all the conditions I shall require for accomplishing my design. Fifteen blows in fifteen seconds will be enough. When the deed is done

I shall not be miserable. I shall feel the same relief that a surgeon would feel after lopping off a mortified limb. But if my nerves should be a little agitated, a quick run home though the fresh evening air will restore my equanimity, and after supper I shall be quite ready for a good night's rest.

From start to finish, C carefully connected Jane's actual murder, and Edmund's movements, with his imaginary "perfect" one. C therefore made his point even more fully than he had the week before: Edmund Pook had committed the perfect murder.

To the Pooks, this was surely a vicious libel and surely actionable. And Henry Pook did take action, firing off a letter to the editor of the *Kentish Mercury*, a young man by the name of Sydney Boate, demanding he reveal C's identity. Boate replied with a letter in which his righteousness fails to disguise his cravenness. "You will pardon me for doubting the wisdom of the course you adopt; but as any man who avows strong sentiments like 'C' should not be afraid of his name being known, Mr. Newton Crosland . . . is the writer whose name you want."

Having thus learned the name of the man who had supposedly written this poison, the Pooks again desisted from legal action. They might have heard of Newton Crosland before: he was a near neighbor living in Blackheath; he was a successful wine merchant; he was a well-known spiritualist. But he was not a writer, and there was an unquestionable literary quality to these letters. The Pooks certainly did know *Mrs.* Newton Crosland, the writer—and Henry Pook, for one, suspected that she was the author of the letters. Chivalrous sentiment might therefore have led them to hesitate. Most likely, however, they simply demonstrated, surprisingly, a bit of common sense. The two letters had so far appeared in a Greenwich local newspaper; no other newspaper had reprinted them, and relatively few people had read them. If the Pooks prosecuted Crosland or the editor Sydney Boate for libel, on the other hand, the most malicious passages from the letters would be read in the courtroom, and newspapers across the country would eagerly—and legally—republish those passages, for millions to read.

For whatever reason, then, the Pooks did not prosecute—until, three weeks later, Newton Crosland left them no choice. On Friday, August 18, a twopenny pamphlet appeared in booksellers and newsagents in Greenwich, throughout the metropolis, and beyond: *The Eltham Tragedy Reviewed,* an expanded version of the *Kentish Mercury* letters, published by Frederick Farrah, a radical publisher on the Strand. Newton Crosland now aimed to spread his attack widely. And the Pooks had to act.

Still they refrained from going after Newton Crosland. "It was not the man who invented the gunpowder, but the man who fired the shot that did the mischief," Henry Pook would later declare in court. They therefore sought to prosecute the *publisher* of the work—or, rather, the publishers. For they considered that *anyone* who disseminated this libel, anyone who sold it as well as anyone who produced it, was a publisher. On the day after the pamphlet first appeared, then, Henry Pook not only obtained a summons at Bow Street Police Court against Frederick Farrah; he also stormed into a little newsagent's shop on Royal Hill, around the corner from the Pooks' home, to order the shop's proprietress, a timid widow by the name of Caroline Horton, to stop selling the pamphlet. "If you sell any after Monday, madam," he snarled, "I shall summons you, and give you three months." "Well, he's anything but a gentleman," Mrs. Horton uttered to a customer. She continued to sell the pamphlet. Two days later Henry Pook attended Greenwich Police Court to obtain a summons against her.

In obtaining those summonses, Henry Pook had placed Edmund Pook, at least potentially, into a difficult situation. Until this point, Edmund Pook had not been obligated to testify under oath concerning Jane Clouson's murder; indeed, as a defendant he was prohibited by the law of that day from doing so. But now that the Pooks were prosecuting Farrah and Horton for publishing the libel that Edmund Pook had killed Jane Clouson, Henry Pook would have to place Edmund in the witness chair to deny that fact. And if he was examined in court, he could be cross-examined: a good lawyer for the defense could trip him up by forcing from him self-incriminating discrepancies or contradictions. Because of the rule against double jeopardy, of course, Edmund could never now face justice as a murderer. But a ruthless and skillful cross-examiner might convincingly demonstrate to the world that he had killed Jane Clouson.

Henry Pook certainly was aware of that danger when on August 22 he appeared with Edmund at Frederick Farrah's examination at Bow Street. He faced the prospect with a show of confidence. "I shall call Edmund Walter Pook, who is ready to be examined," he announced, "and I shall defy the learned counsel to ask him any questions. The time for which the young man has so longed for has at length come, and he will now for the first time have the opportunity of opening his mouth and giving denial to all the charges brought against him." Edmund Pook, however, approached the witness chair with discernible uneasiness.

He need not have worried. Frederick Farrah had made an odd choice for his counsel: Douglas Straight, who had a month before been one of Edmund's own lawyers (and more recently had been Henry Pook's). Straight had advocated Edmund's innocence at his trial; he had no intention of challenging that position now. "I shall ask Mr. Pook no questions," he announced. Without any fear of challenge or contradiction, then, Henry Pook led Edmund through a catechism of denial:

> "Had you any communication with that poor girl?"
> "None whatever."
> "Did you write her a letter?"
> "Never."
> "Did you ever make any appointment to meet her?"
> "Never."

"Was there the slightest act of familiarity between you?"

"None whatever."

"Did you make her a present?"

"Never."

"You have read that pamphlet, Edmund Walter Pook?"

"Yes."

"Do you now, upon your solemn oath, declare that all the charges against you are true or untrue?"

"Untrue in every particular."

"That you solemnly declare before your maker?"

"I do."

Straight then offered the abject submission of his client. Farrah, he claimed, had not scrutinized Newton Crosland's text carefully enough to realize that it was libelous. Now that he realized that it was, Farrah offered to apologize and to suspend publication.

Henry Pook instantly refused that offer; the Pooks, he said, had resolved to prosecute Farrah to the bitter end. The magistrate, Frederick Flowers, declared that in that case he had no choice: the pamphlet was, he was sure, libelous; he committed Farrah on bail for trial at the Old Bailey.

If judicial sentiment at Bow Street lay wholly with the Pooks, popular sentiment there did not. On the street outside the police court, a mass of "half-drunken, ragged loafers" according to one report, howled, hissed, and jostled Henry and Edmund. The two required the assistance of the police to be placed in a cab rather than thrown under it. Their appearance that day only served to whet the public appetite for *The Eltham Tragedy Reviewed*; while they were at court every copy of the pamphlet at Farrah's nearby shop sold out.

One week later, at Caroline Horton's examination in Greenwich for libel, Edmund and Henry Pook experienced a similar victory within the courtroom and a similar rout without. The widow

Horton, despite her limited means, had managed to obtain good counsel. As a young woman she had been a servant in the home of Charles Carttar, a lawyer who now served as coroner for West Kent; he agreed to take on her case. And Carttar, like Douglas Straight, had no intention of challenging Edmund Pook's declaration of innocence. Instead he rebuked the Pooks for aiming to punish Horton rather than Newton Crosland, and sought the sympathy of the magistrate, James Patteson. Horton, he pointed out, was a hardworking widow with a large family; she knew the Pooks and had been supportive of Edmund throughout his ordeal. Because neither the *Kentish Mercury* nor Newton Crosland had been prosecuted for his letters, she considered the pamphlet perfectly legal to sell.

Caroline Horton assisted Carttar by fainting in the middle of his speech. The magistrate was indeed sympathetic, but felt bound by the law. She had indeed sold a work that he was sure was libelous, and he would have to commit her—unless, he emphasized, the Pooks reconsidered. The Pooks—father, solicitor, and Edmund—then conferred, and agreed: they would drop their charge if Caroline Horton apologized. The proceedings ended with rousing cheers—but the cheers were exclusively for the widow. Outside the courtroom the Pooks again faced hissing and the hooting. They escaped by a ruse, the police decoying away the crowd by driving an empty cab around the block, as if they were planning to spirit the Pooks over the back wall.

The rough reception the Pooks got in Greenwich could hardly surprise them. But the rough reception in London almost certainly did. Until recently, the discontent, the rage and ridicule, had been entirely confined to the populace of Greenwich and Deptford. Thanks to *The Eltham Tragedy Reviewed*, but thanks even more to the Pooks' crusade to stamp that pamphlet out, hostility toward the Pooks—all of them—was growing. "The Pook family are becoming a nuisance," two newspapers from outside of London proclaimed several days after Caroline Horton's examination. "It would be quite a mercy if the whole family would emigrate."

And while the rest of the family stayed put, sometime in the last months of 1871 Edmund finally bowed to the pressure, quit his father's employ, and decamped to the East Kent seaside town of Herne Bay; fewer than sixty miles from Greenwich, the place was far enough away from the hurly-burly, but close enough so that Edmund could commute by train for his several court appearances. His rustication was effected so quietly that whom he stayed with, and how he spent most of his time, remains unknown. Only the fact that he sought strength and solace in the church during his stay provides any evidence that he was there at all. In April 1872, the local newspaper reported that the bishop of Dover had laid his hands in the Anglican rite of confirmation upon seventeen youths, "including Mr. Pook, who has been for some time residing in Herne Bay."

In the meantime, contention and commotion continued in Greenwich as if Edmund had never left. Members of the Pook Defence Fund, realizing that the home secretary would not see them and would do nothing to support them, took matters into their own hands: in mid-August they inundated Greenwich and Deptford with placards offering £200 for the detection and conviction of Jane Clouson's *actual* killer. Their opponents derided the offer as a shameful attempt to divert attention from Edmund Pook. And rival committees sprung up to fund legal costs on the other side: an ephemeral Horton Defence Fund and a more successful Farrah Defence Fund. In mid-September, two thousand men, women, and children gathered at a monster meeting on Blackheath in support of the publisher. A number of local radical politicians spoke, extolling the virtues of free speech and castigating the abuses of the Pook trial. Boxes were passed around and a substantial fund raised—a fund, however, offset at the very end of the meeting, when Frederick Farrah's fine gold watch was ripped from its fob and stolen. Superintendent Griffin, on hand to keep order, quickly stepped in to arrest the pickpocket, but not before the thief handed the watch to a confederate, who escaped.

And all this time, *The Eltham Tragedy Reviewed* continued to sell and continued to be read; Frederick Farrah, on bond and awaiting trial, saw no reason why he should not continue publishing the pamphlet until a judge and jury determined it libelous. The Pooks, then, decided they had no choice but to prosecute the one who had invented the gunpowder as well as the one who had fired the shot. And so on September 12, Henry Pook finally sought and obtained a summons for criminal libel against Newton Crosland. Three days later, when Crosland appeared at Bow Street to answer the charge, it became clear that the Pooks finally had a legal battle on their hands. For by Crosland's side was the formidable solicitor George Lewis, junior partner in the firm of Lewis and Lewis.

It would be another five years before George Lewis—with his instantly recognizable furred frock coat, his monocle, and his long Dundreary whiskers—would become the most famous solicitor in England, *the* solicitor of choice to London's high society. But he was already well on his way. Two years earlier, Lewis had been introduced to the Prince of Wales, and just a year before had advised the prince when he became embroiled in the scandalous divorce case *Mordaunt v. Mordaunt*. And he had already developed the abilities that would make him famous: utter discretion, indefatigable service, and a ferocious tenacity at cross-examination. The Pooks would find no submission, no offers to apologize or desist, from George Lewis. And neither Crosland nor Lewis had any intention of shying away from the golden opportunity of subjecting Edmund Pook to a thorough cross-examination.

The confrontation between the two highly passionate and egotistical solicitors was predictably explosive. "Personalities were freely indulged in," remarked the reporter from the *Times*. Henry Pook opened with hyperbole even greater than usual, positing himself as a modern hero of myth—a forensic Jason—taking on his many libelous enemies: he "should meet them as they came, and if there were a thousand dragon's teeth, he would bury them in the earth, and though dug up again, he would face them still, showing that they should not frighten them. Once for all, this matter should be settled." Lewis, for his part, delighted in puncturing the bulging solicitor's bulging ego. When, for example, Lewis complained about Henry Pook's relentlessly ornate speechifying, Pook responded righteously that he did not make speeches for the sake of popularity: he was there in the cause of truth and justice.

He had never imputed to Pook "that he had obtained popularity by his speeches," Lewis responded—"but rather the reverse."

After Edmund Pook, with a remarkable and discernible composure, took the witness chair and Henry Pook guided him through his usual denial that he had murdered Jane Clouson, Lewis rose to cross-examine. He began by establishing that the police did have some grounds for at least considering him a suspect: Jane had lived in his home for twenty-three months, he acknowledged, had become pregnant at that time, and had left only eleven days before her murder. From this line of questioning Lewis quickly turned to Edmund's bloody clothing.

"Do you know how that blood came upon your garments?" Lewis asked him.

"From the fit that I had had," he replied conclusively, eliminating from consideration the possibilities that he had cut his finger in the shop or had bound up a shopboy's cut finger.

When Lewis then asked him where his fit had occurred, Edmund was certain: "at my own house." He was equally certain that he had not had an epileptic fit outdoors for some time—for six or seven months. As to *when* the fit in his home had occurred, he was far less certain. "What is the good of asking me; I know nothing more about it," he protested, when Lewis badgered him on the point. Lewis persisted until Edmund admitted that the fit had occurred no more than two weeks before the murder. With that, Lewis pounced upon a curious anomaly: Edmund claimed to have suffered his fit indoors—while fully dressed for the outdoors.

> "How do you account for the blood on your hat?"
> "By its being knocked off."
> "You do not wear your hat in the house?"

"But you can go in with it, I suppose."

"Then how do you account for it?"

"By its being knocked off, and blood spurting from my mouth on the hat."

"But you said your fit was in the sitting room. You do not wear your hat there?"

"Do you take yours off directly when you go in? I lay on the floor beside it in the fit."

Henry Pook, distinctly discomforted by this line of questioning, here interjected "one would think you were trying the young man over again." Exactly so. Lewis pressed on.

"Was the coat you had on when you were arrested the coat you had on the night of the fit?"

Edmund—whose recollection about the fit to this point was at best vague, was certain on this point: "No."

"Have you looked to see if there is blood on it?"

"No."

"Where is it?"

"At home."

"Has it been examined?"

"The police had all my clothes."

If that coat had been bloody, it seems, the police would have noticed that blood. But they had not. And so, according to his account, he suffered an epileptic fit while dressed in coat and hat, and had bled: bled on his hat, bled on the lower legs of his trousers, but had not bled at all on his coat.

Lewis then turned to Edmund's movements on the night of the murder and elicited from Edmund the claim that he had run from Lewisham to Greenwich "because I felt the fit coming on"—a claim Lewis later dismissed as a physiological absurdity. With that, Edmund left the witness box and Crosland's examination adjourned for a week. Edmund thus braved one of the best cross-examiners in the country, and if he hadn't emerged entirely unscathed, he certainly had not been defeated—he had hardly been exposed as Jane Clouson's murderer. It soon became clear, however, that Lewis would have another chance—and another after that—to shake his story.

On September 19, five days after Lewis examined Edmund, the grand jury convened at the Old Bailey, considered the charge of libel against Frederick Farrah—and ignored the bill. The charge against the pamphlet's publisher thus dropped, Farrah celebrated by issuing a second edition of *The Eltham Tragedy Reviewed*, one in which some of the most striking connections between Edmund Pook and Crosland's imagined perfect murderer were removed. The grand jury offered no reason for ignoring the bill. But its message that the charge did not merit trial at the Old Bailey was perfectly clear. Perfectly clear, that is, to everyone but the Pooks, who refused to admit defeat. Not only did they resolve to press on in their criminal prosecution of Newton Crosland; they also initiated two *more* prosecutions for criminal libel, hoping that the grand jury at the next Old Bailey sessions would consider the matter differently. On the afternoon of September 27, then, Henry Pook hurried from Bow Street to Greenwich Police Court and obtained a second summons against Frederick Farrah on the same basis as before, and then obtained one against yet another Greenwich shopkeeper who had dared sell *The Eltham Tragedy Reviewed*. John Page, tobacconist on Greenwich Road, accepted his summons with ironic honor, displaying it in his shop window next to a particularly ugly likeness of Henry Pook,* and printing up new labels with which to wrap his tobacco. "Happy Jane Maria Clousen. Taken away from the evil to come," they proclaimed, somewhat cryptically, but certainly suggesting that that evil had blasted John Page instead.

---

* Quite possibly this was the image of Henry Pook published in the *Illustrated Police News*: a hideous likeness indeed.

Frederick Farrah, at his examination, had clearly had a change of heart about the prosecution. Thanks to the efforts of the Farrah Defence Fund, and to the moral and financial support of Newton Crosland—who had vowed to fight each and every libel action mounted against his pamphlet—Farrah had dropped the conciliatory Douglas Straight as his counsel. Now, George Lewis represented him. And at *his* examination, John Page, as well, entered police court with both Newton Crosland and George Lewis at his side.

When Lewis cross-examined Edmund Pook at Farrah's Bow Street examination, he took a new tack, questioning Edmund about his trial, and about the testimony of the prosecution witnesses. A pattern quickly emerged. Of William Sparshott, who swore Edmund came to his shop looking to buy an axe, Edmund claimed, "He was an utter stranger to me, and committed perjury in making that assertion." Of the officers who testified to the finding of a whistle near the site of the murder, he said, "Two or three of them committed this perjury, I cannot tell you their names." More than this, "Superintendent Griffin committed perjury . . . Mulvany also committed perjury. Several witnesses, utter strangers to me, committed perjury." Edmund, in short, understood himself to be the victim of a widespread conspiracy of strangers who had no discernible motive to wish him harm. It seemed incredible. And it raised serious doubts, as Crosland had in his pamphlet, about the entire conduct of Edmund Pook's trial.

Two days later, at John Page's examination, Lewis conducted his final cross of Edmund Pook. This time he took Edmund over the same ground as he had before, quizzing him about his bloody clothing and about the improbable roster of supposedly perjuring witnesses. He was here, it seems, acting less the advocate and more the solicitor, preparing a brief for trial: less attempting to convince the magistrate to throw the charge out, but rather seeking out all possible weak points in Edmund's story, weaknesses that a barrister could employ in higher court. And in his probing on this day, Lewis did manage to extract a new and remarkable claim from Edmund. At the end of his testimony, Edmund repeated his assertion that he had seen Jane Clouson walking in public with another man, three days before her murder. And then he added something new: his brother, Thomas, he stated, had seen Jane and a young man walking in public as well—one night before Edmund had seen the two. Edmund then stepped down, and no one in the courtroom seemed to understand how truly astonishing his words were. Had Edmund's brother, Thomas, actually seen Jane and a "swell" together, as Edmund had, he would have had no reason to withhold that information on the day of Edmund's arrest, and every reason to tell it. And yet he had said nothing. More than this, the odds against Edmund and Thomas Pook, and absolutely no one else, seeing Jane walking openly in Greenwich with a young man, on two successive nights, were unbelievably, staggeringly high. Thomas Pook had never claimed to have seen Jane Clouson four days before the murder—almost certainly because he had not done so. George Lewis, it seems, ended his cross by prompting Edmund Pook to lie in order to bolster his case. But it was a lie that even George Lewis did not detect.

If George Lewis, in the course of his three widely reported cross-examinations, succeeded in raising doubts about Edmund Pook's innocence, he did nothing to prevent the magistrates at each examination from committing Crosland, Farrah, and Page for trial. Two of the magistrates were certain, the grand jury's decision on Farrah notwithstanding, that Crosland's pamphlet was libelous; the third thought, at least, that this was a matter for a trial jury to decide. This triumph of sorts was no longer enough for Henry Pook, no longer sure of his chances of winning at the Old Bailey after Farrah's first case collapsed. Libel, he knew, could be fought in civil as well as criminal court. True, the Pooks could never have the vindictive pleasure of seeing their enemies suffer penal servitude if they were convicted in a civil court. But the Pooks could obtain high damages there; they could thus, in particular, inflict a devastating punishment upon wealthy Newton Crosland. And so on October 9, as Newton Crosland walked into Greenwich Police Court to attend John Page's examination, Henry Pook stunned him with a writ from the Court of Exchequer seeking £10,000 damages: not for his pamphlet, but for his two *Kentish Mercury* articles. Henry Pook served similar writs on Sidney Boate, the newspaper's craven editor, and on the proprietor of the newspaper, Boate's great aunt, Christina Hartnoll.

Exactly two weeks afterward, the wisdom of Henry Pook's shift in litigation became apparent, as the grand jury met at the Old Bailey, considered the bills against Crosland, Farrah, and Page—and ignored them all. The Pooks' criminal prosecution of their enemies collapsed in an instant. One week after this, the three celebrated their triumph—of sorts—with a meeting at the Greenwich Lecture Hall to discuss Edmund Pook's trial and to solicit funds—funds no longer for legal defense, but for a monument to Jane Clouson herself. Supporters filled the thousand-seat theater to overflowing, and Newton Crosland, now the undisputed leader of the movement, took the chair. He spoke movingly about the appropriateness of a memorial to the girl; he read out the epitaph for it he had composed himself. (That epitaph, with some changes, was indeed the one chiseled upon the monument.) A collection was taken up and £7 collected—almost all in coppers. But Crosland and several other speakers pressed for more than a statue in Jane's memory: they argued that *R v. Pook* had been a monstrous miscarriage of justice and proposed two legal reforms: the establishment of a public prosecutor and the adoption of the Scottish verdict of "not proven."

Three months of ceaseless litigation had only hurt rather than helped Edmund Pook's and Henry Pook's reputations. Public sentiment at Edmund's acquittal had been, with the exception of Greenwich and Deptford malcontents, entirely on his side. That sentiment had by now evaporated; most would agree, with Greenwich magistrate James Patteson, who declared at John Page's examination that he was "almost sick of the case." At the end of October, George Stiff, editor of the *Weekly Dispatch*, snapped, "The acquitted Mr. Pook got the benefit of the doubt, and certainly silence in the unhappy transaction, rather than litigious vexatiousness, is the wiser procedure. In Scotland the verdict would have been that known as 'not proven;' and something resembling that is precisely what is felt by all in the present case. As people are neither perfectly satisfied, nor fully at ease in their judgment, it is certain that pertinacious persistency in wrangling can only provoke a general irritation." Stiff held Henry Pook responsible for this travesty of justice, litigating simply to achieve "nauseating notoriety." "Really," Stiff concluded, "we recommend Pook to subside."

Henry Pook, however, was never one to subside. Instead, he sued both Stiff and the *Weekly Dispatch*.

<hr />

As the civil cases wound their slow way along—with delays, they would not be argued for another three months—Henry Pook took an inspired legal step, one that surely greatly enhanced his clients' chances of winning their case. He applied at the Court of Exchequer for, and was granted, special juries for his trials against Newton Crosland and the *Kentish Mercury*. Special juries, to put it simply, consisted of men of substantial property: traditionally bankers, merchants, and those who held the rank of esquire. Their higher social status almost guaranteed a more conservative jury, which is why the Crown routinely employed special juries in state and political trials. Such a jury, Henry Pook assumed, might be more amenable to the interests of a solid Greenwich burgher—or of his son.

In the meantime, if tension in Greenwich and Deptford abated, it certainly did not disappear. Edmund Pook remained an exile in Herne Bay. In early December, fourteen-year-old Arthur Thomas paid a price for his mother's inability to state, nine months before, who purchased a hammer from their shop, when a drunken lout with a long memory approached the boy outside the Thomases' ironmongery, shouted incomprehensibly, and felled him with a blow to the side of the head. It was the latest of many attacks upon the Thomases; at the assailant's examination, Arthur's father,

Samuel, noted that the family had for months been "subjected to the greatest annoyance."

One week after this came the news of a far greater fall. "Mr. James Griffin," the newspapers reported in mid-December, "superintendent of the R division of metropolitan police, whose name was often mentioned during the trial for the Eltham murder and the subsequent proceedings, and who is now the defendant in an action brought by the young man Pook for £1,000 damages, has been retired from the force with a superannuation allowance of £200 a year in consequence of ill health." Ill health might indeed have been a cause of Griffin's resignation: managing a police force for months after having entirely lost the confidence of the people of the town could not but have been enormously stressful. But rumors quickly arose that this explanation was a fig leaf to conceal his dismissal for his conduct in the Pook investigation. The *Kentish Mercury* attempted to dispel these by publishing glowing testimonials to Griffin by Commissioner Henderson and other notables. Pressure by the Pooks almost certainly had something to do with Griffin's leaving the force: their lawsuit, pending until the day Griffin retired, vanished completely after that. There would be no *Pook v. Griffin*. The end of Griffin's promising career, it seems, the Pooks accepted as punishment enough.

Newton Crosland entered the Court of Exchequer at Westminster on the first of February, 1872, with an unshakeable sense of foreboding. His astrologer friend, the one who had told him of the great evil to him portended on the date of Jane's death, had again examined his chart and had determined that Crosland was to lose at this trial. And the fact that Chief Baron of the Exchequer Fitzroy Kelly judged the case was additionally inauspicious: Kelly was a good friend of Chief Justice Bovill, whom Crosland had savaged in *The Eltham Tragedy Reviewed*.

Crosland's advocate in the trial was the capable John Humffreys Parry, known for his melodramatic style, his participation in several notable criminal trials, and his reputation for winning. If winning this case entailed establishing that Crosland's assertions about Edmund Pook and his trial were reasonable ones, no one could have done a better job than Parry besides, perhaps, George Lewis—who had briefed him and had briefed him well. In a thorough and lengthy cross-examination of Edmund Pook, Parry forced admission after admission to establish doubt about Edmund's innocence. Edmund acknowledged that the coroner's jury had returned a verdict of willful murder against him, that a magistrate had committed him for trial, that a true jury had returned a true bill against him for murder. He repeated his certainty that many strangers had committed perjury against him, for no clear reason: "with the exception of Inspector Griffin," he testified, "I did not know one of those I charged with perjury." He repeated his callous dismissal of Jane as a "very dirty girl." And he articulated all of the compelling hearsay evidence not admitted at his trial: Fanny Hamilton's claim that Jane was to meet him on the night of the murder, as well as Jane's statement that she was pregnant, and that Edmund was the father. It was the charwoman Jane Prosser who actually had sworn Jane had said this, but Edmund inadvertently rendered the claim more compelling by attributing it to Jane's cousin Charlotte Trott as well as to Prosser.

That hearsay evidence formed the centerpiece of Parry's closing address of the jury on the second day of the trial—an address tailored to be as much a prosecution of Edmund Pook as a defense of Newton Crosland. Crosland had every right to question the exclusion of Jane's words at trial, Parry argued. "There were many circumstances pointing to this young man as the murderer of this girl which he could never get over. If that girl's lips had not been sealed in death, and if she had repeated upon her oath the statements alleged to have been made by her, where would the plaintiff have been now? Why, undergoing penal servitude for life."

That certainly might have been so. But the fact is that Jane's lips *had* been sealed in death, and, for all Parry's sensational marshalling of the evidence, for all his heaping doubt upon Edmund's version of events, he, like George Lewis before him, failed in forcing from Edmund the utterly damning admission that would in an instant have exposed him as guilty, exposed his acquittal as a sham, and vindicated Crosland's attack upon it. Parry failed, in other words, to prove Edmund Pook a murderer. But he certainly did enough to prove to many that Edmund Pook *could have been* a murderer, and that alone should have been enough to win this case. For as both Pook's lawyer—John Huddleston, again—and the judge, Chief Baron Kelly, stated to the jury, the one question at issue was whether Crosland's letters constituted a fair, honest, impartial criticism of the trial, or whether they amounted to an unfair and unwarranted attack upon Edmund Pook. Given the doubts about the case and the trial that Parry had forced from Edmund Pook's own lips, there had clearly been nothing unwarranted about Crosland's criticisms.

But Chief Baron Kelly, and not John Humffreys Parry, had the final words in the trial, and it was with the chief baron's summation, according to Newton Crosland, that everything fell apart. Kelly, Crosland later wrote, "summed up dead against me and said not a word in my favour: he made several mistakes in matters of fact, two of these my counsel corrected, but there was a third which he allowed me to pass. I asked him why he did not correct that also. He replied 'I corrected him twice; if I had done it a third time, I should have put the Judge's back up, and then perhaps it would have been worse for us!'"

Indeed it could have been. The jury retired, consulted for half an hour, and returned to declare Crosland guilty of libel. Edmund, Ebenezer, and Henry had finally won. The damages resulting from the libel, the foreman announced, amounted to £50—not an inconsequential amount in 1871, but certainly not enough to cover Henry Pook's expenses, and a far cry from the £10,000 the Pooks had asked for.

Newton Crosland left the court thoroughly unchastened. And *The Eltham Tragedy Revisited* continued to sell.

⊶

Fifty-two years after the special jury reached their verdict in *Pook v. Crosland,* an elderly judge, who as a young barrister had attended the trial, shared his recollections of it in a letter to the *Times.* That judge, Edward Ridley, had forgotten much in the intervening years. "I forget who were counsel for the plaintiff; I forget even which of the Barons was Judge." He forgot, as well, that Newton Crosland was the defendant in the case—not the *Kentish Mercury,* as he thought. (When Crosland lost his case, the editor of the *Kentish Mercury* quickly settled, and the proprietor's case never came to trial.) While Ridley's grasp of the facts slipped over time, his impression of the true loser in that trial remained clear. "What I do not forget," he wrote, "was that Serjeant Parry was for the defendants. A verdict for them was not possible after the acquittal at the Old Bailey; but Parry, in a deliberate speech of reasoned and stately eloquence, which met with universal admiration, worked through the story piece by piece, and proved the guilt of Pook. The jury gave their verdict for one farthing damages, and Pook's name went down to posterity."

Ridley was of course wrong about the farthing, as well.* But he did capture the shift in public consensus about the Pook case after seven months' litigation, and after first Lewis's and then Parry's cross-examinations. In the eyes of the law, Edmund Pook was an innocent man. But to the public, the law had shown itself in a thousand ways to be an ass. And to the public, Edmund Walter Pook had very likely gotten away with murder.

---

* Six years after this, John Parry was able to obtain damages in exactly that amount—one farthing—for his client the artist James Whistler in the celebrated libel trial *Whistler v. Ruskin.*

CHAPTER SEVEN

VIPER OF KIDBROOKE LANE

On the afternoon of August 7, 1872, an apocalyptic thunderstorm—"the most severe within living memory," reported the *Morning Post*—surged through southeast London. At Woolwich, court suspended so that magistrate and officers could battle rising flood waters. Before the gates of nearby Woolwich Arsenal a three-foot-deep lagoon arose; a foot and a half of water gushed into the shell foundry and destroyed the ordnance stored there. Lowlands became shallow lakes through which trains plodded. Unremitting lightning struck a number of buildings, felled walls, and goaded steamboat passengers on the Thames to jump up "as if electrified or shot." In a market garden in Charlton, just north of Kidbrooke, two girls were struck, one apparently fatally. And in Eltham a thunderbolt battered the police station, exploding its windows.

That deluge was the last and the greatest of a succession of storms that had beset the area that spring and summer, storms that brought with them—at least according to locals—freakish fireballs along with the thunder, the lightning, the flooding. And when some remembered that the very first of these storms had occurred on the first anniversary of Jane's murder, a local superstition grew: the cosmic upheaval would continue until Jane Clouson's murderer was brought to justice.

But Jane Clouson's murderer was never brought to justice.

The £200 reward offered by the Pook Defence Committee, not surprisingly, led to no major breakthrough in the case. And the police of R Division, since Superintendent Griffin's forced departure, and indeed, since Edmund Pook's acquittal, had shown little inclination to continue their investigation. To them the case *was* closed: they behaved as if they knew exactly who had killed Jane Clouson—and behaved as if that killer was now beyond their grasp.

Still, the case continued to force itself upon them, and continued in particular to haunt Detective Inspector John Mulvany. On November 26, 1871, a homeless laborer named Robert Sessions walked into Bagnigge Wells police station and confessed to Jane Clouson's murder. Mulvany was called in to investigate and quickly discovered that Sessions had recently been discharged from the army for attempting suicide while insane, that his father, in a similar fit, had succeeded in killing himself, and that his aunt was presently confined to a lunatic asylum. The charge of murder was dropped and Sessions committed to the insane ward of Clerkenwell Workhouse. Just over a year after this, in Newcastle-upon-Tyne, another itinerant, George King, told the police that he had "kept company" with Jane and had killed her in a jealous rage after he learned that she was carrying Edmund Pook's child. Though King's knowledge of the details of the crime was shaky—he confessed, for one thing, to killing Jane in August 1870 and not in April 1871—he was held for a week so that Scotland Yard could investigate; he was then discharged as a lunatic.

Three months later, in March 1873, a soldier named George Bingham presented the magistrate in the military town of Aldershot with a written confession to Jane's killing. Bingham was a soldier, and perhaps because of rumors early in the case that Jane's murderer was a soldier, his confession attracted a great deal of attention. The Pooks themselves engaged a solicitor—a solicitor from Aldershot, not Henry Pook—to watch the proceedings and to press for a "searching investigation" into the case. Several Pook supporters actually traveled down to observe Bingham's examination. Mulvany traveled down as well and testified that the police could not connect Bingham to Jane Clouson in any way. As with every other confessor to the murder, evidence for Bingham's insanity quickly grew. Jane Thomas was brought from Deptford to swear she could not identify Bingham as the purchaser of the hammer. Two witnesses who had been on Kidbrooke Lane the night of the attack swore as well that they could not recognize Bingham. The charge was dropped, and Bingham then admitted he had concocted the story to get out of the army.

That was the last John Mulvany had anything to do with the case. Later that year he quit Scotland Yard—or, more likely, he was forced out: though a relatively young man of forty-four when he left, and with eight years to live, he described himself in the subsequent census as "Police Inspector Superannuated," that is, dismissed on account of his age. After his failure with the Clouson investigation, Mulvany was never again given charge of a high-profile case. If his star did not fall with Edmund Pook's acquittal, it had certainly stopped rising.

The next confession came seven years after Bingham's, when a mason named Walter Thomas Prince regaled a magistrate in Stratford, in the East End, with an elaborate tale of *assisting* Edmund Pook in murdering Jane. (Prince carried the hammer and disposed of it; Pook actually struck the blows.) Prince then sobered up and confessed instead to being a delusional drunk with a nasty head injury. The magistrate sentenced him to two weeks of hard labor anyway. Two months later Prince made the same confession, and the same retraction, in Wandsworth; he was transferred to Greenwich, where he was let off with a warning.

Finally, in April 1888, four months before the Ripper murders put a stranglehold on public attention, a man who called himself Michael Carroll caused a stir throughout the antipodes by confessing to a police officer in Sydney that he had killed Jane seventeen years before. Wide dissemination of his confession in both Australia and New Zealand prompted a number of letters to local papers by emigrants from southeast London, all very imperfectly recollecting the murder. One British newspaper speculated that Carroll was simply George Bingham, confessing for a second time. Although Carroll's subsequent claim that he had invented and confessed his story while in a drunken stupor did not serve to free him, Scotland Yard did, with a cable declaring his story an utter fiction.

For the Pooks, both solicitor and family, the legal and social storm following Edmund's acquittal eventually passed as well. After their victory against Newton Crosland, Henry Pook still had one lawsuit to mount for Edmund and the family: the libel action against George Stiff, editor of the *Weekly Dispatch*, for daring to claim that Edmund had been lucky in his acquittal—and, incidentally, for pillorying Henry Pook's "litigious vexatiousness." The civil trial, *Pook v. Stiff*, was argued on June 15, 1872, again at the Court of Exchequer, again before a special jury, again with Huddleston leading for the plaintiff and Parry leading for the defense. Again Edmund Pook appeared, to deny killing Jane Clouson. And again the jury found for the plaintiff—this time for £25 damages. With that, the close legal bond that Henry Pook had forged with the Pook family came to an end. The bond of friendship, however, born of desperate need and solidified with heartfelt gratitude, remained. Three months after his trial, Edmund had

presented Henry Pook with a token and an emblem of that friendship: a finely chased silver snuffbox, bearing on its outside Henry
Pook's most appropriate motto, *"ausis nil impossibile"* ("to the
audacious nothing is impossible") and on its inside the inscription
"To Henry Pook, Esq., from Edmund Walter Pook, in commemora-
tion of the 15th of July, 1871, and as a mark of sincere gratitude."
July 15, 1871, of course, was the day of Edmund's acquittal.

Henry Pook thus found himself out of the spotlight and back
in the legal grind. He had certainly hoped that the name he had
made for himself defending Edmund would bring him a higher
class of client and a higher income. But with the exception of a
case or two, this was not to be. For the rest of his admittedly short
career, he generally argued his cases as he had before: at Greenwich Police Court, defending (and very occasionally prosecuting)
for theft, burglary, assault, and other breaches of Greenwich's
peace. In July 1873, Henry Pook sought to capitalize upon his
minor fame in another way, with the death of David Salomons,
one of two Liberal MPs from the borough of Greenwich. (Prime
Minister William Gladstone was the other.) Henry Pook had long
been one of Greenwich's staunchest Conservatives, and when the
local Conservatives selected another man, Thomas Boord, to run
in the by-election, Henry Pook defied them and ran as well. And
Henry Pook thus learned with some embarrassment the meager
political value of his renown. With six candidates running, Boord
won easily with 4,525 votes; Henry Pook tied for last place with
27. He would not have been able to serve very long, in any case; he
died a little over a year later.

Edmund Pook, sitting out the final refrains of Greenwich's
rough music in Herne Bay, returned home to 3 London Street
soon after his March 1872 confirmation into the church. Not long
after that, his brother, Thomas, came home as well. Thomas's
marriage had been on shaky foundations at the time of Jane's
murder; at that time, his wife, Emma, and his infant daughter
(also Emma) had fled Greenwich for her parents' home in the

Kentish countryside. When it became clear that the estrangement was permanent, Thomas gave up his own house and returned to share again Edmund's room and Edmund's bed. And once he returned, Thomas never left. Mary Pook's cousin Harriet Chaplin remained there as well, and so for several years the family configuration at the Pooks' stayed the same as it had been before the murder: father, mother, two sons, cousin. (Also, maids-of-all-work continued to come and go, most of them, it seems, carefully picked from among Mary Pook's poorer relations.)

Ebenezer Pook was the first to break up this domestic arrangement, dying in 1877 of a lingering, painful illness. Mary Pook took over as the printing shop's proprietor. Edmund himself was the next to leave, four years after this, when at the age of thirty he met and married twenty-year-old Alice Swabey, the daughter herself of a prosperous printer, and the two moved into their own house on South Street, around the corner from his mother's. Alice had been ten at the time of Jane Clouson's murder, and had then lived south of Lewisham, close to the cemetery in which Jane was buried. She knew, therefore, about Edmund's legal odyssey and about his unpopularity. None of that mattered to her, apparently.

Less than a year later, Edmund was stunned to read in the newspapers that he had died. According to this report, Edmund Pook had left Greenwich after the murders, changed his name, inexplicably, to John Pook, returned a few years before to London, to Marylebone. He had "lived a solitary and apparently friendless life in private lodgings for the last two years, and kept up no communication with any of his relatives." Newspapers across the country carried this false report; far fewer carried the retraction two days later, when two brothers of the deceased *John* Pook protested that he and they were not related to Edmund, and that they had been "greatly pained" by the news that they were. With little effort, of course, a reporter could have tracked Edmund down; if he was hiding, he was hiding in plain sight. But no one bothered to discover how *he* felt about the mistake.

In September 1882, Alice and Edmund Pook had a son, Edmund Thomas Pook. Three and a half years later, they lost him. They had no children after that. Cousin Harriet died in 1890. Brother Thomas died in 1897. And mother Mary, at age seventy-five, died in 1899. With no family in Greenwich remaining to keep them there, Edmund and Alice nonetheless stayed on for another ten or twelve years. By 1911, however, the two had taken up residence on the island of Guernsey, where sixty-year-old Edmund took a job as a letterpress printer. By 1915 they had moved to the neighboring island of Jersey; Alice Pook died there that year. With her death, Edmund's closest living relative was his brother Thomas's daughter, Emma, who had married a man by the name of Thomas Linforth Spiller and who now lived south of London, in Croydon. And for the last few years of his life, Edmund Pook moved back to south London to live close to his niece and her husband, perhaps even to live with them: they did take boarders.

Edmund Pook died, age seventy, at Croydon Union Hospital. If on his deathbed he had spoken any words about the events of a certain April evening forty-nine years before, no one cared to record them.

A more permanent record exists of Jane Clouson's life, and of her death, thanks to Newton Crosland and to the Clouson memorial committee, dedicated to erecting a monument to honor Jane's suffering, her virtue, and her human value. Their dedication, at first, earned them nothing but ridicule from editorialists who reasoned that monuments were reserved to those who had performed great acts—while Jane Clouson, a lowly maid-of-all-work, had done nothing, it seems, beyond managing to die violently. "It would be difficult," growled a writer in the *Daily News* after the committee gathered funds at the Greenwich Lecture Hall in October 1871, "to imagine a more flagrant breach of good taste, or a greater outrage

on the public opinion and sympathies of a civilized community."
An editorialist for the *New York Times*, after reading of the committee's work in London papers, was equally annoyed. "Was there ever such a display of idiocy outside of Bedlam?" he complained. "It takes a British wiseacre to discover in the simple and common act of dying a merit worthy of sculptured immortality." The committee, ignoring the derision, soldiered on, commissioning a Deptford stonemason, Samuel Hobbs, to sculpt a fine statue of Jane Clouson, set under a dome of stone and over a marble plinth. The pennies of the multitude, and the more substantial contributions of Crosland and others, simply could not bear the cost of such an elaborate production, and when Samuel Hobbs threatened to sue for nonpayment, the committee dropped him and engaged yet another Deptford stonemason, John Lord, for a more generic and affordable production: a suitably funereal depiction of a supplicating young child. That is the monument that now stands over Jane's grave at Brockley and Ladywell Cemetery, adorned with the epitaph that Newton Crosland had composed for it. That epitaph had been edited to take into account public taste; the reference to Jane's cleanliness, in particular, had been removed. It retained, however, Crosland's plea for a resolution, a plea spoken in Jane's voice:

> May God's great pity touch his heart and lead
> My murderer to confess his dreadful deed,
> That when the secrets of all hearts are known,
> Guilt and repentance alike may be shown.

As the years passed, it slowly became a certainty that God's great pity would do no such thing.

A second memorial to Jane Clouson—a memorial of sorts, anyway—had come earlier, and then had quickly and deservedly disappeared. *Pretty Jane: or, the Viper of Kidbrook Lane,* churned out in the spring and summer of 1871 to capitalize upon the murder, was a work that gave new meaning to the term "penny dreadful":

a farrago of sixteen parts containing irrelevant, throwaway wood-cuts to frame execrable prose. Its writer begins with a few pitiful attempts at suspense and horror, but quickly abandons these for hideously inappropriate and mind-numbingly interminable pas-sages of pseudo-comic dialog in the manner of a third-rate Dickens. The very first page of *Pretty Jane* is unquestionably its best: a primitive and yet vivid woodcut, "The First Meeting in the Lane," that depicts what certainly appears to be Edmund Pook, with his wideawake hat and his dark suit, strolling with a doe-eyed Jane Clouson, dressed much as she was in her surviving photograph. But the promise that this illustration offers readers—the promise to get to the heart of the Eltham mystery—would never be ful-filled. The man in the wideawake hat, it quickly becomes clear, is not Edmund Pook at all, but a man named Duchesney, a ludicrous caricature of a vicious aristocrat. Jane *is* Jane Clouson, the reader finally learns for sure on the very last page, but the entire tale, it turns out, allegedly concerns her life *before* she took up service with the Pooks—service in a morally bankrupt manor house of the sort that exists only in the lowest Victorian melodrama and the cheapest gothic fiction. The rest of the work documents Duch-esney's ridiculous and unsuccessful attempts at Jane's seduction. Any reader attaining the incredible feat of reading the serial to the end would have discovered that once Jane kept her virtue and freed herself from Duchesney, "her footsteps unhappily led her to Greenwich, from whence a sad and shrouded fate attended her." And that is the story's only reference to the actual crime. Edmund Pook is never mentioned. The writer and the publisher of the penny dreadful might both have been fools, but they certainly were not so foolish as to court a lawsuit for libel at the hands of Henry Pook.

That such an abysmal production, and such a cheat on its assur-edly meager audience, actually ran its entire course is in itself a minor miracle. Then *Pretty Jane: or, the Viper of Kidbrook Lane* quickly disappeared, almost without a trace. No advertisements for it, and no references to it in either courtroom or newspaper, survive to mark its existence. We know that it *did* exist only because a single copy, apparently, remains on earth today: an incomplete one at the British Library.

A final and nearly as transient memorial to Jane Clouson lay in the clothes she was wearing and the things she carried the night she was murdered. These the metropolitan police kept at Scotland Yard, and, three years later, when Inspector Percy Neame began to assemble exhibits for what became known as Scotland Yard's Black Museum (and is now known as the Crime Museum), he chose Jane's effects for display. The Black Museum was then, as it is now, generally restricted to members of the Metropolitan Police, but in 1877 a reporter for the *Spectator* gained admission. He described seeing on a little wooden shelf "a dirty Prayer-book, a pocket dictionary, a pair of boots, a gaudy bag worked in beads, and the crushed remains of a woman's bonnet, made of the commonest black lace, and flattened into shapelessness"; over the shelf, he saw "a gown and petticoat, of cheap, poor stuff, bearing dreadful, dim stains, and a battered crinoline." Obviously, this collection of Jane's effects had somehow been embellished in the months and years after the murder: she certainly had neither a prayer book nor a dictionary in her possession on the night of her attack. But it is equally clear that the evidence of her clothing was preserved: preserved for a time, anyway. The 1877 description offers the first, and the last, indication that they were in the Black Museum at all. At some point, they were removed to make way for another exhibit; at some point after that, Jane's clothing—the last surviving physical evidence in the case—disappeared altogether.

⚬━⚬

And yet, memories lingered. John Mulvany, James Griffin, and the police of R Division never forgot Jane, and surely never let go of their certainty that they had discovered and arrested her true murderer. They were not the only ones who thought so. In 1924, fifty-three years after Edmund's acquittal—and four years after his death—sleuth-hound Harry Bodkin Poland, then ninety-five years old, spoke out about the case in his memoirs. "Coleridge and I," he remembered, "had no doubt about the guilt of the prisoner." And as far as Poland was concerned, one man alone was responsible for Edmund's escape from justice: that "weak vessel" Chief Justice Bovill, who in his summing-up "had attacked the police who he said, and incorrectly said, had assumed the prisoner's guilt and had strained the evidence to obtain a conviction, and in the result Pook was triumphantly acquitted." Certainly, Chief Justice Bovill's summing-up had destroyed any possible chance of a guilty verdict in *R v. Pook*. But in truth, the case had been decided long before his summation. Harry Poland had failed to give due credit to the masterful work of Edmund's lawyer, John Huddleston, who—well briefed by Henry Pook—thoroughly diffused the prosecution's case by beating down every important prosecution witness, rendering Perren a liar, Lazell a fool, Sparshott muddleheaded, and Dr. Letheby inconsequential. More than this, Poland failed to apportion due blame to John Duke Coleridge for his inability or unwillingness to match Huddleston in energy, persistence, or wit. To be fair, Coleridge's task was far more onerous than Huddleston's; Coleridge was forced to proceed from beginning to end of the trial in the face of the chief justice's carping, his belittling, even his ridicule, while Huddleston enjoyed Bovill's full support. By the third day of the trial, when Huddleston began calling witnesses for the defense, the solicitor general essentially had given up.

Of all these defense witnesses, four of them—the four alibi witnesses from Lewisham—seemed to prove Edmund Pook's innocence beyond doubt. Joseph Eagles, his wife Mary Anne, their lodger William Douglas, and young Eliza Ann Merrett had all, under John Huddleston's examination, given eyewitness accounts placing Edmund Pook miles away from Kidbrooke at the time the prosecution argued that Jane was attacked. And since John Duke Coleridge in cross-examination had done next to nothing to controvert their testimony, their testimony seemed incontrovertible; with their evidence, the jury could naturally conclude that Edmund Pook's alibi was ironclad.

Nothing could be further from the truth. There was a great deal that was suspicious about their claims, and had Coleridge one-tenth of the energy of his opponent at that point of the trial, he could easily have probed those claims, exposed their weaknesses, and left Edmund's alibi in serious doubt. Newton Crosland, for one, professed his deep suspicions in particular of the testimony of Joseph and Mary Anne Eagles and of William Douglas, all of whom claimed that they had seen Edmund Pook lounging outside Alice Durnford's house on the evening of April 25. Each of the three was certain about the time, about the date, and about the man whom they saw. "No one seems," Crosland wrote, "to have called attention to the difficulty or absurdity of attempting to identify a very common-place, conventional-looking young man, said to have been seen lounging on Lewisham bridge—a very frequented spot—on a gloomy April night, at eight o'clock, after eight days had elapsed before there was any special occasion for noticing the incident!" That absurdity increases when one considers that not one of these witnesses came forward when those eight days elapsed and Edmund was arrested for Jane's murder. Nor did they come forward during the next two months, as accounts of the inquest and the police court examinations flooded the newspapers, as portraits of Edmund Pook became public, and as every one of the prosecution witnesses came forward. It was only on Sunday, July 9, three days before Edmund's trial commenced and ten weeks after the night Jane was attacked, that the indefatigable Henry Pook, apparently going door to door in Alice Durnford's neighborhood and hoping against hope to find alibi witnesses, found the Eagleses and heard their accounts of seeing long before a man to whom they still attached no importance—until Henry Pook told them why they should. Having found Joseph and Mary Anne Eagles, Henry Pook had no intention of letting them go. He brought them back to Tudor

House, his home in Greenwich, where, with the greatest interest in their identifying Edmund, he set up his own identification parade, setting before them two photograph albums and some loose photographs of men and women, from which, both Joseph and Mary Anne claimed, they picked Edmund Pook. Later, the Eagleses sent their lodger William Douglas to Tudor House, where he made a similarly successful identification.

Throughout May, Henry Pook had with some justification lambasted the police for the shadiness of their identification parades. Of the shadiness of his own photographic identifications, however, he said nothing. Nor did John Huddleston or Chief Justice Bovill say anything at trial. More surprisingly, John Duke Coleridge himself said little to challenge this identification, thus forsaking a crucial opportunity for the prosecution.

Unlike the Eagleses and Douglas, the fourth Lewisham alibi witness, Eliza Ann Merrett, had come forward early: she had attended both inquest and examination, had made herself known both to Henry Pook and to the police, and had yearned to claim in Edmund's defense that he and she had passed each other as he walked home from Lewisham on the night Jane was attacked. She and Edmund, she professed, were long-standing friends: "I was born in Greenwich," she testified at trial, "and I have always known him." According to her, she and Edmund passed on the street that night; Edmund was walking very slowly, and although the two did not speak, Eliza claimed that she recognized him immediately. One would expect Edmund Pook, similarly, to recognize her, and would expect further that, when the police asked whether he had seen anyone in Lewisham that night, he would eagerly have named her. But Edmund did not; rather, he stated that he had seen no one in Lewisham that he knew or who could prove that he was there. (Later, he remembered that he had seen someone: his family's errand boy, not Eliza Merrett.) More than this, her account of Edmund's slow progress through Lewisham contradicts the several accounts—including Edmund's own—that he was hurrying home to Greenwich that night.

Thomas Pook was the one other important alibi witness at Edmund's trial. But while Thomas and—suspiciously—Thomas alone offered testimony suggesting that Edmund could not have bought the murder weapon on the night before the attack, even he did not offer any evidence of Edmund's specific whereabouts for more than an hour and a half on the night of the attack: that, he left to the Lewisham witnesses. Without the testimony of those witnesses, in other words, Edmund had no verifiable alibi for that night.

But even if John Duke Coleridge had risen to the occasion and established convincingly the weaknesses of Edmund Pook's alibi, he still would hardly have proven beyond a reasonable doubt that Edmund Pook had murdered Jane Clouson: his own case for the prosecution, weakened by obvious false evidence, by ambiguity and contradiction, had by that time collapsed. The most thorough scrutiny of the evidence presented in *R v. Pook* will never satisfactorily answer the question of whether Edmund Pook killed Jane Clouson. To do that, we are forced to look beyond the trial, and to consider evidence not considered there: not simply the evidence actively excluded from the trial, but also the evidence ignored—ignored, because its incalculable value was lost in 1871 upon all of the trial's major participants.

⚬—⚬

Of the evidence excluded at trial, the most compelling by far were the actions performed and the words spoken by Jane Clouson in the days leading up to her encounter on Kidbrooke Lane. Four women—Elizabeth and Charlotte Trott, Emily Wolledge, and Fanny Hamilton—were prepared to testify to these.* All of this

---

* The charwoman Jane Prosser, with her stunning revelation of Jane's awareness of her pregnancy, was on the other hand not set to testify, likely because the police now discounted her story.

evidence, however, Chief Justice Bovill deemed hearsay and absolutely refused to admit. In 1871, hearsay was generally inadmissible because it denied a defendant the possibility of cross-examination, and in particular denied defense counsel any opportunity of testing the veracity of the original speaker. But there were a number of exceptions to the hearsay rule, and underlying those exceptions lay two principles: necessity and probability of trustworthiness. Necessity, according to present-day legal scholar Adrian Zuckerman, occurs when "hearsay provides the only information and it is felt that admitting hearsay is preferable to foregoing the information altogether." Probability of trustworthiness, Zuckerman further states, occurs when "a statement has been made under such circumstances that even a skeptical caution would look upon it as trustworthy." Henry Pook, obviously fearful of what these four had to say, stridently (and surely misogynistically) dismissed their testimony in police court as "the idle tittle-tattle of one woman to another." Chief Justice Bovill agreed. But a closer examination of this testimony than Henry Pook dared to give it, or William Bovill chose to, demonstrates its value, and Jane's words and actions, stifled at trial, demand reconsideration.

The necessity of this testimony is obvious and beyond question: through the Trotts, Wolledge, and Hamilton the police learned of the sexual relationship between Jane and Edmund, and learned that the two almost certainly met on the evening Jane was murdered. Without it, any sense of a motive on Edmund's part disappears, which is exactly what happened at trial. And upon a fuller examination of this evidence, its general trustworthiness becomes clear as well.

Perhaps the strongest indication that these women accurately remembered the gist of Jane's words and actions lies in the fact that there were four of them, that their accounts for the most part accord, and that they often accord without any possibility of collusion. Nowhere is this clearer than in Jane's words to her cousin Charlotte Trott on the Sunday before she disappeared, and her words to her landlady, Fanny Hamilton, two days later, just before she walked off to her death. According to cousin Charlotte, Jane said, "Charlotte, you must not be surprised if I am missing for some weeks, for Edmund says I must meet him at Shooter's Hill either to-morrow night or on Tuesday night to arrange to go with him into the country. He says he will have such a deal to tell me, and we shall have to make all the arrangements." According to Fanny Hamilton, Jane said, "I am going up to Croom-hill to see Mr. Edmund Pook. He has got a great deal to tell me this evening and I cannot stay any longer with you. I'm not going to work at the machine now for he is going to do something better for me." Charlotte Trott and Fanny Hamilton separately shared what they knew when interviewed by the police on May 1, the day Jane's body was identified. They certainly had not met each other between the time Jane had spoken with each of them and the time they spoke to the police; indeed, they had almost certainly *never* met. Even if they had any reason to invent their stories—and what possible reason could that be?—they had absolutely no opportunity to collaborate in that invention.

We cannot expect these women to have had an exact recollection of all that Jane said. When Charlotte remembered that Jane had told her Edmund had given her the locket, for example, she either misheard Jane or Jane misspoke. In either case, that assertion proved to be untrue, to the great embarrassment of the police. Nonetheless, it is clear that their testimony, when considered as a whole, offers a vivid account of the shifts in Jane's mood during the weeks and days before the attack, and offers as well a highly credible explanation for those shifts. "Till within the last few weeks [she] was very cheerful," Elizabeth Trott claimed at the inquest. But then—some time before her leaving the Pooks' employ—she became despondent. By the time she moved in with her friend Emily Wolledge, she appeared "very low spirited," according to Fanny Hamilton. Several days before she disappeared, her mood altered again, and when Charlotte saw her for the last time she observed that Jane was "happier than she had been during the last six or seven weeks." Two days before this, Emily Wolledge witnessed what was almost certainly the cause of Jane's elation: a letter came for Jane in that day's post and Emily had handed it to her. She watched Jane read it, tear it to pieces, and burn it. Afterward, Jane wrote and posted a letter of her own. That Jane, without any obvious anger, so eagerly destroyed the letter strongly indicates that she was instructed to do so by her correspondent, and that in itself indicates the power her correspondent held over her. Emily Wolledge never knew for sure who had written that letter; of the four women who testified about Jane's last conscious days, Emily Wolledge was the only one to whom Jane did not confide the fact that Edmund was her lover. Clearly, however, Edmund at some point had set up an assignation with Jane Clouson and, given the timing and the witnesses' general recognition of Jane's sudden happiness, it was that which Emily Wolledge observed.

Although Emily Wolledge was a witness to hearsay evidence, incidentally, these particular observations of Jane and this letter were not hearsay at all, but eyewitness evidence perfectly admissible in a court of law—evidence that serves to point to the trustworthiness of the hearsay. John Duke Coleridge made a serious mistake in not introducing this hard evidence of a letter at Edmund Pook's trial. Had he done so, he would at the very least have prevented Chief Justice Bovill's unjust attack upon Inspector Mulvany for inventing the fact of a letter in order to entrap Edmund Pook.

On the afternoon of April 25, Jane was "in good spirits," according to Emily Wolledge; "much excited," according to Fanny Hamilton, and she remained so until the moment she left Hamilton at the top of Deptford High Street to walk—eagerly, willingly, happily—to her assignation and to her death. Charlotte Trott and Fanny Hamilton both knew exactly where she was going, knew why she had once despaired, and knew why, on that evening, she was ecstatic. Edmund, Jane had told them—and had repeatedly told Charlotte's mother, Elizabeth—was her lover. They both knew that there had been a domestic explosion between Jane and the Pooks that had caused Jane to flee. Although the Pooks swore that Jane's poor hygiene had led to the breach, Jane's words to her cousin suggested something deeper—something that had left Jane with a particular bitterness toward Mary Pook. "I told Edmund," Jane had said, "that after I was married I should never speak to his mother." Neither Charlotte nor Fanny knew that Jane was pregnant. But it later became clear that the rupture with the Pooks had occurred just around the time that the physiological evidence of her pregnancy would likely have become clear to Jane. Jane's own awareness of her pregnancy further accounts for the depth of her despair as she left the Pooks. Pregnant and abandoned, Jane faced a Victorian woman's worst nightmare: the stigma of a fallen woman and the bleak future that followed. With Edmund's letter and his proposal, that nightmare dissipated instantly, supplanted by a Victorian working girl's dream: respectable marriage, to a man whom Jane might have thought she loved, and hoped loved her, and the elevation to a higher social sphere. Her relief must have been as great as it was sudden; there could have been no stronger enticement to coax her to meet Edmund that night, and to stroll with him to Kidbrooke Lane. Jane, then, walked away from Fanny Hamilton that night blinded by this prospect of happiness. Had she been any less starry-eyed, she surely would have been troubled by the dark undertone of Edmund's commands to her. He told her to burn his letter to her, and she had done so. He cautioned her to speak to no one and to prepare to cut herself off from everyone she knew. "I am not to tell anyone where I am going or write to anyone for some time, as he does not want anyone to know where I am," she confided to Charlotte. By hindsight, no one can consider Jane's words without intimating the impending horror of her murder. But Jane herself was, obviously, blissfully ignorant. And in her blind naïveté lies the strongest proof of her utter sincerity. She understood Edmund Pook to be her lover, her husband-to-be, her savior—not her murderer. The truth about Edmund Pook was beyond her understanding—and Jane simply could not have lied about that which she could not understand.

⚬─┼─⚬

Jane's speech and her actions point to Edmund Pook as her murderer. But they are not alone in this. The blood on Edmund's clothing, too, demonstrates his guilt. The hard evidence of that blood was, unlike Jane's words, most certainly admissible at Edmund's trial—and it was admitted. But in 1871, that evidence spoke in a language that no one could quite understand, although two men, Newton Crosland and Harry Poland, came close. Dr. Henry Letheby could only conclude that the stains were blood—mammalian blood—and that they were relatively fresh. This conclusion held some value at the inquest and magistrate's examination: it allowed Harry Poland to refute Henry Pook's contentions that the stains might be potash, or tobacco, or lemon juice. But it did nothing to shake Edmund's or his family's claims that the blood was not from Jane but from Edmund or a shopboy's cut finger, or from Edmund's tongue, spit out during an epileptic seizure. Since Edmund's clothing has long disappeared, there is nothing whatsoever that can be done to advance Letheby's *chemical* analysis of the blood beyond the limits of 1871 science. But very full descriptions of those stains, by Dr. Letheby and others, do survive, and so a *physical* analysis of the bloodstain patterns is certainly possible. A thorough analysis of the spatter on Edmund's hat, his shirt, and his trousers puts to the lie every pretext given by Edmund and his family for the blood on Edmund's clothing and strongly supports the contention that the blood was indeed Jane's, shed during the attack on Kidbrooke Lane onto the clothes of her attacker.

The most striking feature about the blood on Edmund's clothing to most who saw it at the time was its minuteness, both in terms of overall quantity and in the size of the individual spots. It was a "trifling and insignificant" amount, John Huddleston declared;

much more should have been found on Jane's murderer. All the blood on his trousers, Edmund later testified, was enough "to cover a threepenny bit." "The spots on his hat were so small as to be almost imperceptible," according to Inspector Griffin: Griffin remarked to Inspector Mulvany that he expected to find more there. Although Griffin described the stain on Edmund's right shirt-cuff to be more of a splotch, Henry Letheby, upon closer examination, corrected him: there were six distinct spots there. The coroner at Jane's inquest noted their "minuteness," and a member of his jury exclaimed with surprise that "they could hardly be spots at all, they were so slight, they looked like touches of a rusty iron." Of the many spots on the lower left leg of Edmund's trousers, Chief Justice Bovill scoffed that some of those Letheby had cut out were "the size of pin's heads."

John Huddleston, Chief Justice Bovill, and even, for at least a moment, Superintendent Griffin equated minuteness of the blood with its insignificance. Newton Crosland knew better. "The minute spots of blood on clothes," he wrote, "are sometimes more suggestive than a casual observer would be apt to imagine; their smallness and position may give them additional importance. They may appear not like those drops which fall from a wound caused by an accident to oneself, but rather like particles darted or propelled from a neighboring object—blood sparks struck and scattered from a bloody anvil!" In other words, Crosland understood the distinction between the larger drops of blood that fell directly from a wound and the smaller droplets sprayed from a wound upon contact with another object. The stains on Edmund's clothing could not have been passive blood flow; they were active spatter. Spots of that minuteness simply could not have dripped from Edmund's or a shopboy's cut finger.

Harry Poland understood this early on in the investigation, and before the magistrate at Greenwich Police Court he argued that the blood pattern on Edmund's clothing allowed a reconstruction of the crime. Poland noted a curious fact: there were a multitude of droplets on the left leg of Edmund's trousers, and perhaps only a single droplet on the right. That, he claimed, demonstrated that the blood had fallen upon Edmund as he assumed the stance of an attacker, holding a hammer or an axe: "A person standing and striking at the deceased," Poland declared, "would have the left leg in a forward state, and consequently there would be more blood on the left than the right leg." Two facts bolster Poland's hypothesis. Henry Letheby later determined that there were *no* bloodstains on Edmund's right leg, and many on his left. And all of the bloodstains on Edmund's shirt were on the right cuff—none on the left. Edmund was, of course, right-handed. Together, the blood evidence compellingly supports the case that Edmund bloodied himself during the attack on Kidbrooke Lane. But it was a case that John Duke Coleridge, lacking either the will or the imagination, completely failed to make at Edmund's trial.

More than this, the evidence of the blood on Edmund's clothing does not at all support the one explanation that Edmund offered, excluding all other explanations, when he took the witness chair in the libel action against Newton Crosland. There Edmund asserted that at some point during the month of April—when, exactly, he could not remember—he suffered a *grand mal* (or, as it is more commonly termed today, a tonic-clonic) epileptic seizure in the family's sitting room. He had bitten his tongue and bled on his clothing; his brother, Thomas, had attended to him.* Edmund's prosecutors, both Poland and Coleridge, had always been deeply suspicious of this explanation—incredulous, in particular, about the notion that he could have bled upward and onto the upper brim of his hat during a seizure. In response, Edmund Pook claimed that the hat had been knocked off at the commencement of his fit,

---

* At Edmund's trial Thomas Pook, ever willing to provide his brother with alibis, both supported and contradicted this story: Edmund, he said, indeed had had a seizure in April—on April 6, Thomas claimed—but had suffered it in the printer's shop, not the family's sitting room. [OB testimony of Thomas Birch (sic) Pook.]

and that he then bled on it. But given the physiological process of a tonic-clonic epileptic seizure, that explanation is dubious as well. At the commencement of such a seizure, the body stiffens as all muscles contract: the head generally tips back and the body generally falls backward. A hat worn during such a fall would almost certainly fall off—but would not likely fall to a position directly in front of one's face. And even if this had happened in Edmund's case, Edmund most certainly did not spurt blood onto it: in order to do that, Edmund would have had to have bitten through his tongue to the lingual artery, nearly severing his tongue from his head; in that case he would have saturated the hat with blood, leaving much more than four tiny spots. There is only one possible way that tiny droplets, rather than drops or splashes, could have gotten onto Edmund's hat during a seizure: Edmund would have had to have bitten his tongue, bled into his mouth, and then *expirated* that blood—expelled blood mixed with saliva upon the current of his breath. Blood expirated in this way is generally the same size as impact blood spatter; even today the two can easily be mistaken for each other. But it would have been impossible for Edmund to have breathed directly toward the hat and left the four spots in the configuration discovered by Henry Letheby. Letheby made it clear in testimony that those spots were evenly distributed around the crown of the hat—both in the front and in the back. Edmund could have left spots in that configuration only if he had been lying on his back and expirating upward, droplets of blood flowing with the breath in an arc, up and then down, a trajectory that likely would have given one of the stains—the one on the vertical plane of the hatband—a distinctive tadpole-tailed shape. No one who described the stains on the hat described any such thing.

Though it is unlikely that Edmund expirated blood onto his hat in this way, it is possible. On the other hand, it was simply not possible for Edmund to have expirated the blood found on his trousers during a tonic-clonic seizure. During the first, or tonic, phase of this type of seizure, as muscles stiffen and the body falls and as the head and chin generally tip upward, the legs stretch outward, away from the head. And during the second, or clonic, phase, the body's muscles repeatedly relax and contract, leading to rhythmic jerking movements. In order to expirate blood to the bottom of his trousers during a seizure, Edmund would have had, in his unconsciousness, to turn his face toward his legs, nearly touching his chin to his chest. With the repeated tensing of neck muscles during the clonic phase of a seizure, that posture is absolutely impossible to assume.*

Every explanation, then, that Edmund and his family offered for the blood on his clothing falls to the ground. On the other hand, the blood evidence—what there was of it—is consistent with the prosecution's claim that it was Jane's, shed during the attack. But there was so *little* blood, and that in itself seemed to argue against the prosecution's claim. If Edmund had so brutally attacked Jane with a plasterer's hammer, shouldn't he have been saturated by her blood? That was what Henry Pook and John Huddleston argued; that is what Chief Justice Bovill and eventually the jury believed. Where, then, was all that blood?

It is possible that Jane's attacker was *not* saturated with her blood—possible, ironically, that the very viciousness of the attack might have lessened the amount of bloodshed. Both Henry Letheby and Michael Harris testified that a *fully*-severed artery will bleed less than a partially-severed one, because the muscle wall of a fully-severed artery contracts and partially cuts off the flow of blood. More than this, if Edmund had been facing Jane when he attacked her, and struck her with side swings, as her injuries suggested, the direction of force would have been away from him, and little impact spatter would have fallen upon him. If, on the other hand, Edmund struck at Jane's head while she lay upon the ground—as her assailant surely did—the majority of spatter would be found

---

* One other possibility is worth considering: that Edmund, sitting up after his seizure, expirated blood upon his trousers. But the multitude of droplets on his left leg, and the entire absence of droplets on his right, argues against this.

exactly where it was found upon Edmund—on his lower left leg and the end of his right arm. Attacking Jane would surely have left Edmund bloody—but not necessarily so bloody as to stop him from ducking into Mrs. Plane's shop to collect himself before going home the night of the attack.

Nonetheless, the fact that all the blood found on Edmund was found at the periphery of his body—hat, lower legs, shirt-cuff—and none found elsewhere is simply explained: the rest of the blood—what there was of it—was spattered upon Edmund's coat, a coat that disappeared before the police came to search for it. Edmund himself claimed that he was wearing a coat on the night of the attack, and the witnesses on Kidbrooke Lane agreed that the man they saw was wearing one. Edmund might have gotten a great deal of blood on his coat; he might have gotten very little on it. But that he got no blood whatsoever on that coat is unthinkable. And yet, of all the articles of clothing Edmund handed over as having worn on the night of the attack, there was only one upon which Henry Letheby found not a single spot of blood: the coat. More than this, when Inspector Mulvany and Superintendent Griffin first came to the Pooks' house, they asked Ebenezer Pook to see *all* of Edmund's coats and Ebenezer Pook had shown them all: Griffin testified that "every facility" had been given him and Mulvany in their search. That eagle-eyed John Mulvany could have detected the tiny spots on Edmund's hat and trousers and have somehow missed spots on his coat is inconceivable. A bloodied coat—bloodied from the attack or even from an epileptic fit—should have been in the house; that it was not strongly suggests that Edmund, who never saw the stains on his hat, his shirt, or his trousers, *did* see the stains on his coat, and, in the week he had between the attack and his arrest, hid or more likely disposed of that incriminating evidence.

Both that missing evidence, and the remaining, existing blood evidence all point to the attack on Kidbrooke Lane: blood spattered upon Edmund Pook as, in a frenzy but the same time with intent, he chopped and battered Jane Clouson into something no longer recognizably human. Jane, Edmund had surely determined, had left him no choice. He was the young master; he was a gentleman with prospects. She was his servant, and she had served him as innumerable young female servants had served innumerable young masters in the past; what they had done was more a social transaction than a relationship. But then Jane had become pregnant, and with that Jane, never more than a convenience, became distinctly inconvenient; she suddenly threatened Edmund's prospects of marriage, either with Alice Durnford or with his cousin Louisa, and threatened his reputation among the important people of Greenwich. Jane had made clear she would not go away; she had, therefore, to be disposed of. And so he arranged to meet her. He explored Kidbrooke Lane to choose the best spot for the attack. He hurried to Deptford—a short walk or even shorter train ride away—to buy the hammer at a shop where he surmised he would not be recognized. Then he met Jane and coaxed her to Kidbrooke and surprised her with the hammer, the axe, perhaps eliciting from her the shocked scream that William Norton and Louisa Putman interpreted as ecstatic. And then, he destroyed her.

He ran home and dined with his family and then went to bed. No one at his home was alarmed. When the police came, six days later, he was polite and cooperative. He protested when they arrested them, but after that he slipped into the imperturbable demeanor that he maintained throughout the turbulent days that followed: calmly reading his *Pickwick*, patiently enduring imprisonment at Maidstone and then Newgate, coolly observing the proceedings at Greenwich Police Court and at the Old Bailey. He refused to conform to anyone's notion of a guilty murderer. And his calmness served him well, complementing the passionate and effective case made for him first by Henry Pook and then by John Huddleston. Calmly, Edmund Pook contended with the Victorian system of law and order—if not in all its majesty, then in all its variety. And he triumphed, triumphed so absolutely that upon his acquittal it seemed as if Edmund Pook and not Jane Clouson had been the innocent victim at the heart of *R v. Pook.*

Edmund's placid demeanor, then, was a tactic. But it was not a ruse. Edmund Pook knew he was guilty of the girl's murder. But there is little evidence he *felt* guilt at her murder. She had once been useful to him, but when he killed her she had outlived her usefulness. She was a thing of no value to him; she mattered to him as much as did the mud of Kidbrooke Lane in which he left her dying. Inspector Mulvany and Superintendent Griffin realized how little she had meant to him on the day they arrested him—at the moment, perhaps, that the two first *knew* that he was involved with her murder. When Mulvany informed Edmund that Jane had been murdered, Edmund did not even pretend to have sympathy or at least empathy for the girl. "She was a dirty girl," he told them. That is why she left them. Edmund had a reason to dismiss her so churlishly: he wished to convey that he had had no motive to kill her because he had no connection to her. But that he could so characterize the young woman who had lived with him for nearly two years, and had suffered unimaginably, suggests that beneath the pretense was an absolute sincerity: Jane Clouson meant nothing to him.

In Greenwich and Deptford, however, and in Blackheath and Lewisham, those who knew Jane, those who knew of her, and those who learned of her and immediately felt for her, refused to dismiss her as something without value. Even before they knew the identity of the woman battered in the lane, they traveled to the place where she had been battered, and they traveled there not to glorify in bloodshed, but to contemplate the horrible end of one of their own. In the pouring rain they lined the streets from Deptford to Brockley to pay their respects to her as she passed. They responded angrily, inside and outside the courtroom, to the Pooks' claim that she was dirty. They gathered outside the police court and coroner's court to demonstrate their sympathy with her and to vent their anger at the one they couldn't help but conclude had killed her. And when Edmund Pook was acquitted, they refused to let the case rest; for five days they howled their disappointment. Even after that, they refused to go away: they gathered in a mass on Blackheath and crowded the Greenwich Lecture Hall both to support the men—Edmund Pook's supposed libelers—who kept her case alive. And at those meetings they supported enthusiastically a monument for the girl. The newspapers ridiculed them for that plan. But to them, there was nothing ridiculous about memorializing a seventeen-year-old working girl. She had been, they believed, affectionate and amiable. In her short life, she had worked hard as a maid-of-all-work, as the prop of respectability to a middle-class family that in turn denied her the respect *she* was due. She had lived dutifully in this hard world and had died seeking in vain for something better. She was one of them.

Edmund Pook, shocked out of his imperturbability by their anger on his journeys back and forth from Maidstone to Greenwich, and beleaguered by their rough music in the days after his acquittal, could not have escaped learning the lesson they taught him. And while during the forty-nine years left to him, years he had taken away from Jane, he never did, never could, share that lesson with another soul, it was a lesson he surely could not forget.

Jane Maria Clouson meant something.

Jane Clouson *mattered*.

ACKNOWLEDGMENTS

Many, many thanks to:

—Charlie Olsen at Inkwell Management;

—Claiborne Hancock, Richard Milbank, and the folks both at Pegasus and at Head of Zeus;

—the always helpful staffs at the British Library, the London Metropolitan Archives, the Greenwich Heritage Centre, the Local History and Archives Centre at Lewisham, the National Archives at Kew, and the University of Colorado's Norlin Library, as well as the now-dispersed staff at the British Newspaper Library at Colindale;

—Peter Burgess, talented mapmaker and creator of the well-known *Tubular Fells* map of the Lake District, for the map at the front of this book;

—Michael Guilfoyle, whose words to me four years ago led to all of this;

—my good and supportive friends in London: Linda Gough, Steve, Nina, and Jean Button, Tracey Ward, Steve Terrey, John Watts, Geoff Youldon, and Lawrence Goldman;

—my good and supportive friends and family in the USA: my children, Daniel and Miranda; my mother, Olive Murphy; my siblings, Regina Collins, John, Jim, and Bill Murphy, and Cathy Murray and all their families; Din, Amelia, and Hazel Tuttle, John Jostad, Scott Woods, Chris Morrison, Don Eron, Suzanne Hudson, Paul Levitt, and Elissa Guralnick;

—and my wife, Tory Tuttle, whose never-ending editorial and moral support for this project has left me with a debt I can never, never repay. But, at least—I can try.

NOTES

Abbreviations used in the notes:

NEWSPAPERS AND JOURNALS:
A: The Age (Melbourne, Victoria, Australia).
AMG: Aldershot Military Gazette (Aldershot, Hampshire).
AS: Auckland Star (New Zealand).
BA: Bendigo Advertiser (New South Wales, Australia).
BC: Berkshire Chronicle (Reading).
BDP: Birmingham Daily Post.
BM: Bristol Mercury.
BMJ: British Medical Journal.
BN: Belfast News-Letter.
BO: Bradford Observer.
CC: Chelmsford Chronicle.
DC: Dundee Courier.
DN: Daily News (London).
E: Era (London).
EN: Essex Newsman (Chelmsford).
FJ: Freeman's Journal (Dublin).

G. *Graphic* (London)

GDC: *Greenwich and Deptford Chronicle* (Deptford).

GH: *Glasgow Herald.*

HA: *Hampshire Advertiser* (Southampton).

HC: *Huddersfield Chronicle.*

IPN: *Illustrated Police News.*

KM: *Kentish Mercury* (Greenwich).

L: *Lloyd's Newspaper* (London).

LA: *Lancet.*

LC: *Leicester Chronicle.*

LG: *Lancaster Gazette.*

LM: *Leeds Mercury.*

LTA: *Luton Times and Advertiser.*

MC: *Manchester Courier and Lancashire General Advertiser.*

MEN: *Manchester Evening News.*

MP: *Morning Post* (London).

MT: *Manchester Times.*

NC: *Newcastle Courant.*

NE: *Northern Echo* (Darlington).

NG: *Newcastle Guardian and Tyne Mercury.*

NYT: *The New York Times.*

PIP: *Penny Illustrated Paper* (London).

QT: *Queensland Times* (Ipswich, Queensland, Australia).

RN: *Reynolds's Weekly* (London).

S: *Standard* (London).

SI: *Sheffield Independent.*

SLC: *South London Chronicle.*

SM: *Samford Mercury* (Samford, Suffolk).

SP: *Spectator* (London).

T: *The Times* (London).

TE: *Telegraph* (London).

WD: *Weekly Dispatch* (London).

WDP: *Western Daily Press* (Bristol).

WG: *Wrexham Advertiser* (Wrexham, Wales).

WM: *Western Mail* (Cardiff).

WT: *Whitstable Times and Herne Bay Herald* (Whitstable, Kent).

WW: *Wagga Wagga Advertiser* (New South Wales, Australia).

YP: *Yorkshire Post and Leeds Intelligencer* (Leeds).

TRIAL TRANSCRIPTS:

OB: Tim Hitchcock, Robert Shoemaker, Clive Emsley, Sharon Howard and Jamie McLaughlin, et al., *The Old Bailey Proceedings Online, 1674–1913* (www.oldbaileyonline.org, version 7.2). Unless otherwise noted, references to this site are to the trial of Edmund Pook for murder, July 12–15, 1871.

CHAPTER ONE: LET ME DIE

1:      half an hour before the sun rose: World-timedate.com lists sunrise in London on April 25, 1871, as occurring at 4:41:31 a.m.: "Sunrise Sunset Calendar of London, England: (April, 1871)."

1:      his beat . . . smaller town of Eltham: *KM* May 6, 1871, 5.

1:      few carriages or wagons traveled that way: "The lane is so little frequented that it is completely overgrown with grass": *DN* May 1, 1871, 3; July 13, 1871, 6 (solicitor general's summing up at trial).

2:      the place where he had grown up: distant Caithness: *Census Returns of England and Wales, 1871*, for Donald Gunn.

2:      Gunn had made his first circuit of Kidbrooke Lane two and a half hours before: *OB*, testimony of Donald Gunn.

2:      The moon had set long before this: at 12:59 a.m. on April 26, 1871. "London, United Kingdom—Moonrise, moonset and moon phases, April 1871."

2:      it was standard issue for all metropolitan police officers: Dell 19–20.

2:      he did not use it: *OB*, testimony of Donald Gunn; *MP* May 5, 1871, 8.

2:      he could see her head . . . as she moaned softly, "piteously.": *OB*, testimony of Donald Gunn; *T* July 13, 1871, 11.

2:      He immediately concluded that she was drunk: *SI* May 6, 1871, 9.

2:      "Oh, my poor head; oh, my poor head": *S* July 13, 1871, 6.

3:      he looked at her and saw . . . a battered and bloody mass: *OB*, testimony of Donald Gunn and Michael Harris.

3:      "Let me die": *T* May 5, 1871, 11; *OB*, testimony of Donald Gunn.

3:      a small pool of blood, cold and clotted into the mud: *OB*, testimony of Donald Gunn.

3:      Two feet from the woman was a pair of women's gloves: *OB*, testimony of Donald Gunn. A full description of Jane's clothes is given in *KM* April 29, 1871, 4.

3:      Gunn looked up and down the road: *OB*, testimony of Donald Gunn.

3:      his sergeant, Frederick Haynes, happened to be there: *OB*, testimony of Donald Gunn and Frederick Haynes.

4:      Haynes . . . jumped to the conclusion . . . assaulted sexually: *DN* May 5, 1871, 6.

4:      the blood had ceased to flow from many of her wounds: *MP* May 5, 1871, 8.

4:      She had obviously lain here for several hours: *OB*, testimony of Frederick Haynes.

4:      "Oh, save me!": *MP* May 5, 1871, 8; *T* May 5, 1871, 11.

4:   police surgeon and medical officer of health for the district: *Census Returns of England and Wales, 1871*, for David King; *BMJ* September 6, 1873, 295; *LA* November 11, 1865, 554.

5:   both were fresh out of Guy's Hospital's medical school: *BMJ* August 18, 1928, 325; *Census Returns of England and Wales, 1871*, for Michael Harris and Frederic Durham; Wilks and Bettany 488.

5:   a nurse stripped off her clothing: *OB*, testimony of Michael Harris; *Times* May 31, 1871, 12.

5:   She was completely unconscious and perceptibly cold from loss of blood: *S* July 13, 1871, 6.

5:   Most of her wounds were deep and cleanly cut: Harris divulged his notes about Clouson's injuries at both her inquest and at the magistrate's hearings on the case, but his fullest account is in the official transcripts of Edmund Pook's trial: *OB*, testimony of Michael Harris.

5:   inflicted by a weapon both sharp and heavy: *DN* April 27, 1871, 3.

5:   this woman had fought her attacker face-to-face: One early newspaper report (*DN*, May 1, 1871, 3) claimed that the doctors at Guy's Hospital considered that the first blow was to the back of the head with a blunt instrument, rendering the woman immediately insensible. No other reports confirm this claim, and Dr. Harris's various testimonies soundly contradict it.

5:   her temporal bone was bashed inward: *OB*, testimony of Michael Harris; *KM* May 6, 1871, 5.

6:   a horizontal three-inch trench of smashed bone . . . swollen brain bulged through: *OB*, testimony of Michael Harris; *Daily News* May 1, 1871, 3.

6:   like all of the other wounds, recently inflicted: *KM* May 6, 1871, 5.

6:   the doctors found no signs whatsoever that she had been assaulted sexually: *KM* May 6, 1871, 5.

6:   Harris and Durham estimated that she was between twenty-three and twenty-five years old: *DN* April 27, 1871, 3, April 28, 1871, 6; *S* April 28, 1871, 3.

6:   the thick calluses . . . a servant: *DN* May 1, 1871, 3.

6:   And she was dying: *DN* April 27, 1871, 3; May 1, 1871, 3.

6:   Dr. Harris ordered that . . . day and night: *MP* May 5, 1871, 8.

6:   Sergeant Haynes examined her clothing: *T* May 31, 1871, 12; *IPN* May 6, 1871, 4; *KM* May 6, 1871, 5.

6:   They were the walking-out clothes of a servant girl: *DN* April 28, 1871, 6; *MP* April 29, 1871, 3; *T* May 12, 1871, 5; *OB*, testimony of Michael Harris.

7:   two small keys to boxes or suitcases: *OB*, testimony of John Mulvany.

7:   James Griffin . . . had already come to Kidbrooke Lane: *T* May 31, 1871, 12.

7:   Griffin was a twenty-five-year veteran of the Metropolitan Police: In Griffin's January 1, 1846 marriage record he describes himself as a "gardener";

but by June of that year the newspapers begin reporting his activities as a police constable. *Church of England Parish Registers, 1754–1921* marriage record for James Griffin; *S* June 30, 1846, 4.

7:      appointed superintendent of Greenwich Division four years earlier: Griffin became superintendent between January 4, 1867, when a police report designates him Inspector, and January 21, 1868, when another reports him as superintendent. *MP* January 4, 1867, 7; January 21, 1868, 3.

7:      the forensic value of footprint evidence was well known by 1871: Critchley 160.

8:      He, at least, realized that the footsteps told a story: *DN* May 1, 1871, 3; *T* May 5, 1871, 11.

8:      He walked north up the lane another three hundred yards: while Haynes stated during the coroner's inquest that the brook was only ninety or a hundred yards from the scene of the crime, at both the magistrate's hearing and the trial of Edmund Pook he claimed it to be three hundred yards away. *Manchester Evening News* May 5, 1871, 2; *T* May 5, 1871, 11; July 13, 1871, 11; *OB*, testimony of Frederick Haynes.

8:      Haynes crossed the brook on a little plank, where he observed on the far bank a stone: *T* May 5, 1871, 11; *WM* May 31, 1871, 2; *OB*, testimony of Frederick Haynes.

8:      The assailant, Haynes thought, had stopped on his flight northward: *MT* May 13, 1871, 3; *S* May 2, 1871, 7.

8:      Another of the many officers . . . more potential evidence in the mud: *OB*, testimony of Edwin George Ovens.

9:      At eight o'clock that morning . . . in Greenwich: *OB*, testimony of Thomas Layzell [sic].

9:      Their cottage was about a third of a mile from the spot: *T* May 17, 1871, 12.

9:      Lazell's father, prostrate with gout: *DN* May 5, 1871, 6.

9:      It was . . . a bloody white handkerchief: *OB*, testimony of Thomas Layzell [sic].

10:     he had found the cloth . . . north from the spot where the woman had been found: *OB*, testimony of James Griffin. Transcripts of Lazell's trial testimony in the *Daily News* (July 15 ,1871, 5) suggest that the cloth was found outside of Lazell's own garden, but that location is speculation by Edmund Pook's defense attorney, not a fact spoken by Lazell.

10:     Later that morning, he made his way down the lane: *DN* May 5, 1871, 6.

10:     Willis and the police thought the cloth far less valuable: *DN* May 5, 1871, 6.

10:     the police kept the cloth . . . dog whistle: *OB*, testimony of James Griffin; *DN* May 5, 1871, 6.

11:   he spied it lying on a bed of leaves: *IPN* May 6, 1871, 4; *T* July 13, 1871, 11; *S* July 13, 1871, 6; *OB*, testimony of Thomas Brown.

11:   Its sixteen-inch handle . . . a string was looped: *T* May 3, 1871, 11; *MP* May 17, 1871, 7.

11:   Stamped onto the steel . . . "J Sorby" and a trademark: *T* May 31, 1871, 12.

11:   a magnificent almshouse . . . attributed to Christopher Wren: Joyce 1.

11:   Brown found the hammer five yards from that footpath: *IPN* May 6, 1871, 4; *S* July 13, 1871, 6.

12:   Thomas Brown carefully took up the hammer and carried it to his neighbor: *OB*, testimony of Thomas Brown, Lucy Brown, and Thomas Hodge.

12:   Mulvany . . . had joined the force in 1848: *London, England, Births and Baptisms, 1813–1906; London, England, Marriages and Banns, 1754–1921.* In John Mulvany's 1829 baptismal record his father, Michael Mulvenny, is listed as a "servant"; in the register for Mulvany's 1850 marriage, his father is listed as a "coachman." Payne 27; Cobb 108.

12:   As a detective . . . chased Irish revolutionaries—Fenians—in Liverpool and Paris: *S* July 31, 1865, 7; *MP* September 2, 1865, 7; *T* December 21, 1865, 11; *MP* February 22, 1869; *T* June 3, 1870, 11; *T* June 18, 1870, 11; Payne 79–80, 85.

12:   Mulvany had already been to Eltham that afternoon: *OB*, testimony of Frederick Haynes and John Mulvany.

13:   Indeed he would, the next day, show it to his supervisor, Dolly Williamson: *OB*, testimony of Frederick Adolphus Williamson.

13:   The hammer . . . delivered into the hands of Inspector Mulvany: *OB*, testimony of Charles Wilson.

13:   plasterers had been at work . . . place of assault: *MP* April 29, 1871, 3.

14:   "take hold of my hand": *DN* April 28, 1871, 6; *KM* April 29, 1871, 4.

14:   "Emily, don't beat me so cruelly": *S* April 28, 1871, 3.

14:   "Oh, Emily—Oh, Ned, don't": *MP* April 29, 1871, 3.

14:   "Oh Edward, don't murder me!": *Sheffield Independent* May 6, 1871, 9; *Morpeth Herald* May 6, 1871, 3.

14:   sighing "Emily" or "Sarah": *S* April 28, 1871, 3; *MP* May 1, 1871.

14:   when asked her identity, she weakly uttered "Mary Shru—": *DN* May 1, 1871, 3; *T* May 1, 1871, 5.

14:   Michael Harris . . . under his care: *MP* May 5, 1871, 8; *DN* May 5, 1871, 6.

15:   another young woman . . . a little pond in Lee: *DN* April 28, 1871, 6; *KM* April 29, 1871, 4.

15:   Any fears . . . the woman found in the pond: *MP* April 29, 1871, 3; *S* April 29, 1871, 3.

15:   the woman's parents in Peckham: *Census Returns of England and Wales, 1871*, for James W. and Mary A. Surridge.

15:     . . . police suspicion at first centered on Woolwich: *DN* April 28, 1871, 6;
        MP April 29, 1871, 3; *BDP* April 29, 1871, 8.

15:     one soldier there was soon arrested: *DN* April 29, 1871, 2; *BDP* April 29,
        1871, 8; *GH* April 29, 1871, 5.

15:     A rifleman from Woolwich, claimed another report, had been spotted
        early that Wednesday morning: *MP* April 28, 1871, 7.

15:     a sergeant of a Scotch regiment entered an Eltham beer shop: *DN* April
        28, 1871, 6; *MP* April 28, 1871, 7.

16:     Several came, but no one succeeded in recognizing her for certain: *GH*
        April 29 ,1871, 5.

16:     George Evans . . . the comatose woman at Guy's Hospital: *S* April 28,
        1871, 3, April 29, 1871, 3; *DN* April 28, 1871, 6.

17:     Mary Caladine slept . . . in the adjacent slum of St. Giles: *Census Returns
        of England and Wales, 1871*, for Mary Caladine.

17:     That Christian charitable institution . . . "reclamation": Ranyard 265–6;
        "Sketches from the Great City," 13.

17:     "lured . . . in an unwary moment": Ranyard 269.

17:     Jeanie Kay, came to Guy's on the Friday . . . : *MP* April 29, 1871, 3; *S* April
        29, 1871, 3; *Census Returns of England and Wales, 1871*, for Jeanie Kay.
        (The newspapers state the matron's name was "Mrs. Key," but the census
        entry for Jeanie Kay is conclusive.)

18:     the sad story of Alice, her surname withheld: *S* May 1, 1871, 6; *MP* May
        1, 1871, 4; *DN* May 1, 1871, 3.

18:     she "fell from the path of virtue . . ." : *S* May 1, 1871, 6.

18:     The matron of the home implored Alice to leave the soldiers: *S* May 1,
        1871, 6.

19:     "a companion of soldiers at Woolwich": *MP* May 1, 1871, 4.

19:     The chaplain of the Alice's Greenwich home . . . the battered woman: *MP*
        May 1, 1871, 4; *S* May 1, 1871, 6.

19:     the "lowest dens of infamy in Woolwich": *S* May 1, 1871, 6.

19:     'a brown barège, trimmed with brown fringe': *S* May 1, 1871, 6.

19:     they had already scoured the shops: *DN* May 1, 1871, 3.

20:     the police had tracked down the London agent for J Sorby hammers: *S*
        May 31, 1871, 6; *MP* May 31, 1871, 3.

20:     a Sorby #2 hammer was hanging by a string in the shop window: *T* May
        31, 1871, 12; *OB*, testimony of Jane Mary Thomas.

20:     she hadn't heard about it: *KM* May 20, 1871, 5.

20:     neat entries, all of them written in her hand: *OB*, testimony of Jane Mary
        Thomas.

20:     The two of them scanned the book: *OB*, testimony of Jane Mary Thomas.

20:     the larger #3 hammer sold for two pennies less than the smaller #2: *T*
        May 17, 1871, 12.

20. they were interrupted by a woman who needed a compass saw: *OB*, testimony of Jane Mary Thomas.

21: important enough to bring Detective Inspector Mulvany to the shop: *KM* June 3, 1871, 5; *OB*, testimony of Samuel Thomas.

21: —On the evening of Saturday, the 22nd of April: *KM* May 6, 1871, 5.

22: And on this Sunday, April 30 . . . thousands came: *MP* May 6, 1871, 5.

22: footprints in the slushy mud had obliterated the crime scene: *SI* May 6, 1871, 9.

22: still visible in defiance of rainshowers of the days before: *DN* May 1, 1871, 3.

22: everyone sought out a souvenir: *MP* May 6, 1871, 5; *DN* May 6, 1871, 3.

22: Someone placed a rudely constructed cross at the site: *MP* May 6, 1871, 5.

22: These "pilgrims," it was obvious, were overwhelmingly working-class: *GDC* May 13, 1871, 2.

23: "There are among us . . . large numbers of men and women": *DN* May 8, 1871, 5.

23: "The neighborhood of Eltham at present offers a spectacle": *PMG* May 10, 1871, 4.

23: "If in other and less favoured countries": *DN* May 8, 1871, 5.

24: When she died, the woman was two months pregnant: *T* July 13, 1871, 11.

CHAPTER TWO: JANE

25: the same hour, the same minute: 9:15, according to the *Times* May 2, 1871, 10.

25: Trott's home was hard by the Thames: *Census Returns of England and Wales, 1871*, for William Trott.

25: His father had been a lighterman . . . his sons would become lightermen: *Census Returns of England and Wales, 1861*, for John Trott; *Census Returns of England and Wales, 1871*, for William Trott, Alfred Trott, and William Trott Jr.; *Census Returns of England and Wales, 1881*, for Thomas Trott, Henry Trott.

25: That was the path . . . Trott's daughters would take: *Census Returns of England and Wales, 1841*, for Elizabeth Hancock [Trott]; *Census Returns of England and Wales, 1871*, for Charlotte Trott; *Census Returns of England and Wales, 1881*, for Charlotte [Trott] Ives, Alice Trott.

26: two thousand descriptions of the victim: *DN* April 29, 1871, 2.

26: ". . . Aged about twenty-five years . . .": *R* April 30, 1871, 5. The radical and sensational *Reynolds's Weekly* was one of the most popular Sunday newspapers of the day and particularly popular among the working class. And *Reynolds's* was the one Sunday newspaper that week which carried a full description of the victim at Guy's. It was, therefore, almost certainly the Sunday newspaper that William Trott read on the evening of April 30.

27: Charlotte thought she knew where Jane had been last week: *MEN* May 5, 1871, 2.

27: her mood had altered completely: *BM* May 5, 1871, 3, records that Charlotte claimed of Jane "that she seemed happier than she had been during the last six or seven weeks." Other reports, however, note that a headache she had that evening dampened her spirits: *KM* May 6, 1871, 5.

27: they set out with their two items after midnight: *KM* May 6, 1871, 5; *DN* May 5, 1871, 6.

27: important enough to impel him to swift action: *KM* May 6, 1871, 5.

28: Jane had often spent her days off with her aunt and uncle Trott: *KM* May 6, 1871, 5.

28: Griffin ordered the victim's clothes sent from the station house: *RN* May 7, 1871, 6.

28: the scrap of imitation Maltese lace they brought matched the lace on her jacket perfectly: *KM* May 6, 1871, 5.

28: Jane's birthmark—a mole on her right breast: *KM* May 6, 1871, 5; *SI* May 5, 1871, 3.

29: In any case, it was clearly Jane's photograph, and it matched the body before them: *L* May 14, 1871, 10.

29: "very stout and well-looking": *T* July 13, 1871, 11.

29: Jane's father, James, had been a fisherman before taking up work closer to home: *Board of Guardian Records, 1834–1906*, and *Church of England Parish Registers, 1754–1906*, for Maria Cecilia Clouson; *Census Returns of England and Wales, 1861*, for James Robert Clouson.

29: a son who died as an infant: *England and Wales Civil Registration Indexes*, death record for Charles James Elias Clouson.

29: Jane was a "religious and virtuous" and "good handsome" girl: *S* May 2, 1871, 7.

30: a diligent student both at a local day school and at Sunday school: William Trott described her Sunday school as "Wesleyan Baptist School." He likely meant the school attached to the Wesleyan Methodist Chapel in Deptford. *S* May 2, 1871, 7; *GDC* May 13, 1871, 2.

30: In 1863 tuberculosis killed Jane's thirteen-year-old sister, Sarah: *S* May 2, 1871, 7.

30: In 1866, it killed her mother: *England and Wales Civil Registration Indexes*, death record for Jane [Elizabeth] Clouson; *GDC* May 13, 1871, 2.

30: He slipped across the Thames to the Isle of Dogs: *Census Returns of England and Wales, 1871*, for James Robert Clouson.

30: she is listed as a "visitor" with a family in Croydon: *Census Returns of England and Wales, 1871*, for Maria C. Clouson.

30: Jane then began her working life: *GDE* May 13, 1871, 2; *WDP* May 23, 1871, 3.

30: the captain's many children and grandchildren: *Census Returns of England and Wales, 1871,* for Archibald Thomas Taylor.

30: Griffin knew Ebenezer Pook and he knew him well: *OB,* testimony of Ebenezer Pook; *KM* June 3, 1871, 5.

31: Of the 1.2 million English servants recorded in the 1871 census, 780,040, or roughly two-thirds, were "general domestics," or maids-of-all-work: Horn 232.

31: most . . . moved on by their twenties: Dawes 86; Beeton 1005.

32: "The general servant, or maid-of-all work . . . commiseration": Beeton 1001.

32: Their battles against dirt . . . eighty hours a week or more: Burnett 171; McBride 55.

32: Her duties, as elaborated by Beeton: Beeton 1001–1005.

32: cleaning the privy or water closet: At several points in her diaries, Hannah Cullwick, who worked at this time as a maid-of-all-work, describes this as one of her regular tasks. Cullwick.

32: she, too, was expected to be clean and so reflect her employer's cleanliness: Beeton 1002, Dawes 85.

32: She generally interacted almost entirely with her mistress: Beeton 1002, 1003.

33: ". . . subject to rougher treatment than either the house- or kitchen-maid": Beeton 1001.

33: The Pooks were relatively new to the middle class: *Census Returns of England and Wales, 1851 and 1861,* for Ebenezer Pook.

33: they might have been playmates: Indeed, many years later, in 1888, a cousin of the Pooks claimed that Jane and Edmund actually *were* playmates when young. Geography argues against this. *AS* March 20, 1888, 5.

33: the need to observe and preserve that distance became that much greater: Horn 14.

33: Maids-of-all-work were generally prohibited from having "followers": Dawes 36.

34: Any serious moral breach . . . grounds for instant dismissal: Dawes 12.

34: an otherwise eminently appropriate suitor by the name of James Harley Fletcher: *DN* May 5, 1871, 6; *Census Returns of England and Wales, 1861,* for James Harley Fletcher; *Census Returns of England and Wales, 1871,* for Mary Ann Fletcher.

34: She and Edmund were now keeping company, she told them: *S* May 5, 1871, 7.

35: Aunt Elizabeth . . . tried repeatedly to dissuade Jane from seeing Edmund: *T* May 5, 1871, 11.

35:    she had been miserable for weeks: *BM* May 5, 1871, 3.

35:    on April 13, Jane abruptly left the Pooks and moved in with Emily Wolledge: *OB*, testimony of Elizabeth Trott; *T* May 3, 1871, 11.

35:    Jane told Charlotte that she had left by choice: *KM* May 6, 1871, 5.

35:    "Charlotte . . . you must not be surprised if I am missing for some weeks": *MEN* May 5, 1871, 2.

36:    The Trotts offered up one other scrap of information to the police: *S* May 2, 1871, 7. William Clark himself spoke with the police about meeting Mary Smith and Edmund Pook—but he gave that information after nine o'clock that night. Griffin and Mulvany must have been aware of Mary Smith before that, as they suggested to Ebenezer Pook that his son was sexually involved with her. Since William Trott spoke of Mary Smith to reporters that day, I conclude that the Trotts were aware of Clark's story and shared it with Griffin and Mulvany. I have been unable to find in the 1871 England Census a clear candidate for a William Clark who lived in Deptford and who was roughly Jane Clouson's age. I have, however, discovered a twenty-year-old waterman by the name of William *Cleak*, who lived with his mother and stepfather just two doors down from the Trotts. Phonetically, the names are far apart—but for a newspaper compositor, transcribing a reporter's handwritten notes, the error is a simple one.

36:    they arranged that Jane's body would follow them: *T* May 9, 1871, 12.

37:    William Trott made his way to the newspapers: *S* May 2, 1871, 7.

38:    he immediately identified the body as his battered, murdered child: *KM* May 6, 1871, 5.

38:    The police gathered at the end of London Street: *KM* May 20, 1871, 5.

38:    while consulting, the police enjoyed at least one round of beer: *T* May 15, 1871, 2.

38:    they chose to meet at this place purely for refreshment: *T* May 15, 1871, 13.

39:    Mrs. Matilda Wolledge, in whose room Jane had stayed, knew nothing: *KM* May 6, 1871, 5.

39:    that month she attended day and night to a woman and her newborn twins: *Census Returns of England and Wales, 1871*, for Matilda A. Wolledge.

39:    She knew that Jane had been depressed, often in tears: *KM* May 6, 1871, 5; *S* May 2, 1871, 7.

39:    Jane received a letter in the post: *KM* May 6, 1871, 5; *T* May 5, 1871, 11.

39:    Jane revealed both these things, however, to the Wolledges' landlady: *T* May 5, 1871, 11; *L* May 14, 1871, 10; *OB*, testimony of Fanny Hamilton.

40:    she was going to meet Edmund Pook at his request: *S* May 5, 1871, 7.

41:     Inspector Mulvany swore that they had no intention of arresting Edmund
        Pook: *KM* May 20, 1871, 5.

41:     Mulvany, as detective, would do most of the talking: *OB*, testimony of
        James Griffin.

42:     Introductions were made, hands shaken: *OB*, testimony of James
        Griffin.

42:     they could hear the chatter and laughter of the Pook family at their
        midday dinner: *T* July 14, 1871, 11.

42:     Jane Clouson had not slept alone while working there: *OB*, testimony of
        Harriet Chaplin.

43:     He was sorry to hear it was so, he said: *OB*, testimony of Ebenezer Pook.

43:     "terms of intimacy": *T* July 13, 1871, 11.

43:     With both of them "he did as he liked": *OB*, testimony of Ebenezer Pook.

43:     "Ah, it is a very painful matter, but it is too true": *OB*, testimony of
        Ebenezer Pook.

43:     "a minute longer than we thought he should be": *OB*, testimony of
        Ebenezer Pook.

43:     Thomas Pook was married and had his own home in Greenwich: *Census
        Returns of England and Wales, 1871* for Thomas B. Pook.

43:     his wife had left them with their daughter: *OB*, testimony of Ebenezer
        Pook.

43:     "I am positive it is not the case": *OB*, testimony of Ebenezer Pook.

44:     Jane was a slovenly girl: *OB*, testimony of John Mulvany.

44:     he and Griffin watched Mulvany go to work: *OB*, testimony of John
        Mulvany.

44:     His inspection . . . was not as thorough as it could have been: *T* May 31,
        1871, 12; *KM* June 3, 1871, 5.

44:     He found no blood: *KM* May 19, 1871, 5.

44:     He was slightly built: *PIP* May 6, 1871, 291, *IPN* May 20, 1871. Two sketch
        portraits of Edmund Pook appeared on the front pages of the *Illustrated
        Police News* of May 13 and May 27, 1871. The first, the newspaper later
        admitted, was not drawn from life and hardly looked like Edmund Pook.
        The second was much more accurate.

44:     "Good Morning Mr. Griffin, I know you": *T* July 15, 1871, 11; *OB*, tes-
        timony of Ebenezer Pook. Later, Superintendent Griffin denied that he
        and Edmund shook hands: *KM* May 6, 1871, 5.

44:     "We have come to inform you . . . Jane Clouson": A number of accounts
        of the conversation between Edmund Pook and the police on May 1 exist,
        differing in small details but adding up to a coherent script. Most of the
        verbatim quotes are from James Griffin's testimony at Edmund Pook's
        trial at the Old Bailey.

45:     "She was a dirty girl": *S* July 13, 1871, 6; *T* May 3, 1871, 7.

45: "Do they? Have you the letter? If it is in my handwriting, that will prove it": *KM* May 6, 1871, 5.

45: ". . . I saw her in the town, talking to a young *gent* . . .": *KM* June 3, 1871, 5.

45: "Is it necessary to mention her name?" *OB*, testimony of James Griffin.

45: "That would bring you by Arthur's House": *OB*, testimony of James Griffin.

46: "By-the-bye, I saw our boy . . .": *OB*, testimony of James Griffin, John Mulvany, and Ebenezer Pook; *WDP* July 13, 1871, 3.

46: "Call up my brother": *T* July 11, 1871, 11; *OB*, testimony of Ebenezer Pook.

46: ". . . I remember his coming home, and saying he had seen her with a *swell*": *OB*, testimony of John Mulvany.

46: he had worn an overcoat that night: *OB*, testimony of John Mulvany.

47: On it Mulvany discerned minute spots: *OB*, testimony of James Griffin.

47: Edmund sarcastically asked them whether they wanted to see the waist-coat and tie: *DN* Oct. 7, 1871, 6.

47: He walked out and called her: *OB*, testimony of Ebenezer Pook.

47: Griffin . . . agreed it was blood: *OB*, testimony of James Griffin and John Mulvany.

47: "Yes, there is blood on his things": *OB*, testimony of James Griffin.

47: "I shall have to take you into custody . . .": *OB*, testimony of John Mulvany.

47: "Very well . . . I shall go anywhere you like with you": *OB*, testimony of James Griffin.

48: they did not give him the usual caution against self-incrimination: *MP* May 12, 1871, 6; *DN* May 12, 1871, 2.

48: Edmund asked the police whether he could bring a book with him: *DN* May 12, 1871, 2.

48: At the station, Inspector Mulvany signed the sheet: *KM* May 6, 1871, 5.

CHAPTER THREE: TITTLE-TATTLE

52: The procedure that Griffin followed had been established long before: Beattie, 107–8, documents examples from as early as 1757 of Bow Street Runners setting suspects among other men and instructing witnesses to examine the group and touch the one they recognized upon the shoulder.

53: Their ages and their general appearance weren't very important: Eric R. Watson, in his descriptions of the notorious identification parades for the woefully misidentified Adolf Beck in 1895 and 1904, makes it clear that at those times and before, the Metropolitan Police had little concern about choosing participants that looked like the suspect [34, 36].

53: A terrified Jane Thomas walked into the room: *TE* May 17, 1871, 3; *L* May 21, 1871, 4.

53: he, too, recognized no one: *T* May 17, 1871, 12.

53: Henry Pook, in spite of his name, was not related: *T* May 3, 1871, 11; *TE* May 3, 1871, 2.

53: The son of an innkeeper: *Census Returns of England and Wales, 1851* and *1861*, for Henry Pook.

53: suffered bankruptcy at least twice: *BC* January 11, 1862, 5; *RM* April 9, 1864, 4.

53: He once pleaded for the life of a condemned man: *SLC* May 2, 1868, 2.

54: this "sensational drama": *KM* May 6, 1871, 5.

54: "The prisoner was now before him, and that was sufficient": *KM* May 6, 1871, 5.

55: with "utmost composure": *TE* May 3, 1871, 2.

55: The state could intervene in cases of special importance: Mathew, 9–10. For a full description of the process in police court at this time, and particularly of private prosecutions, see Kurland and Waters.

55: a local solicitor by the name of John Lenton Pulling: Pulling resided in nearby Lee, according to the *Census Returns of England and Wales, 1871*, for John L. Pulling.

56: he was unprepared: *KM* May 6, 1871, 5.

56: Most of the testimony Pulling obtained from the witnesses that day: For reporters' transcripts of Edmund Pook's examination at Greenwich Police Court on May 2, see *T* May 3, 1871, 11; *KM* May 6, 1871, 5; *TE* May 3, 1871, 2; *IPN* May 6, 1871, 4; *MP* May 3, 1871, 6; *S* May 3, 1871, 3; *DN* May 3, 1871, 6.

56: Inspector Mulvany had shown him that clothing before the inquest: *KM* May 6, 1871, 5.

56: "She said she was going to Crooms Hill . . .": *KM* May 6, 1871, 5.

56: a forty-eight-year-old charwoman and costermonger's wife: *Census Returns of England and Wales, 1871*, for Jane Prosser.

57: "There was no evidence whatever . . .": *MP* May 3, 1871, 6.

57: "had power . . . no one would be safe": *KM* May 5, 1871, 3.

58: They discovered Smith in Tottenham: *SI* May 4, 1871, 4; *LTA* May 5, 1871, 3; *L* May 14, 1871, 7.

59: the public filling whatever seats were not taken by the doctors of Guy's: *TE* May 5, 1871, 5.

59: The inquest began at noon: For reporters' transcripts of the first sitting of the inquest (May 4), see *T* May 5, 1871, 11; *MP* May 5, 1871, 8; *TE* May 5, 1871, 3; *KM* May 5, 1871, 3; *DN* May 5, 1871, 6; *L* May 14, 1871, 10.

59: they left Jane's body in the hands of undertaker William Billington: *GDC* May 6, 1871, supplement; *KM* May 13, 1871, 5; *TE* May 9, 1871, 3.

60: he had a reputation for partisan combativeness: Atlay.

60: "I have heard her say that she was keeping company with her young master": *MP* May 5, 1871, 8.

60: "I'm not going to work at the machine now": *MP* May 5, 1871, 8.

60: "it is evidence": *MP* May 5, 1871, 8.

61: he was cursed by a defect of the lip: *S* May 20, 1871, 6.

61: a "smirking sneer": *L* May 7, 1871, 12.

61: "Don't laugh. It's not a laughing matter": *L* May 7, 1871, 12.

61: "the most important evidence we have had": *L* May 7, 1871, 12.

61: "You have the audacity to come here with this pretty tale": *MP* May 5, 1871, 8.

61: "twice in a twelvemonth": *T* May 5, 1871, 11.

62: "You seem rather warm": *MP* May 5, 1871, 8.

63: numbers that . . . "overwhelmed" R Division: *BM* May 20, 1871, 9.

63: William Sparshott became one of the many: for Sparshott's claims see his testimony in police court on May 19 (*T* May 20, 1871, 11; *TE* May 20, 1871, 3; *KM* May 20, 1871, 4) and also his testimony at trial.

64: James Conway . . . at Samuel Thomas's shop: for Conway's claims see his testimony at the second sitting of the inquest on May 11 (*T* May 12, 1871, 5; *TE* May 12, 1871, 3; *KM* May 13, 1871, 5).

64: "something like a gentleman": *T* May 12, 1871, 5.

64: Mulvany had personally knocked on Letheby's door bearing in a parcel Edmund's trousers, shirt, hat, and coat: *TE* May 15, 1871, 6. Neither this account, nor any other, mentions the delivery of the coat. Letheby delivered all Edmund's clothing on this day, however, and Letheby made clear in his testimony that he did indeed examine Edmund's coat.

64: a highly reputed expert witness: a search for Henry Letheby as a witness, at *The Proceedings of the Old Bailey* website, reveals that between 1847 and 1871 Letheby appeared in thirty-one Old Bailey trials.

65: He had a surer test for blood than this: For Letheby's procedure in examining bloodstains, see *TE* May 15, 1871, 6, and Letheby.

67: "Ah, now he is off to Calcraft": *T* May 10, 1871, 11.

67: "I am most certainly astonished at the people": *T* May 10, 1871, 11.

68: "I am not disposed to extend those thanks": *T* May 10, 1871, 11.

68: In the courtroom . . . for nothing: *MP* May 8, 1871, 7; *T* May 8, 1871, 11.

68: "the sleuth-hound of the Treasury": Bowen-Rowlands 57; *PMG* Sept. 16, 1877, 5.

69: "Ignorant constables": *TE* May 8, 1871, 3.

69: "the tittle-tattle of one woman to another": *MP* May 8, 1871, 3.

69: "not be running about in other directions merely to fix the guilt on this young man": *KM* May 13, 1871, 5.

69: That man was older than Edmund, between twenty-six and thirty-four: *MP* May 9, 1871, 6, in which Yearsley is incorrectly identified as Ormond *Earsley*.

69:     Henry Pook introduced . . . Henry Humphreys. *OD*, testimony of James Griffin; *T* May 8, 1871, 11; *TE* May 8, 1871, 3.

70:     Henry Humphreys was thirty years old and married: *Census Returns of England and Wales, 1871*, for Henry Humphreys; Board of Guardian Records, 1834–1906 and Church of England Parish Registers, 1754–1906, for Henry Humphreys.

70:     "one link of the supposed chain of evidence . . .": *MEN* May 8, 1871, 2.

70:     inviting Superintendent Griffin to come to Tudor House: *MP* July 19, 1871, 7; *KM* July 22, 1871, 5. Henry Pook claimed that Griffin drank a second glass of whiskey on this night; Griffin, by the first account, states he could have—and by the second, denies it.

71:     the coffin holding Jane Clouson's body: For accounts of Jane Clouson's funeral, see *GDH* May 13, 1871, 2; *KM* May 13, 1871, 5; *T* May 9, 1871, 12; *TE* May 9, 1871, 3.

71:     magnificent funerals were the norm even among the working class: Curl 195, 209; Litten 165.

71:     burial insurance—generally called "life insurance": Strange 112, 115.

72:     Having peers of the deceased hold the pall was the custom for Victorian funerals: Litten 14–15.

72:     a service "of an unusually solemn and impressive nature": *KM* May 13, 1871, 5.

73:     They converged on London Street: *T* July 19, 1871, 11; *KM* July 22, 1871, 5.

73:     he would "either go mad or do mischief to somebody": *DN* July 19, 1871, 2.

73:     Lucas was a rogue, a liar, and . . . a police snitch and spy: *KM* July 22, 1871, 5.

73:     Deputy Coroner William John Payne considered himself greatly put upon: For reporters' transcripts of the second sitting of the inquest (May 11), see *KM* May 13, 1871, 5; *S* May 12, 1871, 7; *T* May 12, 1871, 5; *TE* May 12, 1871, 3.

74:     "I understand . . . about to take this case up . . .": *T* May 12, 1871, 5.

74:     "let me go, let me go": *T* May 12, 1871, 5.

74:     Norton served as coachman . . . and Putman a maid-of-all-work: *Census Returns of England and Wales, 1871*, for John Norton and Louisa Putman. In the census, Norton—coachman to John Gamble, as reported in the newspapers—is listed as *John*, not *William*. But in all of the many newspapers that named him in connection with the case, he is called William.

74:     "of about my stamp": *T* May 12, 1871, 5.

74:     "I thought . . . some young woman there": *S* May 12, 1871, 7.

75:     "You know that when you have got a young girl out with you she often screams": *S* May 12, 1871, 7.

75: "A great amount of difficulty might have been obviated had the witnesses been allowed to see the prisoner": *S* May 12, 1871, 7.

76: Lazell replied, in confusion, "No," then "I don't—I don't believe I did" and then "I think I did": *S* May 12, 1871, 7.

77: They had obviously attempted to entrap Edmund Pook: *KM* May 13, 1871, 5.

77: "Do you interrogate prisoners then?": *T* May 10, 1871, 11.

78: He hoped in the future that Mulvany and the police would remember Cockburn's words: *TE* May 12, 1871, 3.

78: the Thomases, Samuel and Jane, once again pored over their sales ledger: The Thomases's discoveries are largely reconstructed from their testimony at the third sitting of the inquest, May 16, 1871: *KM* May 20, 1871, 5; *T* May 17, 1871, 12; *TE* May 17, 1871, 3.

78: Thomas Wittard returned to remind them: In *KM* May 20, 1871, 5, this customer's name is transcribed as "Willan." But the Census for 1871 is clear: the man living at the address stated in Samuel Thomas's testimony is Thomas Wittard.

79: William Norton failed to recognize Pook: *TE* May 17, 1871, 3.

79: Louisa Putman failed as well: *TE* May 17, 1871, 3.

79: Thomas Lazell . . . touched him on the shoulder: *TE* May 17, 1871, 3.

80: James Conway, too, also touched Pook: *KM* May 20, 1871, 5.

80: Cronk then scrutinized the twenty men's backs: *KM* May 20, 1871, 5.

80: Three of these witnesses testified in court that day: For reporters' transcripts of the third police court examination (May 13) see *T* May 15, 1871, 13; *TE* May 15, 1871, 6; *KM* May 20, 1871, 5; *MP* May 15, 1871, 6.

80: "Can you say any person in court was the man you picked out from several others this morning": *T* May 15, 1871, 13; *TE* May 15, 1871, 6.

80: "If that was all the learned counsel could produce . . .": *T* May 15, 1871, 13.

81: that blood was "common to all animals": *KM* May 20, 1871, 5.

81: "such a fallacy . . . examination of the spots . . .": *KM* May 20, 1871, 5.

81: "wouldn't you expect . . . saturated with blood?": *TE* May 15, 1871, 6.

81: "that if the temple artery is cut through it does not bleed": *T* May 15, 1871, 13.

82: "similar in quality to that found?": *T* May 15, 1871, 13.

82: "blood from a self-inflicted wound . . .": *S* May 15, 1871, 4.

82: His mood could not have been helped by the first two witnesses: For reporters' transcripts of the third sitting of the inquest (May 16), see *T* May 17, 1871, 12; *KM* May 20, 1871, 5; *TE* May 17, 1871, 3; *L* May 21, 1871, 4; *MP* May 17, 1871, 7.

82: "I want some further particulars . . .": *KM* May 20, 1871, 5.

83: "Is it not a fact that you would sell it twopence cheaper . . .": *L* May 21, 1871, 4.

83: "If I could get a few pence to get away to the north . . .": *S* May 17, 1871, 6.

84: "Because the learned counsel . . . browbeat the witness" *MT* May 20, 1871, 3.

84: Several members of the jury immediately concurred: *FJ* May 17, 1871, 7.

84: She began to receive anonymous, threatening letters: *T* July 14, 1871, 11; *MP* May 26, 1871, 7.

84: "a woman named Merritt was sentenced to death upon your evidence . . .": *FJ* May 17, 1871, 4.

85: "the character of Dr. Letheby is too high in this country . . .": *TE* May 17, 1871, 3.

85: cell 33 of Maidstone Jail: *T* May 10, 1871, 11.

85: the books in the jail's library were "dry." *T* May 9, 1871, 12.

86: Her testimony was a crushing disappointment to him: For reporters' transcripts of the fourth police court examination (May 19) see *T* May 20, 1871, 11; *KM* May 20, 1871, 4; *TE* May 20, 1871, 3; *S* May 20, 1871, 6; *R* May 20, 1871, 5.

86: "we did not part very good friends": *T* May 20, 1871, 11.

86: "sit down, sir!": *S* May 20, 1871, 6.

86: Edmund wrote an anxious letter to Thomas Pook: *DN* July 15, 1871, 6.

87: Sparshott had easily picked Edmund Pook from a dozen other men: *KM* May 20, 1871, 4.

87: "Now tell us: have you not seen a photograph of the prisoner?": *S* May 20, 1871, 6.

87: The newspaper itself . . . apologized for the terrible likeness: *IPN* May 27, 1871, 2.

88: the police had run out of bombshells: For reporters' transcripts of the fourth sitting of the inquest (May 25), see *T* May 26, 1871, 12; *KM* May 27, 1871, 5; *TE* May 26, 1871, 3; *MP* May 26, 1871, 7; *S* May 26, 1871, 6.

89: "very substantial and astounding": *T* May 26, 1871, 12.

89: "not because they could not, but because they would not": *S* May 26, 1871, 6.

90: "would be very unsatisfactory . . . for nothing": *T* May 26, 1871, 12.

90: "If you return an open verdict . . . it will very much weaken the case . . .": *S* May 26, 1871, 12.

91: Edmund Pook experienced the terror of a near lynching: *DN* May 31, 1871, 2.

91: Police and prosecution . . . offered up in Southwark five days before: For reporters' transcripts of the sixth police court examination (May 30) see *T* May 31, 1871, 12; *KM* June 3, 1871, 5; *TE* May 31, 1871, 3; *DN* May 31, 1871, 2.

91: "been plentiful in indulging theories which had broken down": *KM* June 3, 1871, 5.

91: Dr. Letheby himself shot off a letter that appeared in the *Times*: *T* June 2, 1871, 8.

92: "would not be deemed sufficient . . . 5s. in a County Court": *T* May 31, 1871, 12.

CHAPTER FOUR: SOCIAL CONFUSION AND MORAL CORRUPTION

94: Newgate was no longer an emblem of hell on earth: Griffiths 562, 566.

94: Frederick Lloyd-Jones: *ILN* May 6, 1865, 427.

94: Lloyd-Jones apparently made sure that Pook was transferred: *KM* June 3, 1871, 5.

94: the Pooks . . . lost no time in feeding the news to the press: the *PMG* (June 3, 1871, 6) reported that "A great point is to be made of his having bitten his tongue while so seized."

94: The last two of these were mainstays at the Old Bailey: *T* June 5, 1914, 10, in an obituary of Douglas Straight.

95: "admirable in the conduct of a cause . . .": *T* Dec. 6, 1890, 9.

95: Huddleston declared himself eager to begin at once: *SI* June 8, 1871, 3.

95: a witness who could give "very material" evidence: *T* June 8, 1871, 11.

95: Poland scoffed at that last argument: *BO* June 8, 1871, 8.

96: twenty-six-year-old Perren managed his mother's livery stables: *London, England, Births and Baptisms 1813–1906*, baptism record for Walter Richard Perren ; *PMG* June 10, 1871, 6; *T* July 14, 1871, 11.

96: The *Times* would later disparage him as a "donkey-driver": *T* June 12, 1871, 10.

96: Perren said that for three or four years he had known Pook slightly: *T* July 14, 1871, 11.

96: Pook spoke first: *TE* July 14, 1871, 5.

97: Perren somehow realized that he might be a crucial eyewitness: *S* July 14, 1871, 5.

97: Detective Mulvany hustled him to the Old Bailey: *DN* July 14, 1871, 5.

97: He then went to the exercise yard at Newgate: *TE* July 14, 1871, 5.

97: He had, in other words, a "perfect answer" to Perren: *T* June 8, 1871, 11

98: "He is perfectly calm": *MEN* July 3, 1871, 3.

98: a thousand pounds in all, by one estimate: *TE* June 10, 1871, 3.

98: A fund was quickly got up: *GDC* June 10, 1871, 3; *MEN* June 12, 1871, 2.

98: the Treasury submitted to Henry Pook a list of the witnesses: *TE* 3 July 1871, 3.

98: Mary Ann Love and Alice Langley . . . utterly inconclusive: *DN* July 15, 1871, 5; *T* July 15, 1871, 11.

99.   Henry Pook found three neighbors to the Durnfords willing to testify: *DN* July 15, 1871, 6; *T* July 15, 1871, 11; *OB*, testimony of Joseph and Mary Anne Eagle [sic].

99:   There he had each one scrutinize two albums holding thirty photographs: *DN* July 15, 1871, 6; *OB*, testimony of Joseph Eagle [sic], Mary Anne Eagle [sic], and William Douglas.

99:   he managed to engage in a spell of international diplomacy: *KM* June 24, 1871, 6; *T* June 19, 1871, 5; *TE* June 19, 1871, 6.

100: "The interest felt in this case . . .": *T* June 12, 1871, 10.

101: The pilgrimage there reached its peak on Whit-Monday, May 29: *DN* May 30, 1871, 2; *G* June 2, 1871, 3; *GDC* June 3, 1871, 6.

102: foreign correspondents began to submit their dispatches not by post but by telegraph: Williams 114.

103: It was the worst civil bloodletting in all of Europe and during all of the nineteenth century: Tombs 10.

103: fifteen-year-old Agnes Norman: *S* April 14, 1871, 2.

104: Mullard revealed what he had learned at the inquest: *PMG* April 18, 1871, 6.

104: the coroner would not let any of them speak: *RN* Apr. 23, 1871, 6.

105: John William Beer angrily vowed to pursue the case further: *PMG* April 18, 1871, 6.

105: a detective arrested Norman for Beer's murder: *TE* May 1, 1871, 2.

105: At every appearance Agnes Norman stood absolutely indifferent: *S* June 1, 1871, 7; *TE* May 8, 1871, 2, May 19, 1871, 3.

105: Agnes Norman obtained her first place in Camberwell in January 1869: *DN* May 19, 1871, 6.

105: Mrs. Milner worked away from home: *DN* May 19, 1871, 6. She worked as an envelope folder.

105: Less than a month after she had arrived, Agnes fetched a neighbor: *S* May 26, 1871, 7.

105: The neighbor found Tommy Milner on a bed: *DN* May 13, 1871, 3.

105: the jury ruled Tommy Milner's death natural: *DN* May 13, 1871, 3.

105: Agnes, he said, had sent him away to buy a halfpenny sweet: *S* May 26, 1871, 7. Arthur Milner is misnamed "John" in this account. And according to Elizabeth Milner's testimony, Arthur's older brother, Ralph, apparently knew something about Agnes's behavior on this day, as well, though he doesn't appear in Arthur's account.

106: "Minnie is dead": *S* May 26, 1871, 7.

106: Agnes Norman obtained—without a reference—a place in nearby Brixton: *DN* May 19, 1871, 6.

106: Again, there was an inquest; again, the jury ruled the death natural: *DN* May 19, 1871, 6.

106: giving her a good reference, noting her "sobriety and civility": *DN* May 19, 1871, 6.

106: By July Agnes had found a place as a maid-of-all-work for the Brown family: *MP* May 13, 1871, 3.

106: One parrot miraculously survived: *S* May 26, 1871, 7.

106: the boy awoke to find Agnes Norman kneeling upon him: *DN* May 19, 1871, 6.

107: with the recommendation of a neighbor's servant-girl: *S* May 26, 1871, 7.

107: the Beers engaged Norman for three shillings a week: *OB*, testimony of John William Beer.

107: before the inquest could take place, a cat and a canary followed: *MP* May 13, 1871, 3.

107: nearly 30 percent of all English children never lived to see their tenth birthday: *Mortality in England and Wales: Average Life Span*, 2010, 7–8.

107: "Have you witnesses to say she murdered your child?": *RN* April 23, 1871, 6.

108: "every charge must rest upon the specific evidence relating to it": *DN* June 6, 1871, 3.

108: "No, not much": *DN* May 19, 1871, 6.

109: "too well known to a large part of the London world . . .": *T* July 17, 1871, 11.

109: PC Charles Futerall was called by a doctor to 23 Newton Road, in Bayswater: *T* May 26, 1871, 12.

109: a seven-inch poultry-carving knife: *T* May 30, 1871, 5.

109: "The person was in the house": *S* May 26, 1871, 6.

109: wildly excited: *S* May 26, 1871, 6.

109: Futerall immediately told her to consider herself under arrest: *OB*, trial of Hannah Newington alias Flora Davey, testimony of William Fewtrell [sic].

109: She was thirty-eight years old, tall, stout, and muscular: *T* May 29, 1871, 6.

109: More than once she had stated that she thought she had done it: *S* May 26, 1871, 6; *MP* June 2, 1871, 3; *T* July 14, 1871, 6; *TE* July 14, 1871, 11.

109: George Lewis, solicitor of choice for London's elite: Juxon 31, 92; McKenna 286.

110: the home, it turned out, that Captain Davy owned: *T* May 30, 1871, 5.

110: Mansfield declared he had been "grossly deceived": *T* May 29, 1871, 6.

110: "I forfeited husband and character": *T* June 17, 1871, 10.

110: she had placed herself under the protection of Captain Davy: *S* May 30, 1871, 7.

110: Apparently, neither man quite knew the extent of the involvement of the other: *S* June 9, 1871, 6; *T* May 30, 1871, 5.

111: "a sort of quicksand of social confusion and moral corruption": *T* July 17, 1871, 11.

111: for a time, she could pretend to be "Mrs. Moon." *MP* June 2, 1871, 3.

111: the aliases she adopted: *S* May 30, 1871, 7.

111: long separated from Mr. Toynbee: *Census Returns of England and Wales, 1871*, for Anne M. Toynbee and for Thomas Toynbee.

111: she served Davy as a friend and not a hireling: *S* May 30, 1871, 7; *OB*, trial of Hanna Newington alias Flora Davy, testimony of Ann Marsden Toynbee.

111: Mrs. Davy shared her bed with two men: *T* May 29, 1871, 6.

111: "found there no one knows how or why": *T* July 17, 1871, 11.

111: they were the daughter and niece of a woman with whom Flora Davy had once lodged: *T* June 2, 1871, 8; *OB*, trial of Hanna Newington alias Flora Davy, testimony of Catherine Dulin. Laura Pook, the niece, was of no relation to either Pook family of Greenwich.

111: a not quite respectable flirtation: *T* June 17, 1871, 10.

112: Flora Davy was volatile and imperious: *S* June 16, 1871, 7, May 30, 1871, 7; *T* June 2, 1871, 8.

112: a dipsomaniac, according to her doctors: *T* May 30, 1871, 5; *TE* June 2, 1871, 3.

112: Captain Davy, for whatever reason, began to spend less and less time at 23 Newton Road: *T* May 30, 1871, 5.

112: vowed to pay her off and have done with her: *T* June 17, 1871, 10.

112: "No, you are not . . . and what is more, you never will be . . .": *T* June 2, 1871, 8; *DN* June 2, 1871, 2.

112: that evening Moon came to the house in a dark mood: *T* June 17, 1871, 10.

112: in self-defense, she claimed: *T* June 17, 1871, 10.

112: "He was my very all": *T* June 17, 1871, 10.

113: its ability to generate a full-fledged popular movement: McWilliam 172.

113: "Great numbers of persons believe . . . imposed upon . . .": *DN* Nov. 16, 1866, 3.

114: The last time that the indisputable Roger Charles Tichborne had been seen alive: general details about the Tichborne Claimant and his case can be found in Gilbert's, Maugham's, McWilliam's, and Woodruff's accounts.

114: the dowager Lady Tichborne, a temperamental—many thought unbalanced—Frenchwoman: Gilbert 33.

114: promising "A handsome REWARD": Gilbert 34.

115: a hundred or so witnesses prepared to testify in favor of the Claimant's claim, and more than 250 prepared to testify against it: Woodruff 189.

116: "he would pull at the organ stop labelled 'pathos . . .'": Woodruff 168.

116: "a stream of silvery mediocrity": Woodroffe 237.

116: the record-setting twenty-one-day opening speech for the defense: Gilbert 172.

116: Coleridge's cross-examination of the Claimant established a record for length: Gilbert 170.

116: his relentless protestations of "I don't know" and "I have forgotten": Gilbert 152.

117: "would it surprise you to know": Woodruff 199.

117: the "ruffian's ignorance": Coleridge 2.417.

117: "It is Greek to you, anyhow": TE June 14, 1871, 6.

117: "Do you mean to swear before the Judge and jury . . . that you seduced this lady?" TE June 6, 1871, 5.

118: "I pity you, Mr. Solicitor": TE July 1, 1871, 5.

118: "He will kill me before I do him": Coleridge 2.418.

118: public consensus held that this trial helped kill him: DN November 3, 1873, 2.

118: "the honest opinion of lawyers concerning the lamented judge . . .": "Sir W. Bovill" 27.

118: He was notorious, for one thing, for his partiality: Hamilton; Woodruff 166.

118: Bovill gave a speech at a Lord Mayor's dinner: TE June 9, 1871, 5.

118: a "patent want of sympathy with the Bar": DN Nov. 3, 1873, 2.

119: "I have not a moment's peace of mind from morning till night . . .": TE June 6, 1871, 5.

119: "the arduous and unaccustomed duties of master of the ceremonies": Ballantine 421.

119: "It weighs upon me": Woodruff 393.

119: "I am only enabled to attend to this case by going down to Brighton to get a little fresh air": TE June 29, 1871, 6.

120: he declared himself "utterly exhausted": TE July 8, 1871, 6.

CHAPTER FIVE: TALLY-HO

121: "excellent as the utterly inadequate accommodation of the Court will permit": TE July 13, 1871, 5.

121: those inside the courtroom were discernibly better dressed: T July 13, 1871, 11.

122: He was certain that spirits in the millions swarmed the metropolis: for Crosland's particular spiritualist beliefs, see his *Apparitions* in both its original (1856) and revised (1873) editions, as well as his autobiography, *Rambles Round My Life* (1898).

122: "To doubt the reality of these manifestations": Crosland, *Apparitions* [1856] 6.

122: Newtonian physics Crosland thought "old-fashioned, clumsy, mechanical, vulgar": Crosland, *Apparitions* [1873] 33.

122: "the most colossal, dazzling, infidel mass of ignorance . . .": Crosland, *Rambles* 29.

123. "They are certainly very curious": Crosland, *Rambles* 276.

123: "a great deal that was very unpleasant": Crosland, *Rambles* 276.

123: six for the prosecution—four barristers, two solicitors: *MP* July 13, 1871, 3.

125: "nothing of the hang-dog, cowering look . . .": *TE* July 13, 1871, 5.

125: Pook calmly but emphatically pleaded that he was not guilty: *T* July 13, 1871, 11.

125: "some observations were made by Jane Clouson . . .": *T* July 13, 1871, 11.

126: The first, written to Edmund from Wales by an aunt: *TE* July 13, 1871, 6. Edmund's aunt was named Rebecca Winston; his cousin, Louisa Parton Stevens. The letter was written from Sennybridge, on the Welsh border. It is clear from trial testimony that police and prosecution did not know any of these things.

126: "If I am remanded . . . of course I must 'grin and bear it'": *TE* July 13, 1871, 6.

127: "I don't think he was on duty up to 10 o'clock": *OB*, testimony of Donald Gunn.

127: "So that this lonely place is left without a policeman till a quarter-past two?": *TE* July 13, 1871, 6.

128: "Where there are such wounds as these, I should expect blood to spurt forth": *OB*, testimony of Michael Harris.

128: "She was not dirty, quite different to that altogether . . .": *OB*, testimony of Elizabeth Trott.

128: her daughter agreed: *TE* July 13, 1871, 6.

128: "she told me where she was going" *OB*, testimony of Fanny Hamilton.

128: Huddleston objected immediately, citing the then-standard argument against hearsay: *The Queen v. Edmund Walter Pook*, day 1, 133; *OB*.

129: "the question," he noted, "was not ably argued." Crosland, *Eltham Tragedy Reviewed* 22.

129: "It seems to me . . . that the question asked . . .": *WDP* July 13, 1871, 3.

130: "He seemed . . . out of condition, irritable, nervous . . .": Crosland, *The Eltham Tragedy Reviewed* 18.

131: The Judge (angrily): "Might have been! . . .": Crosland, *The Eltham Tragedy Reviewed* 18.

131: "This unjust aspersion upon Mr. Mulvany soon became epidemic": Crosland, *The Eltham Tragedy Reviewed* 19.

131: Edmund "had made no reply": *T* May 31, 1871, 12.

131: "I do not remember his saying 'It is not true'": *OB*, testimony of James Griffin.

132: "How could you possibly say upon your oath . . . matter referred to." *S* July 13, 1871, 6.

132: The Chief Justice (to Witness): You are the principal officer: *TE* July 13, 1871, 6.

133: Bovill's humble opinion was a patent legal absurdity: Legal scholar David Bentley actually cites *R v. Pook* and Bovill's opinion here as the nineteenth century's most extreme expression of the concept of legal discovery. (Bentley mistakenly attributes the opinion not to Bovill but to Alexander Cockburn, Lord Chief Justice of the Court of Queen's Bench.) The doctrine, Bentley notes, did not take root. Bentley 40.

133: "I must say that Crown prosecutions ought not to be conducted in this manner": *TE* July 13, 1871, 11.

134: "I hope never again . . . in this country": Crosland, *The Eltham Tragedy Reviewed* 28.

134: "deeply pained": *TE* July 14, 1871, 5.

134: "I protest . . . kept back in this case.": *TE* July 14, 1871, 5.

134: "I did not intend to imply the slightest imputation upon you, Mr. Solicitor": *TE* July 14, 1871, 5.

135: "I have no doubt whatever that he is the man": *S* July 14, 1871, 5.

136: it was a "sort of sensational Newgate Calendar": *DN* July 14, 1871, 5.

136: "It was most improper that portraits should be given . . .": *TE* July 14, 1871, 5.

136: "Her Majesty's government are now engaged in very arduous duties": *KM* July 15, 1871, 3. According to the *Telegraph*, however, Coleridge's reply was acquiescent rather than sarcastic: "There cannot be two opinions as to the impropriety of such publications" [*TE* July 14 1871, 5].

136: "He had on a lightish pair of trousers": *OB*, testimony of Rowland Renneson.

136: "Light trousers; I remember that": *OB*, testimony of Alfred Sparshott.

137: the same feeling that Superintendent Griffin had had nearly three weeks before: *LS* July 13, 1871, 6.

137: "a young woman breaking her parasol over my head": *OB*, testimony of Walter Richard Perren.

137: "I won't swear it, I might have been . . .": *OB*, testimony of Walter Richard Perren.

138: "there are a great many persons who know me in the concert business . . .": *OB*, testimony of Walter Richard Perren.

138: "Well, I believe that I did . . . Is that what you want?": *TE* July 14, 1871, 5.

138: "It is a farce to ask you any more questions": *TE* July 14, 1871, 5.

138: "Did you say to Mr. Field . . . at the police court . . .": *TE* July 14, 1871, 5.

138: I have given you every opportunity of explaining yourself": *TE* July 14, 1871, 5.

139: "I thought . . . clearing our character": *TE* July 14, 1871, 6.

139: "All I can say is the detectives would be doing good service to society by finding out who sends these letters." *TE* July 14, 1871, 6.

139: The screams they had heard were "of a person in fun, and not in pain or anguish": *OB*, testimony of William Norton.

140. "I do not speak to his face": *OB*, testimony of William Cronk.

140: "I thought she addressed the man by the Christian name of *Charley*": *OB*, testimony of William Cronk.

141: she could only say it was "something like" the one Edmund had carried: *T* July 14, 1871, 11.

141: "the prosecution could not be accused of suppressing that piece of evidence": *TE* July 14, 1871, 6.

141: "a pretty, good-looking young woman": *OB*, testimony of Thomas Lazell.

142: "How often have you seen the prisoner before?": *DN* July 15, 1871, 5.

142: "If the duster . . . the most outrageous thing in the world": *KM* July 15, 1871, 4.

143: "Did you send it to Dr. Letheby?": *T* July 15, 1871, 11.

143: a "ragged dirty piece of rubbish": *OB*, testimony of James Griffin.

143: "I have not the least idea who the stackmaker is . . .": *OB*, testimony of James Griffin.

143: "most essential witness": *TE* July 15, 1871, 5.

144: "To what does this all tend?" *DN* July 15, 1871, 5.

144: "Two of the holes are hardly perceptible . . .": *TE* July 15, 1871, 5.

144: "I suppose these points of similarity might occur in the hair of five thousand people?": *DN* July 15, 1871, 6.

145: it was in their power ". . . not guilty": *DN* July 15, 1871, 6.

145: "I felt sure . . . among things forgotten": *TE* July 15, 1871, 6.

145: the Crown's case "crumbled to nothing": *TE* July 15, 1871, 6.

145: "Like dogs after game": *T* July 15, 1871, 11.

146: "only known to the inquisitions of old": *DN* July 15, 1871, 6.

146: "It is the life of this young man": *TE* July 15, 1871, 6.

146: "quiet, well-conducted man": *T* July 15, 1871, 11.

146: "If I had any one call in the evening . . ." *The Queen v. Edmund Walter Pook*, day 3, 231.

147: "I kept proper order in my house": *OB*, testimony of Mary Pook.

147: "even if he was in his bedroom . . . made about him": *DN* July 15, 1871, 6.

147: "if there had been any intimacy I should certainly have discovered it at once": *OB*, testimony of Harriet Chaplin. According to the *Telegraph*, Chaplin actually said "if I had seen any intimacy I should have *discouraged* it at once": *TE* July 15, 1871, 6.

147: "If there had been any familiarity . . . must have seen it": *OB*, testimony of Alfred George Collins.

147: "We were not separated for five minutes": *OB*, testimony of Thomas Birch [sic] Pook.

148: an assistant in the shop had scraped the flesh off the back of his knuckles: *TE* July 15, 1871, 6.

148: he had seen Jane walking out with a "swell": *T* July 15, 1871, 11; *OB*, testimony of Thomas Birch [sic] Pook.

148: he had obtained lotion to treat his partially blind eye on that day: *OB*, testimony of Joseph Ambrose Eagle [sic].

149: had "always" known him: *OB*, testimony of Eliza Ann Merritt [sic].

149: "I thought he was waiting for somebody": *OB*, testimony of Eliza Anne Merritt [sic].

149: "a piece of lining full of holes . . .": *TE* July 15, 1871, 6.

149: "Gypsies throw away rags . . .": *TE* July 15, 1871, 6.

149: "All I can say is this": *TE* July 15, 1871, 6.

149: The police "ought to have investigated into the circumstance . . .": *TE* July 15, 1871, 6.

150: "That . . . is where the injustice lies": *TE* July 15, 1871, 6.

150: "It shows . . . the necessity that exists for a public prosecutor": *TE* July 15, 1871, 6.

151: "an exceedingly well-conducted man at all times": *TE* July 15, 1871, 6.

151: "The accused had borne a character . . . son to bear": *TE* July 15, 1871, 6.

151: Matthew Crawford, a pastry cook . . . next-door neighbor to the Sparshotts: *Census Returns of England and Wales, 1871*, for William Crawford.

151: He had since moved from Deptford: *MP* July 17, 1871, 2.

151: "I could not alter my statement on any account . . .": *OB*, testimony of William Sparshott.

152: "Mr. Sparshott's evidence before the magistrate was not positive . . .": *DN* July 17, 1871, 5.

152: He would "wait with anxiety": *DN* July 17, 1871, 5.

152: "rather a personal matter": *T* July 17, 1871, 12.

152: "Policemen . . . were not to be set up in the box like schoolboys' cockshies . . .": *TE* July 17, 1871, 5.

153: "there was an end of the case, and the prisoner ought to be acquitted": *MP* July 17, 1871, 2.

153: "Outrages of this description . . . could not go unrevenged . . .": *TE* July 17, 1871, 5.

153: "deliberately and wilfully false": *TE* July 17, 1871, 6.

154: "then they were left in doubt . . .": *TE* July 17, 1871, 6.

155: a small amount of gas could "produce an explosion and blow them all up." *MP* July 17, 1871, 2.

155: giving a "tinge" to their words: *TE* July 17, 1871, 6.

155: "You and I . . . would have been made instruments in fixing guilt upon the prisoner . . .": *The Queen v. Edmund Walter Pook*, day 4, 400.

155: "Sensation" enveloped the courtroom: *TE* July 17, 1871, 6.

155: "It is cruel indeed": *The Queen v. Edmund Walter Pook*, day 4, 400–401.

156:    he chatted with his guards, and was seen to smile: *DN* July 17, 1871, 6; *L* July 23, 1871, 8.

156:    the "loose manner" in which they had presented their case: *L* July 23, 1871, 8.

CHAPTER SIX: ROUGH MUSIC

157:    the crowd that had been gathering outside the Old Bailey: *S* July 17, 1871, 5.

157:    betting with one another: *LM* July 17, 1871, 6.

157:    Over the next few days . . . the "stupid" and "reprehensible" police: *T* July 18, 1871, 9; also *DM* July 19, 1871, 5; *S* July 17, 1871, 4; *PMG* July 17, 1871, 2–3, and July 24, 1871, 10–11; *TE* July 17, 1871, 4–5; *R* July 23, 1871, 4; and *WDP* July 18, 1871, 2.

158:    "It would, indeed, be hardly possible . . . our present system": *T* July 18, 1871, 9.

158:    They burst into sustained and raucous celebration: *TE* July 17, 1871, 6; *T* July 17, 1871, 12.

158:    Flora Davy could find some solace in having escaped the gallows: *TE* July 12, 1871, 3.

159:    she had repeatedly stated, "I fear I did it": *TE* July 14, 1871, 6; *T* July 14, 1871, 11.

159:    Hardinge Giffard and the prosecution had anticipated this strategy: *OB* trial of Hannah Newington alias Flora Davey [sic].

159:    "Life in this country would not be safe if that were not manslaughter": *TE* July 14, 1871, 6.

160:    Flora Davy then launched with wild-eyed distress into a semi-coherent declaration: *TE* July 17, 1871, 2.

160:    Poland, then, forced a ruling on this issue as quickly as he could: *TE* July 17, 1871, 2.

161:    After this considerable recess, he returned with a decision—of sorts: *TE* July 17, 1871, 2.

161:    He began to call his witnesses: the fullest testimony of these witnesses appears in the *OB* trial of Agnes Norman.

161:    they simply did not have enough evidence to convict Agnes Norman: *T* July 17, 1871, 13.

162:    "I was woke up in the morning by somebody strangling me . . ." *OB* trial of Agnes Norman, testimony of Charles Parfitt.

162:    In response . . . a ten-year-old's recollection: *TE* July 17, 1871, 2.

163:    "mob of the lowest class": *MP* July 17, 1871, 2.

163:    "roughs of Greenwich": *HA* July 22, 1871, 3.

163:    Newsboys ran among them: *KM* July 22, 1871, 4; *MP* July 17, 1871, 2.

163:    A number of men and boys in the crowd had prepared for just this moment: *TE* July 17, 1871, 6.

163: Their solicitor was not as fortunate: *MP* July 17, 1871, 2; *TE* July 17, 1871, 6.

164: "Greenwich is at present suffering from high fever": *LM* July 20, 1871, 5.

164: "I have always considered . . . English nation": *TE* July 20, 1871, 2, and widely republished.

165: At six o'clock that evening, a cart was wheeled up to the Pooks' shop windows: *DN* July 18, 1871, 3.

165: "Pook the Butcher": *DN* July 18, 1871, 3; *G* July 22, 1871, 6.

165: a group of Pook supporters . . . destroyed the effigies: *DN* July 18, 1871, 3. The *Daily News* reported that the police might have assisted the Pook supporters in their destruction, but this is unlikely.

165: These were later resurrected and, Guy-like, employed to solicit donations: *KM* July 22, 1871, 3.

165: At least three thousand strong, they . . . unleashed a "perfect Babel": *BDP* July 19, 1871, 4; *PMG* July 18, 1871, 6. The *Daily News* estimated a crowd of five thousand to six thousand (July 18, 1871, 3), and *Reynolds's* one of eight thousand to ten thousand (July 23, 1871, 8).

165: according to one report, a mock funeral for Edmund Pook was planned: *L* July 23, 1871, 2.

166: "As I have been unable to get redress from the police here": *TE* July 20, 1871, 2.

166: he would give "the necessary directions to the police on the street": *TE* July 20, 1871, 2; *IPN* July 22, 1871, 3.

166: "Last night . . . a few policemen might be seen hovering near the spot . . .": *DN* July 19, 1871, 2.

166: one man began to incite children to attack the Pooks' house: *KM* July 22, 1871, 3.

167: E. P. Thompson notes that . . . the tradition of rough music was strongest in the southeast: Thompson 520. He cites an example, complete with effigy and band, which occurred in Woolwich in 1870.

167: "none of its members . . . reproach and remark": *LM* July 20, 1871, 5.

167: "My name has been brought into most unenviable notoriety . . .": *TE* July 17, 1871, 2; with slight differences also in *T* July 17, 1871, 14, and *MP* July 17, 1871, 2.

168: Leopold de Breanski . . . the mob on London Street: *TE* July 24, 1871, 3; *KM* July 29, 1871, 5.

169: "Sir I would be very much thankful if you let the publice a large . . . ": *YP* July 18, 1871, 7.

169: "as for Perrin [sic], Conway, and Lazell . . . ": *TE* July 17, 1871, 2; *T* July 17, 1871, 14; *MP* July 17, 1871, 2.

169: They would seek those summonses at London's Guildhall: *T* July 21, 1871, 11.

170. Eight officers of R Division testified to Henry Pook's fist-shaking and obscenity-laden conduct: *KM* July 22, 1871, 5; *TE* July 19, 1871, 2

170: Douglas Straight . . . coaching his officers on their testimony: *KM* July 22, 1871, 5.

170: Partridge ruled, "with great regret," that Henry Pook was guilty: *TE* July 19, 1871, 2.

170: "I feel deeply the insult to which Mr. Pook has been subjected": *S* July 20, 1871, 7.

171: What steps then . . . would he take to protect the public: *T* July 21, 1871, 7.

171: While their cases were pending . . . prejudice them: *S* July 21, 1871, 3.

171: Henry and Ebenezer Pook had marched into Guildhall: *KM* July 22, 1871, 5; *T* July 21, 1871, 11.

172: Edmund had "made no reply": *MP* July 25, 1871, 7.

172: *"people said* that he had written a letter to her.": *T* July 13, 1871, 11.

173: so "just and conscientious a judge": *T* July 27, 1871, 11.

173: seeking twenty thousand pounds' damages on two charges: *T* Feb. 2, 1871, 11. Edmund revealed in later testimony that he had sued Griffin for £10,000 damages; most likely his father had sued Griffin for the same amount.

173: Henry Bruce gushed unqualified praise for both officers: *T* August 1, 1871, 7.

173: The Pook Defence Committee . . . did their best to force the matter: *S* Aug. 7, 1871, 7; Sep. 2, 1871, 6.

174: Henry Bruce, however, refused to see them: *S* Aug. 12, 1871, 7.

174: "As there is a general opinion abroad . . . ": *KM* July 22, 1871, 4.

175: I shall prepare myself for my diabolical task: *KM* July 29, 1871, 4.

176: "You will pardon me for doubting the wisdom of the course you adopt": *MP* Sept. 13, 1871, 7.

176: Henry Pook, for one, suspected that she was the author of the letters: *T* Sept. 16, 1871, 9. Newton Crosland wrote to the *Times* to deny his wife had written the pamphlet: *T* Sept. 18, 1871, 10.

177: Frederick Farrah, a radical publisher on the Strand: *DN* Aug. 23, 1871, 2.

177: "It was not the man who invented the gunpowder . . .": *MP* Aug. 23, 1871, 3.

177: "If you sell any after Monday, madam . . . I shall summons you . . .": *KM* Sept. 2, 1871, 5.

178: "I shall call Edmund Walter Pook, who is ready to be examined": *S* Aug. 3, 1871, 2.

178: Edmund Pook, however, approached the witness chair with discernible uneasiness: *TE* Aug. 23, 1871, 2; *FJ* Aug. 25, 1871, 4.

178: "I shall ask Mr. Pook no questions": *MP* Aug. 23, 1871, 3.

178: Had you any communication with that poor girl?: *MP* Aug. 23, 1871, 3.

179: The magistrate, Frederick Flowers, declared that in that case he had no choice: *T* Aug. 23, 1871, 9.

179: a mass of "half-drunken, ragged loafers": *FJ* Aug. 25, 1871, 4—excerpted from the *Evening Telegraph*.

179: while they were at court . . . sold out: *FJ* Aug. 25, 1871, 4.

180: Instead he rebuked the Pooks: *T* Aug. 31, 1871, 9.

180: "The Pook family are becoming a nuisance": *NG* Sept. 2, 1871, 5; *WA* Sept. 2, 1871, 4.

181: "including Mr. Pook, who has been for some time residing in Herne Bay.": *WT* Apr. 27, 1872, 4. Church records confirm that this Mr. Pook was indeed Edmund Walter Pook: *England, Select Births and Christenings, 1538–1975* for Edmund Walter Pook.

181: in mid-August they inundated Greenwich and Deptford with placards: *MP* Sept. 6, 1871, 4.

181: Their opponents derided the offer: *IPN* Sept. 23, 1871, 3.

181: Frederick Farrah's fine gold watch was ripped from its fob and stolen: *IPN* Sept. 23, 1871, 3; *KM* 23 Sept. 1871, 5.

182: just a year before had advised the prince: Davenport-Hines; Juxon 93.

182: "Personalities were freely indulged in": *T* Sept. 16, 1871, 9.

182: he "should meet them as they came . . .": *TE* Sept. 16, 1871, 2.

183: He had never imputed to Pook "that he had obtained popularity . . .": *TE* Sept. 16, 1871, 2.

183: Edmund Pook, with a remarkable and discernible composure: *S* Sept. 16, 1871, 7.

183: "Do you know how that blood came upon your garments?": *S* Sept. 16, 1871, 7.

183: "How do you account for the blood on your hat?": *S* Sept. 16, 1871, 7.

185: the grand jury convened at the Old Bailey: *MP* Sept. 20, 1871, 7.

185: John Page . . . accepted his summons with ironic honor: *KM* Oct. 7, 1871, 5. Page was actually one of two shopkeepers summoned by the Pooks at this time, but Page was the only shopkeeper examined.

185: "Happy Jane Maria Clousen. Taken away from the evil to come": One copy of this tobacco paper actually survives, in the John Johnson Collection of Printed Ephemera at Oxford University: Tobacco Papers 4 (16).

186: Newton Crosland . . . every libel action mounted against his pamphlet: *BN* Oct. 10, 1871, 3.

186: "He was an utter stranger to me, and committed perjury in making that assertion": *DN* Oct. 5, 1871, 6.

187: his brother, Thomas, he stated, had seen Jane and a young man walking in public: *TE* Oct. 7, 1871, 3.

188: Henry Pook stunned him with a writ: *DN* Oct. 10, 1871, 3.

188.   Henry Pook served similar writs: *KM* Oct. 14, 1871, 5. In the end, only the suit against Hartnoll reached the point of settlement.

188:    the grand jury met at the Old Bailey: *MEN* Oct. 24, 1871, 4.

188:    a meeting at the Greenwich Lecture Hall: *L* Nov. 5, 1871, 4; *LT* Nov. 4, 1871, 7; *T* Oct. 31, 1871, 5.

188:    he was "almost sick of the case": *T* Oct. 7, 1871, 11.

188:    "The acquitted Mr. Pook got the benefit of the doubt . . .": *WD* Oct. 29, 1871, 8.

189:    He applied at the Court of Exchequer for . . . special juries: *T* Nov. 24, 1871, 11.

189:    Special juries, to put it simply, consisted of men of substantial property: Bentley 89. A year before, with the 1870 juries act, a higher property qualification was added to the traditional restriction to bankers, merchants, and esquires.

189:    the Crown routinely employed special juries in state and political trials: Hostettler 141.

190:    "subjected to the greatest annoyance": *KM* Dec. 16, 1871, 6.

190:    One week after this came the news of a far greater fall: *MP* Dec. 16, 1871, 5, and a number of other newspapers. James Griffin later found employment as an agent of the Charity Organisation Society [*Census Returns of England and Wales, 1881* for James Griffin].

190:    The *Kentish Mercury* attempted to dispel these by publishing glowing testimonials: *KM* Dec. 23, 1871, 5.

190:    His astrologer friend . . . had again examined his chart: Crosland, *Rambles* 281.

191:    "with the exception of Inspector Griffin . . . charged with perjury": *MP* Feb. 2, 1872, 7.

191:    He repeated his callous dismissal of Jane as a "very dirty girl": *MP* Feb. 2, 1872, 7.

191:    "There were many circumstances pointing to this young man . . .": *T* Feb. 3, 1872, 11.

192:    Kelly . . . "summed up dead against me and said not a word in my favour . . .": Crosland, *Rambles*, 278.

193:    "I forget who were counsel for the plaintiff . . .": *T* April 28 ,1924, 8.

CHAPTER SEVEN: VIPER OF KIDBROOKE LANE

194:    "the most severe within living memory": *MP* Aug. 8, 1872, 5.

194:    "as if electrified or shot": *CC* Aug. 9, 1872, 4.

195:    And when some remembered . . . first anniversary of Jane's murder: *PMG* August 9, 1872, 4. The *Pall Mall Gazette* actually reported calm weather in England on the anniversary of Jane's *death*—April 30, 1872—but did report of April 25, 1872, a year to the day after Jane was attacked, that "rain has been very general, and thunder and lightning were reported in several parts of England" (*PMG* May 1, 1872, 7; Apr. 26, 1872, 9).

195: On November 26, 1871 . . . Bagnigge Wells police station: *MEN* Dec. 1, 1871, 2.

195: The charge of murder was dropped: *GH* Dec. 1, 1871, 5; *SM* Dec. 8, 1871, 3.

195: Just over a year after this . . . carrying Edmund Pook's child: *DN* Dec. 20, 1872, 3; *S* Dec. 20, 1872, 6.

195: he was held for a week so that Scotland Yard could investigate: *DN* Dec. 20, 1872, 3; *SI* Dec. 30, 1872, 4.

196: Three months later . . . a written confession to Jane's killing: *T* March 21, 1873, 12.

196: Several Pook supporters actually traveled down to observe Bingham's examination: *AMG* March 15, 1873, 3.

196: Mulvany traveled down as well: *MP* March 14, 1873, 7.

196: evidence for Bingham's insanity quickly grew: *HA* March 15, 1873, 7; *L* March 16, 1873, 3.

196: Two witnesses . . . swore as well that they could not recognize Bingham: *T* March 28, 1873, 12. Neither of these witnesses had testified at trial. One was John Walker, Thomas Lazell's Kidbrooke landlord, who professed to have seen the couple Lazell had seen that evening; the other was a man named John James Brown, never mentioned in connection with this case before or after this.

196: Bingham then admitted he had concocted the story: *MP* March 28, 1873, 6.

196: Later that year, he quit Scotland Yard—or, more likely, he was forced out: "Retirement from the Metropolitan Police: John Mulvany."

196: "Police Inspector Superannuated": *Census Returns of England and Wales, 1881,* for John Mulvany.

196: The next confession came seven years after Bingham's: *T* June 14, 1880, 13; *PMG* April 14, 1880, 10.

197: Two months later Prince made the same confession . . . in Wandsworth: *T* June 14, 1880, 13.

197: a man who called himself Michael Carroll . . . seventeen years before: *T* April 28, 1888, 10; *WW* March 15, 1888, 3; *BA* March 22, 1888, 2; *A* March 23, 1888, 5.

197: Wide dissemination . . . emigrants from southeast London: *AS* March 20, 1888, 5; *QT* March 20, 1888, 3; *TA* March 24, 1888, 8.

197: One British newspaper . . . George Bingham: *DC* May 7, 1888, 3.

197: Scotland Yard did, with a cable declaring his story an utter fiction: *MC* May 5, 1888, 11.

197: the libel action against George Stiff: *T* June 15, 1872, 11.

197: "litigious vexatiousness": *WD* Oct. 29, 1871, 8.

198: *"ausis nil impossibile"*: *KM* Oct. 14, 1871, 5.

198: With six candidates running, Boord won easily with 4,525 votes: *T* Aug. 5, 1872, 5.

199: Also, maids-of-all-work continued to come and go: *Census Returns of England and Wales, 1881* for Caroline Burch; *Census Returns of England and Wales, 1891* for Ada C. Burch.

199: Ebenezer Pook . . . dying in 1877 of a lingering, painful illness: *S* May 9, 1877, 1.

199: Alice Swabey, the daughter herself of a prosperous printer: *Census Returns of England and Wales, 1881,* for Thomas Swabey.

199: Alice . . . then lived south of Lewisham: *Census Returns of England and Wales, 1871,* for Alice Maria Swabey.

199: "lived a solitary and apparently friendless life . . .": *MEN* April 25, 1882, 4, and a host of other newspapers.

199: they had been "greatly pained" by the news: *HC* Apr. 27, 1882, 4.

200: Alice and Edmund Pook had a son, Edmund Thomas Pook: *London, England, Births and Baptisms, 1813–1906* for Edmund Thomas Pook.

200: Three and a half years later, they lost him: *England and Wales Civil Registration Indexes,* death record for Edmund Thomas Pook.

200: Cousin Harriet died in 1890: *Board of Guardian Records,* burial record for Harriet Chaplin.

200: Brother Thomas died in 1897: *England and Wales Civil Registration Indexes,* death record for Thomas Burch Pook.

200: And mother Mary, at age seventy-five, died in 1899: *England and Wales Civil Registration Indexes,* death record *1837–1915* for Mary Pook.

200: By 1911, however, the two had taken up residence on the island of Guernsey: *Census Returns of England and Wales, 1911* (Channel Islands Census), for Edmund Walter Pook and Alice Maria Pook.

200: By 1915 they had moved to the neighboring island of Jersey: Principal Probate Registry for Alice Maria Pook.

200: Emma, who had married a man by the name of Thomas Linforth Spiller: *Census Returns of England and Wales, 1911,* for Thomas Linforth Spiller and Emma Nellie Spiller.

200: Edmund Pook died, age seventy, at Croydon Union Hospital: Principal Probate Registry for Edmund Walter Pook.

200: "It would be difficult . . . flagrant breach of good taste . . .": *DN* Oct. 31, 1871, 5.

201: "Was there ever such a display of idiocy outside of Bedlam?": *NYT* Nov. 20, 1871, 4.

201: commissioning a Deptford stonemason, Samuel Hobbs: *MP* Oct. 8, 1872, 7.

201: the committee dropped him and engaged yet another Deptford stonemason: "Tomb of Jane Mary Clouston" [sic]. The sculpture was based upon Luigi Pampaloni's *Samuel in Prayer* (Freidus).

202: a farrago of sixteen parts: *Pretty Jane: or, the Viper of Kidbrook Lane.*

202: "her footsteps unhappily led her to Greenwich . . .": *Pretty Jane: or, the Viper of Kidbrook Lane* 136.

203: Inspector Percy Neame began to assemble exhibits: "The Crime Museum."

203: He described seeing on a little wooden shelf "a dirty Prayer-book . . . ": *SP* Oct. 6, 1877, 11; *T* Oct. 8, 1877, 10.

203: at some point after that, Jane's clothing . . . disappeared altogether: Paul Bickley, Curator at the Crime Museum, confirms their disappearance. [Private correspondence.]

204: "Coleridge and I . . . had no doubt about the guilt of the prisoner": Bowen-Rowlands 95.

205: "No one seems . . . to have called attention to the difficulty . . .": Crosland, *Eltham Tragedy Reviewed* 28.

206: he set up his own identification parade: *OB*, testimony of Joseph Ambrose Eagle [sic] and Mary Ann Eagle [sic].

206: the Eagleses sent their lodger William Douglas to Tudor House: *OB*, testimony of William Douglas.

206: "I was born in Greenwich": *OB*, testimony of Eliza Ann Merritt [sic].

206: Later, he remembered that he had seen someone: *T* May 31, 1871, 2; *TE* May 2, 1871, 2.

208: "hearsay provides the only information": Zuckerman 201.

208: "the idle tittle-tattle of one woman to another": *MP* May 8, 1871, 7.

209: "Charlotte, you must not be surprised if I am missing for some weeks . . .": *MEN* May 5, 1871, 2. Other transcriptions of this testimony have Jane meeting Edmund on Monday, not on Monday or Tuesday.

209: "I am going up to Croom-hill to see Mr. Edmund Pook . . .": *MP* May 5, 1871, 8.

209: "Till within the last few weeks [she] was very cheerful": *KM* May 6, 1871, 5.

209: she appeared "very low spirited": *S* July 13, 1871, 6.

209: Jane was "happier than she had been . . . ": *BM* May 5, 1871, 3.

210: Emily Wolledge witnessed . . . Jane's elation: *L* May 14, 1871, 10.

210: Jane was "in good spirits," . . . "much excited": *KM* May 6, 1871, 5; *TE* May 5, 1871, 3.

211: "I told Edmund . . . to his mother": *DN* May 5, 1871, 6.

211: "I am not to tell anyone . . . for some time . . .": *MEN* May 5, 1871, 2.

212: It was a "trifling and insignificant" amount: *DN* July 15, 1871, 6.

213: enough "to cover a threepenny bit": *DN* Oct. 5, 1871, 6.

213: "so small as to be almost imperceptible," *S* July 13, 1871, 6.

213: there were six distinct spots there: *T* July 15, 1871, 11.

213: The coroner at Jane's inquest noted their "minuteness": *PMG* May 13, 1871, 8.

213: Chief Justice Bovill scoffed . . . "the size of pin's heads": *DN* July 15, 1871, 5.

213: "The minute spots of blood on clothes . . . apt to imagine . . .": Crosland, *Eltham Tragedy Reviewed* 19. Crosland demonstrates a remarkable prescience here; the first significant study of bloodstain pattern analysis would not appear for another twenty-four years. [James *et al.*, 3]

214: "A person standing and striking at the deceased . . . in a forward state . . .": *PMG* May 13, 1871, 8.

214: And all of the bloodstains . . . none on the left: *T* July 15, 1871, 11. Superintendent Griffin claimed at trial that there was blood on both cuffs, but Chief Justice Bovill both corrected him and censured him for making that claim [*S* July 17, 1871, 5].

215: At the commencement of such a seizure: For the physiology of tonic-clonic seizures, see Appleton and Marson, 10–12, and Eadie and Bladin, 8.

216: Both Henry Letheby and Michael Harris testified: *DN* May 20, 1871, 4; *OB* testimony of Michael Harris. Their point about partially and wholly severed arteries is still understood to be valid [James *et al.* 13].

216: the direction of force would have been away from him: James et al. 127–8 describes just such a scenario.

217: Griffin testified that "every facility" had been given him: *T* July 31, 1871, 12.

219: "She was a dirty girl": *S* July 13, 6; *T* May 3, 1871, 7.

WORKS CITED

Appleton, Richard, and Anthony Marson. *Epilepsy*. Oxford: Oxford University Press, 2009.

Atlay, J. B., "Willis, William (1835–1911)." Rev. Eric Metcalfe. *Oxford Dictionary of National Biography*. Oxford: Oxford University Press, 2004. Online ed. Ed. Lawrence Goldman, 2004.

Ballantine, William. *Some Experiences of a Barrister's Life*. Revised edition. New York: J. M. Stoddart, 1883.

Beeton, Isabella. *The Book of Household Management*. London: S. O. Beeton, 1861.

Bentley, David. *English Criminal Justice in the Nineteenth Century*. London: Hambledon, 1998.

Board of Guardian Records, 1834–1906 and Church of England Parish Registers, 1754–1906. London Metropolitan Archives, London.

Bowen-Rowlands, Ernest. *Seventy-two Years at the Bar: A Memoir*. London: MacMillan, 1924.

Burnett, John. *Useful Toil: Autobiographies of Working People from the 1820s to the 1920s*. Harmondsworth, UK: Penguin, 1984 [1974].

Burney, Ian A. *Bodies of Evidence: Medicine and the Politics of the English Inquest 1830–1926*. Baltimore and London: Johns Hopkins University Press, 2000.

Census Returns of England and Wales, 1841. Kew, Surrey, England: The National Archives of the UK, 1841.

Census Returns of England and Wales, 1851. Kew, Surrey, England: The National Archives of the UK, 1851.

Census Returns of England and Wales, 1861. Kew, Surrey, England: The National Archives of the UK, 1861.

Census Returns of England and Wales, 1871. Kew, Surrey, England: The National Archives of the UK, 1871.

Census Returns of England and Wales, 1881. Kew, Surrey, England: The National Archives of the UK, 1881

Census Returns of England and Wales, 1911. Kew, Surrey, England: The National Archives of the UK, 1911.

Christiansen, Rupert. *Paris Babylon: The Story of the Paris Commune.* New York: Viking, 1994.

Church of England Parish Registers, 1754–1921. London Metropolitan Archives, London.

Cobb, Belton. *Critical Years at the Yard: The Career of Frederick Williamson of the Detective Department and the C.I.D.* London: Faber and Faber, 1956.

Coleridge, Ernest Hartley. *Life and Correspondence of John Duke Lord Coleridge, Lord Chief Justice of England.* London: William Heinemann, 1904. 2 vols.

"Confessions." *The American and English Encyclopædia of Law.* Ed. John Houston Merrill. Northport, NY: Edward Thompson 1887. 3.483-484.

"The Crime Museum." Metropolitan Police website. http://content.met.police.uk/Article/The-Crime-Museum/1400015334971/1400015334971.

Critchley, T. A. *A History of Police in England and Wales.* Montclair, NJ: Patterson Smith, 1972. Second edition.

Crosland, Newton. *Apparitions: A New Theory.* London: Effingham Wilson, 1856.

———. *Apparitions: An Essay, Explanatory of Old Facts and a New Theory.* London: Trübner & Co., 1873.

———. *The Eltham Tragedy Reviewed.* Third edition. London: F. Farrah, 1871.

———*Rambles Round My Life. An Autobiography (1819–1896).* London: E. W. Allen, 1898.

Cullwick, Hannah. *The Diaries of Hannah Cullwick, Victorian Maidservant.* Ed. Liz Stanley. New Brunswick, NJ: Rutgers University Press, 1984.

Curl, James Stevens. *The Victorian Celebration of Death.* Thrupp, Stroud, Gloucestershire, UK: Sutton, 2000.

Davenport-Hines, Richard. "Lewis, Sir George Henry, first baronet (1833–1911)." *Oxford Dictionary of National Biography.* Oxford:

Oxford University Press, 2004. Online ed. Ed. Lawrence Goldman. May 2010.

Dawes, Frank. *Not in Front of the Servants: Domestic Service in England 1850–1939*. London: Wayland, 1973.

Dell, Simon. *The Victorian Policeman*. Princes Risborough, Buckinghamshire, UK: Shire, 2004.

Eadie, M. J., and P. F. Bladin. *A Disease Once Sacred: A History of the Medical Understanding of Epilepsy*. Eastleigh, Hampshire, UK: John Libbey & Co., 2001.

England and Wales Civil Registration Indexes. London, England: General Register Office.

England, Select Births and Christenings, 1538–1975. Salt Lake City: FamilySearch, 2013 Ancestry.co.uk.

Freidus, Robert. "Monument for Jane Maria Clouson." *The Victorian Web*. http://www.victorianweb.org/sculpture/funerary/148.html.

Galton, Francis. *Inquiries into Human Faculty and Its Development*. London: J. M. Dent, 1907.

"Galton Whistle, Europe, 1876–1920." Science Museum, London. *Brought to Life*. https://www.google.com/url?sa=t&rct=j&q=&esrc=s&source=web&cd=5&ved=0CCsQFjAEahUKEwjM1cOJsY7JAhXIJYgKHRCpBqc&url=http%3A%2F%2Fwww.sciencemuseum.org.uk%2Fonline_science%2Fexplore_our_collections%2Fobjects%2Findex%2Fsmxg-432708&usg=AFQjCNHyU8A4CcVm1xzqR5MEk8Oe-WL5cQ.

Gilbert, Michael. *The Claimant*. London: Constable, 1957.

Griffiths, Arthur. *The Chronicles of Newgate*. London: Chapman and Hall, 1884.

Hamilton, J. A. "Bovill, Sir William (1814–1873)." Rev. Mary Heimann. *Oxford Dictionary of National Biography*. Oxford: Oxford University Press, 2004. Online ed. Ed. Lawrence Goldman.

Hamlin, Christopher. "Letheby, Henry (1816–1876)." *Oxford Dictionary of National Biography*. Oxford: Oxford University Press, 2004. Online ed. Ed. Lawrence Goldman.

Horn, Pamela. *The Rise and Fall of the Victorian Servant*. Stroud, Gloucestershire, UK: Sutton, 2004.

Hostettler, John. *A History of Criminal Justice in England and Wales*. Hook, Hampshire, UK: Waterside Press, 2009.

James, Stuart H., Paul E. Kish, and T. Paulette Sutton. *Principles of Bloodstain Pattern Analysis*. Boca Raton, Fla.: Taylor & Francis, 2005.

Juxon, John. *Lewis and Lewis*. New York: Ticknor & Fields, 1984.

Kurland, Philip B. and D.W.M. Waters. "Persecutions in England, 1854–79: An Essay in English Legislative History." *Duke Law Journal* 1959.4 (Fall 1959), 493–562.

Law Reform Commission. *Search Warrants and Bench Warrants.*
[Consultation Paper.] Dublin: Law Reform Commission, 2009.

Letheby, Henry. "Dr. Letheby on Spectrum Analysis." *Clinical Lectures and Reports by the Medical and Surgical Staff of the London Hospital.*
London: J. Churchill, 1866.

Litten, Julian. *The English Way of Death: The Common Funeral since 1450.*
London: Robert Hale, 1991.

London, England Births and Baptisms 1813–1906. London Metropolitan Archives, London.

"London, United Kingdom—Moonrise, moonset and moon phases, April 1871." timeanddate.com.

Mathew, Theobald. *The Office and Duties of the Director of Public Prosecutions.* London: Athlone Press, 1950.

Maugham, Frederick H. *The Tichborne Case.* London: Hodder & Stoughton, 1936.

McBride, Theresa M. *The Domestic Revolution.* New York: Holmes & Meier, 1976.

McKenna, Neil. *Fanny and Stella: The Young Men Who Shocked Victorian England.* London: Faber and Faber, 2013.

McWilliam, Rohan. *The Tichborne Claimant: A Victorian Sensation.* London: Hambledon Continuum, 2007.

Mortality in England and Wales: Average Life Span, 2010. Office for National Statistics, 2012. (http://www.ons.gov.uk/ons/dcp171776_292196.pdf.)

"Obituary. Mr. Serjeant Payne." *The Solicitors' Journal & Reporter,* March 2, 1872, 331.

Payne, Chris: *The Chieftain: Victorian True Crime through the Eyes of a Scotland Yard Detective.* Stroud, Gloucestershire, UK: The History Press, 2011.

Pretty Jane: or, the Viper of Kidbrook Lane. N.p.; n.d. [1871].

Principal Probate Registry. *Calendar of the Grants of Probate and Letters of Administration Made in the Probate Registries of the High Court of Justice in England.* London, England.

The Queen v. Edmund Walter Pook. National Archives, Kew. PRO DPP 4/7.

Ranyard, Ellen [L. N. R.]. *Life Work, or, the Link and the Rivet.* London: James Nisbet & Co., 1861.

"Retirement from the Metropolitan Police: John Mulvany." PRO MEPO [Public Records Office, Records of the Metropolitan Police Office] 21/11/3775.

"Sir W. Bovill." *Law Times* 56 (1873–74), 27.

"Sketches from the Great City." *The Scottish Sabbath-School Teachers' Magazine.* N.s. 1 (1861), 11–14.

St. Giles, Camberwell, Register of Baptisms, September 1838–September 1845. London Metropolitan Archives.

Strange, Julie-Marie. *Death, Grief and Poverty in Britain, 1870–1914.* Cambridge, UK: Cambridge University Press, 2005.

"Sunrise Sunset Calendar of London, England: (April, 1871)": world-timedate.com.

Thompson, E. P. *Customs in Common.* New York: New Press, 1991.

"Tomb of Jane Mary Clouston [sic]." http://www.britishlistedbuildings.co.uk/en-472748-tomb-of-jane-mary-clouston-brockley-ceme#.VkZcEvmrTIU

Tombs, Robert: *The Paris Commune 1871.* London and New York: Longman, 1999.

Watson, Eric R. *Adolf Beck (1877–1904).* Edinburgh and London: William Hodge & Co., 1924.

Wilks, Samuel, and G. T. Bettany. *Biographical History of Guy's Hospital.* London: Ward, Lock, Bowden & Co., 1892.

Williams, Kevin: *Read All About It!: A History of the British Newspaper.* London: Routledge, 2010.

Woodroffe, W. L. "Lord Coleridge and the English Law Courts." James Parton, ed., *Some Noted Princes, Authors, and Statesmen of Our Time.* Norwich, Conn.: Henry Bill, 1885. 237–241.

Woodruff, Douglas: *The Tichborne Claimant: A Victorian Mystery.* London: Hollis & Carter, 1957.

Zuckerman, A.A.S. *The Principles of Criminal Evidence.* Oxford: Clarendon, 1989.

INDEX